JESUS
"The Way" the
Truth and the Life

Dennis Ryan

JESUS "The Way" the Truth and the Life
Dennis Ryan

© 2021 Amazon Publishing

All rights reserved. No part of this publication may be reproduced, stored in a retrieval system or transmited in any form or by any means, electronic, mechanical, photocopying, recording or otherwise without the prior permision of the publisher or in accordance with the provisions of the Copyright, Designs and Patents Act 1988 or under the terms of any licence permitting limited copying issued by the Copyright Licensing Angency.

Published by:
Amazon Publishing
551 Boren Ave N,
Seattle, WA 98109, USA

Cover Design and Typesetting: Rachel Rifat

ISBN: 9798713450342

Imprint: Independently published

Printed in USA

Dedicated to my God and heavenly Father, to my Saviour and Lord, Jesus and to His precious Holy Spirit, for giving me the revelation and insights in this work. Also, to my beautiful wife, Christine, who has supported me wholeheartedly throughout our journey together and whose love, faithfulness and dedication has kept me strong. Lastly, to all our church who have stood by me, who have loved and supported me and my family throughout the years. Thank you all so much.

Finally, to every spiritual leader that desires to build according to the divine heavenly pattern. May you come under a fresh anointing of the Spirit in revelation and inspiration.

Contents

Chapter 1

The Way Defined 27

Chapter 2

The Way Defiled 45

Chapter 3

The Way Destroyed 56

Chapter 4

The Way in Type and Shadow 64

Chapter 5

The Temple 74

Chapter 6

The Way Modelled 85

Chapter 7

The Missional 92

Chapter 8

The Way Recovered 100

Chapter 9

From Type and Shadow 105

Chapter 10

The Heavenly Tabernacle 124

Chapter 11

The Way Renewed 133

Chapter 12

The Spiritual Temple 143

Chapter 13

Two Priesthoods 154

Chapter 14

The Way Revealed 180

Chapter 15

The Early Church and Prayer 190

Chapter 16

Prayer for the Nations 199

Chapter 17

God's Business 212

Chapter 18

Praying with All Prayer 231

Chapter 19

Hindrances to Effective Prayer. 248

Chapter 20

The Way Experienced 257

Chapter 21

Spiritual Gifts 274

Foreword

My name is Reverend Heather Dube. I was born and brought up in a Christian family. My family were Catholics but when I grew up, I started attending Evangelical churches. I studied a Bachelor of Divinity degree at the University of London and became an Ordained Minister of Religion in October 2010. I have had the privilege of serving as a Pastor in an Evangelical church from January 2002 to December 2009. I also served under Prison Chaplaincy from 2010 till 2016. In 2017 I worked under Hospital Chaplaincy for a year. I was with Church of England till May 2018 when the Lord directed my footsteps to Trafford Christian Life Centre.

This is when I met Pastor Dennis Ryan. I enjoyed my ministry work but never got a job satisfaction in all I did. I always felt like I was missing something spiritually. I felt emotionally void until I came across Pastor Dennis. From the onset, I liked his preaching and teaching. As an academic, I paid full attention to his preaching on Sundays and came to the conclusion that Pastor Dennis was teaching sound doctrine and everything he said was Bible centred.

He then told me about his Christian journey and how he has always been committed to winning souls and serving God. He told me that his teachings originated from the revelation he had from seeking God. This revelation prompted him to write this book, Jesus, the Way, the Truth and the Life. It was from this revelation that he started teaching the 'approach to prayer.' This was indeed an eye-opener to me, even though I had worked as a Pastor, I felt I was still praying amiss. It was only after applying Pastor Dennis' teaching that I learnt how to pray more effectively.

When I began applying the correct approach to my personal circumstances, I started seeing a massive change. The clarity in his teaching made everything easy to understand from spiritual gifts, different types of prayer and discerning the voice of God. I consider myself really blessed to be serving under Pastor Dennis' ministry. This revelatory teaching has empowered church members, including myself, to grow spiritually, and has sparked personal revival in prayer. I am now able to live and walk in the Spirit.

It is my prayer that Church Leaders and the wider Christian community, not only from the UK, but globally would read this book and benefit from the wealth of knowledge about living as overcomers and rising to the enthroned life. This teaching clearly lays out how to approach the Throne of God and build an intimate relationship with God through prayer. I believe that this book will help to change the way churches are operating at the moment, from a religious way to a spiritual way. This book is filled with biblical truths which will not only cause you to grow spiritually but will also point your ministry in the right direction towards the coming of our Saviour Jesus Christ.

This book has impacted my life and faith in a positive way. Christianity has always been like running a race without a finishing line, but after reading this book, the reader will know what they are called to do by God and how their work will advance the Kingdom of God in this perishing world. Jesus is the only Way (access) to God, in heaven, the only true measure of righteousness, and the source of both physical and spiritual life.

Preface

In 2015 the Lord changed my walk. Prior to this I had gone through the worst period of my life, of which I will come to in a moment. I got saved in December 1983 when I was 20 years old. I was playing bass guitar in our family Irish showband. I had joined them when I was fifteen years old. The band included my mother and father, as well as my eldest brother, eldest sister and brother in-law. By the way I have four brothers and six sisters.

I met my wife, Christine on a gig, in a pub. We courted, got engaged and were married when I was 19. Christine was 18. We wanted to start our family early so that we wouldn't be too old when they were becoming independent, and so, Debra our first child was born in 1983. Dennis Jr. and Sandra followed.

Up to this point, Christine was out on every gig and we were always together. We were young, madly in love and madly jealous of each other too. This led to many a quarrel and fight. When Debra was born Christine stayed home and I was out gigging on my own. This intensified the arguments and because of our insecurity and immaturity we were breaking up every other week.

My conversion came about through an older sister and her husband whom we hadn't seen for years due to family issues. They visited us one evening when we had just watched a movie called 'The Day After' which was about nuclear war and the devastation and the death toll on human life. This opened us up to the question of life after death and so it was a perfect opportunity for them to share the gospel with us both.

I was gigging that very evening and so I had to leave to be on stage and ready to play for 9pm.

As I was driving to the venue I prayed and invited the Lord to make Himself known to me. I walked into that pub a different person. I knew something had happened to me but I couldn't explain it. I felt different, like a new person. When I got home that night, I didn't say anything to Christine about my experience and just went to bed. The next day, when I got up, my sister and her husband had left a NIV bible with us as a gift. I immediately began reading and I was mesmerised as I read. I couldn't put it down. Christine was reading it as well, and so we would argue about reading time.

Over a few days, Christine asked me if I was ok? I said, 'Yes, why?' She went on to say that she had noticed that I hadn't swore for three days (I'm from an Irish family and I picked it up really young!) It was then I shared my experience with her and to my surprise Christine had her own experience with the Lord that very same night. There's so much more to my conversion that I could write another book on that alone. But sufficient for now that was my conversion and beginning with the Lord.

We began attending a small pioneer church with about 8 members and got involved in everything the church was doing from street evangelism to bible studies and services. The church grew to about 150 people and was a mother church to three other churches. We got involved in music ministry and bible studies and general church life. We had an insatiable appetite for the things of God and so it wasn't long before I was leading bible studies and then preaching. We had on the job training and six years on we were associate pastors in that mother church.

We learned so many great things in that church but unfortunately over time the church had become increasingly legalistic with an unhealthy control over members. It was with much sadness that we made the decision to leave for our own spiritual welfare. The response of our spiritual leaders and church family toward us left us very hurt to the point that for a time we didn't attend any church as we had become discouraged and disillusioned with that brand of Christianity.

From day one, I have had special encounters with the Lord and numerous prophecies about the Lord's calling on my life. A year or more after we had left our first church, the Lord used a dear pastor friend, Bill Davidson, to restore us and help us recover from our sour experience. This led to a prophecy that the Lord spoke to us about starting a new church in our home town of Stretford. I didn't realise how pertinent and powerful this prophecy would be in my life and ministry. But in it the Lord said that He would stabilise me, that he would give me fresh revelation and vision, that he would cause me to walk in the Spirit and that in time He would commission me to go forth renewed.

With the help of Pastor Bill and his church we launched Stretford Christian Fellowship in March 1993. By the end of the first year, we had around 40 people with us. I knew that we couldn't do church the way we had experienced it before but I wasn't sure as to what direction to go in. I needed fresh revelation and vision.

It was at that time another pastor friend from California sent me the book: The Purpose Driven Church by Rick Warren. I read and reread that book seven times over. We attended the Saddleback conference in Southern California and I brought back all the materials that would help me bring this direction to our church. I began to implement that pattern of turning the church into the purpose driven direction. I thought that this was the fresh revelation and vision that the Lord had for me but over time, I realised that it wasn't working the way that I thought it would and so I slowly stopped pushing it in the church.

I was in neutral and coasting along not really knowing what to do next. It was somewhere in this period that I experienced the worst period of my life to date. I had become sick with a virus that the doctor couldn't diagnose or treat. I was told to take paracetamol and water. I'd lost all my energy and was spending most days in bed. I'd get up for Sunday and mid-week services and then return back to bed when I got back home. I managed a brave face but it was taking its toll.

As well as the virus I was becoming disillusioned with church. I was becoming more aware of how aimless and powerless the church was. I was becoming disillusioned with everything in my life; pastoring, marriage, family life and responsibilities. I started withdrawing from everyone and everything. I didn't want to be married, I didn't want family life and responsibility, I didn't want to pastor, I wanted out and I was giving up! I was sinking into depression. I was wiped out spiritually, physically, mentally and emotionally. I'd had enough! I felt I couldn't go on.

As I began analysing my life, I was overwhelmed with how my walk with the Lord had been dogged by a besetting sin that I just couldn't gain mastery over. I had this ongoing cycle of victory and then defeat time and again. I wanted to die and go to heaven. This is where the Lord stepped in. I had just woken up and my wife, Christine, (who I owe my whole life and a huge debt of gratitude to, because through it all, she was the one that stood by me and refused to give up. By the way I very nearly lost her during that period.) She had made a cup of coffee for me and brought it into the bedroom that morning. I sat up on the edge of the bed and was getting ready to face yet another day as before. I was in such a bad place I told the Lord I'd had enough and asked if He would take me to heaven.

Then suddenly, something happened. The Lord was with me and spoke to me very clearly and distinctly. '*Reckon yourself dead!*' Wow! It hit me like a ton of bricks, the revelation of it, the truth of it, and the power of it. In that moment I was changed into another man. 'Oh my God! The old Dennis is dead! He was crucified with Christ over 2000 years ago' I said. And in that moment the Lord delivered me from everything that was against me as the old Dennis was put to death. I had read it for years. I knew it and had even preached it but hadn't really experienced it. In an instant everything changed. I was renewed in Christ. I experienced the divine exchange! When Christ died, I died. When Christ rose, I rose. And when Christ ascended, I ascended.

I began to realise that what I had experienced was a mixture of divine and demonic work against me. The Lord was bringing me to the end of my old self and renewal in him, and the demonic was trying desperately to take advantage of my weakness by severe spiritual attack. I was surprised at how quickly I recovered. I felt spiritually alive in a way I'd never known before. My mind was released, my energy came back and I was ready for the next step. I began to pray and seek the Lord.

I was lying on the bed one morning and as I closed my eyes, I saw a pair of tramp's boots in front of me. They were a mustardy colour, all tattered and worn with no laces and holes in the soles. As I looked, they were transformed before my eyes. From top to bottom they were overlaid with gold and I heard the voice of the Lord say, *'Dennis, I'm changing your walk, you are going to walk in the Spirit!'* I was flabbergasted!

The next day, I was walking across the floor of my living room praying. I had my eyes closed, and as I looked down (with my spiritual sight) I was wearing those tramps' boots. I stood still and watched as they were overlaid with gold and were transformed. Again, the Lord said, *'Dennis, I'm changing your walk. You are going to walk in the Spirit!'*

In the prophecy I received in 1992 the Lord had said that I would walk in the Spirit. From that time, every time I closed my eyes the Lord gave me visions and words and began teaching me and opening up Scriptures to me in jaw dropping experiences that has led to the writing of this book.

The very first thing the Lord taught me was the 'enthroned life.' I found a small book of the same title in my library and to this day I don't know how it got there. I really don't remember buying it. It was a used book that someone had marked when they were reading it. As I read it my spirit soared. The book emphasised that we have been raised with Christ and are now seated in heavenly places (Ephesians 2:6). The Lord gave me revelation about the cross and the divine exchange. I began to realise what it meant to live and to walk in the Spirit (Galatians 5:25).

I realised that when Jesus died on the cross, I died with him. The sixth chapter of Romans had come alive and the more the Lord showed me the more liberated and empowered I became. My sin nature was crucified! The devil, the ruler of this world was also taken to the cross and defeated and so his power over me was broken too (John 12:31)! Not only that, but the world was taken to the cross and so now all that is in the world, the lust of the eyes, the lust of the flesh and the pride of life (John 2:15) was broken as well. Hallelujah! Also, all the handwritings that were against me were also nailed to the cross. I was a free man, and he who the Son sets free is free indeed (John 8:36)! All of this was by the Spirit of God, and where the Spirit of the Lord is, there is liberty (2 Corinthians 3:17).

This was huge, because I was delivered the moment, I applied the word. Hallelujah! I was now finally overcoming the body of sin because I had applied the cross and gave it a decent burial. The apostle Paul in Romans 7:24, 25 stated, 'O wretched man that I am! Who will deliver me from this body of death? I thank God — through Jesus Christ our Lord!' I experienced supernatural deliverance. I was set free in my body and my mind from a besetting sin that caused more condemnation in me than I care to admit. This besetting sin gave the enemy a foothold in my life and I know that my life, my family and my ministry had suffered because of it!

I began to meditate on these truths daily and as I did, I felt my spirit begin to rise. If I was seated in heavenly places then I was going to set my mind on things above and not on the things of the earth (Colossians 3:1-3). I was determined to take my place in the heavenly places. I began to establish life in the Spirit. I thanked God for the divine exchange every time I came before him. I rehearsed it all the time. When

Christ died, I died, when Christ rose, I arose. So, I rose up in newness of life, justified, sanctified and glorified to the throne of God. I rose up in resurrection life and thanked God for the gift of righteousness and the abundance of grace in the Lord Jesus Christ, and I asked Him to help me reign in Life (Romans 5:17). I did all of this in a meditative state of prayer.

In fact, the Lord led me into meditative prayer. I would lay on my bed and seek the Lord and I would come into visions and words of which I will share later. The Lord was leading me in a *way* I hadn't been before and was so new to me. He was leading me in *truths* that had been there all along but had been hidden from me. He was leading me into *spiritual life* that I hadn't experienced before.

I was so excited I wanted to shout it from the rooftops. But then again, as I shared my experiences with others, I very quickly realised that I had to take it slowly as I could tell I was coming across as super-spiritual, a term that has had bad press in the church for decades, oh, and has kept believers from living and walking in the Spirit for too long!

I can say that my walk with the Lord has become very per-sonal, very powerful and so refreshing that I can't wait to spend time in His kingdom and His presence. My life has changed on every level. The greatest thing for me in all of this is that the Lord has birthed a message and a divine pattern in me. For the last five years I've been in download mode as the Lord has poured His word into me. He has shown me things that I never saw before. Nearly everything that I had learned and knew and believed has been challenged and changed.

Now, every message I preach and every teaching is filled with the revelation of Christ, the cross and the divine exchange, living and walking in the Spirit, His finished work and His present and continuing ministry as High priest of heaven. Through everything the Lord has done and is doing, I'm learning to hear and know His voice and be obedient and a doer of the word! The gifts of the Spirit have begun to flow too! It is my prayer and desire that as you read this book it will ring true and register with you in your spirit and soul, and that you will be inspired to live and walk in the spirit too.

Introduction

> *"I am the way, the truth, and the life. No one comes to the Father except through Me."* John 14:6

These words spoken by Jesus are amongst the most popular Scriptures quoted by believers. But have we really understood them? And have we really grasped all that they imply. There are many ways that are presented to believers about how to come before God, such as come as you are or come as a child etc. If Jesus is claiming to be the way, is there a definite prescribed way that we as believers are to come to the Father. I think so, and I think that the way is clearly mapped out in the Bible. Proverbs 14:12 says, *'There is a way that seems right to a man, but its end is the way of death.'* If we get the way wrong it can hinder us spiritually in so many ways.

Let's take a brief look as we begin our journey.

Jesus is the way. The way to where and what? Is this simply a comforting Scripture that gives us hope when we die, encouraging us that we will be with the Lord *one day*? Or is there deeper truth that we have missed? Jesus is the way back to the Father's holy city, to the throne and the altar, and the inheritance of every spiritual blessing. Hebrews says that Jesus has passed through the heavens and that he has opened a new and living way (Hebrews 4:14; 10:20). We don't have to wait until we die!

Jesus is the truth. Jesus said, *'you shall know the truth and the truth shall make you free'* (John 8:32). But have we understood the truth? Are we walking in the full light of the truth? Or has the truth been hidden, blocked, hijacked, twisted or even lied about? The truth will not only set you free but will restore you to every promise of God's Word.

Jesus is the life. What kind of life? Jesus stated in John 10:10 that the thief (the devil), came to kill, to steal and to destroy.

But that He came to bring life, and life more abundant. Abundant life is a quality of life that includes spiritual, eternal, and physical life. This life is experienced through Jesus. But are we really experiencing abundant life? Jesus is the way back to spiritual life, and to the tree of life and the river of life! These sources are in the Father's house and Jesus has opened up a new and living way to experience them once again. Adam didn't lose physical life, or at least not immediately. But he did lose spiritual life. It's our spiritual life that Jesus came to restore. His truth, when understood, grasped and applied, will lead you in the way that leads to a fully restored spiritual and abundant life.

These are extremely important statements and questions and must be faced and asked. As we embark on our journey to uncover and discover fresh truth about Jesus, get ready to encounter 'The Word' in a new and exciting way that will bring you into the full knowledge and full measure of the Son of God bringing about spiritual maturity and perfection in Christ (Ephesians 4:11). Only then, can we truly enter into *the* work of the ministry which for the church is to display the manifold wisdom of God to principalities and powers in the heavenly places; to bring the enemy under the written judgment and the footstool of God and finally, gather all things both in heaven and in earth together into Christ!

The devil is the arch enemy of God and His kingdom. He hates everything about it and is opposed to all that it represents: righteousness, peace and joy in the Holy Ghost (Romans 14:17). The devil has set up his own opposing kingdom which is built on the same pattern as God's kingdom. Remember that the devil is a created being and has nothing original about him. All that he has established and all that he does is based upon his knowledge of heaven. He possesses inside information about God's kingdom, God's throne and altar and the workings of heaven's order, as he was attendant to God's throne for eons. His own kingdom is but an evil twist of the kingdom of God and of heaven.

However, we must not underestimate the devils' skills and abilities to rule and reign with terror over the world of men, nations, churches, cities, families and individuals, nor his intention to steal, kill and destroy. Satan and his kingdom of darkness are doing everything in their power to obstruct, hinder, deceive and keep hidden the way, the truth and the life. Because when the church comes into the truth of them, she will rise up and be the glorious church that she is and defeat and spoil his kingdom and bring about the restoration of all things at Christ's return. What you are about to read has the potential to lift you out of religiosity, spiritual confusion, darkness, barrenness and impotence and bring you into a new and living way accomplished by Jesus on the behalf of All believers whom He has called, and chosen for Himself.

The church is a laughing stock in the eyes of the world and principalities and powers. She is full of doctrines of demons, man's wisdom and manmade programmes that have brought a certain kind of growth and success but she lacks real power and purpose, as well as the glory of God. Dogged by spiritual impotence, moral failures, hypocrisy and division within the local church and the wider church, she is not making the kind of progress we see in the life and ministry of Jesus or the early church. Something is missing! She has lost her way! She has lost the truth and she is not experiencing abundant spiritual life! Please bear with me as I know how this sounds. I'm speaking in a general way and not of every church. There are some churches doing better than others. Please read on and allow me to share the revelation of who the church is and what God is seeking to do in this season.

The church is about to undergo a radical transformation that will see her become a glorious church, without spot and blemish and rise to become a temple and habitation for God in the Spirit. Jesus promised that he would build His church and that the gates of hell would not prevail against it. We are in that time right now. The church is being lifted up from ground based, humanistic ways and ideas, and from man's wisdom and demonic wisdom and into living and walking in the Spirit. The Lord is calling her upward, to fulfil the heavenly call of God and to where he has established her, positioned her, authorised her and gifted her to minister.

As the church rises in the Spirit, she is going to come under the glory of God and the inspiration, revelation and power of the Holy Spirit. She is going to manifest the manifold wisdom of God to principalities and powers in the heavenly places and will bring *All* Gods' enemies under the written judgment and the footstool of the Lord. Finally, she is going to gather in the final harvest in the most glorious display of ministry ever seen or witnessed by human eyes. Finally, she will usher in the coming of the Lord for the restoration of all things (Acts 3:21).

Ephesians 5:27; 2:21,22; 3:10; Matthew 16:18; Hebrews 3:1; 10:13; Ephesians 1:10; Colossians 1:20

THE BIG PICTURE:

Developing a Biblical Worldview

When putting a jigsaw puzzle together it helps massively to see the big picture on the box. Without the big picture in view the puzzle is so much more difficult. Once we see the big picture and keep it in view, the individual pieces come together easier and we complete the puzzle. The bible is like a jigsaw puzzle. It's made up of so many different truths, themes, topics, doctrines, teachings, and precepts, that it can be a major task to know where to start and how to piece it together. If we get this wrong, we can go on for many years with various pieces here and there and out of place so that we still have no clear picture before us.

The church has presented so many steps and keys along the way that have helped to a degree but without the big picture in view we can still find ourselves aimless and helpless. We have steps to a better marriage, steps to a better life, keys to more effective ministry and it goes on and on. Of course, none of this is bad; it's just that without the big picture in view we can be missing the point. The church is the most over conferenced, over seminared and over taught institution in the world! She has been juggling all the pieces for decades and is still void of the glory of God!

On top of this, we have a very cunning and deceitful enemy in the devil, who has a highly ordered kingdom that is in constant opposition against the kingdom of God and its aims and objectives. He has been very clever in mixing the pieces of the jigsaw up for the church because he knows if he can keep her confused and unsure of the big picture, she won't know her true design and calling, resulting in a state of continual defeat and frustration or smugness and self-satisfaction.

The devil is a master deceiver. After all, he was able to sway a third of the Lords' angels and gather support for his rebellion in heaven. This means that he is no fool and neither is he a pushover.

From the very beginning we see the devil twisting the word of God and putting his slant on it (Genesis 2:1–5). Did you know, that the devil has written a commentary on the bible? He presents these thoughts, comments, and interpretations to the people of God every day!

Remember his battle with the Lord! When Jesus said, 'It is written!' the devil came back to him with words from his commentary and he even used the written word against Jesus (see Matthew 4: 1–11). Much of what the church believes to-day has come from the devil's commentary and unfortunate-ly, it has robbed the church of her true inheritance and call-ing. Paul spoke of doctrines of demons at work in the church in latter times (1 Timothy 4: 1). I realise that this is a strong statement, but please bear with me and please read on.

After the Lord had given me a vision of the tramps' boots transformed into gold, and told me he was changing my walk, I began seeking the Lord daily. At various times I would withdraw to my bedroom and lay on the bed to pray. My prayer life was being transformed. My prayer life was becom-ing more meditative as I lay on my bed. By the way, this was practiced by King David as we read in the Psalms and Daniel had visions as he lay on his bed! Jesus too, was accustomed to meditative prayer. This explains why he could spend hours and all night in prayer!

As I was seeking the Lord, after I had seen the vision of the golden boots and the Lords' words that he was changing my walk, I was lying on my bed and the Lord gave me this vision. I saw in front of me a stronghold with four open square win-dows in it. Sticking out of the windows were four trumpets. I asked the Lord what it meant and He told me that the first trumpet was the revelation of the Old Testament; the second trumpet was the revelation of the gospels; the third trumpet was the revelation of the New Testament letters and the fourth trumpet was the revelation of Revelation.

He went on to say that the revelation of the trumpets had been stolen by four demons who had obviously created false doctrines with them: the first one was Deception; the second one was Disbelief; the third one was Doubt and the fourth demon was Fear. I asked the Lord what could be done about it and He told me to approach the wall, rebuke the demons and call for angels to recover the trumpets and bring them back to Zion where they should be sprinkled with His blood and presented to the Father.

I immediately obeyed and did as the Lord directed me. Then the Lord said to me that he was going to release the revelation of the four trumpets into my life and ministry. From that moment my eyes were opened and the Lord began to take me on a journey that has instilled within me a biblical worldview that has changed the way I think, pray, study, teach and minister. As I've grown in this worldview, I have a clearer picture of what it is the Lord has called His church to be and do.

I began writing down the visions and words the Lord was giving to me so I wouldn't forget. My prayer times were becoming more and more powerful and I was growing in life in the Spirit. I began asking the Lord to teach me more and more about the spiritual realm. I asked Him to open my eyes and ears in greater ways so that I could learn from Him and He didn't disappoint me.

The prophecy of 1993 was now coming to pass in my life. The Lord had stabilised me and He was causing me to walk in the Spirit and now, He was giving me fresh revelation and vision. All I can say is that the more I sought the Lord, the more revelation I would receive. I always approached the Lord through the cross and the divine exchange, exercising my faith in the word of God. As I did, I would rise in the Spirit and meet with the Lord and receive revelation.

The church has been playing around with the jigsaw pieces for too long, with a piece here and a piece there that the puzzle is no clearer than when we started. Both discipleship and the work of the ministry have suffered because of this. You see, it's the big picture that helps us to see what we are aiming at with evangelism, discipleship and ministry. What is the ultimate aim of discipleship? It is Christlikeness! And Christlikeness is not simply displaying a few godly traits; more love, kindness, etc. But true Christlikeness is thinking like Christ, talking like Christ, behaving like Christ, praying like Christ and ministering like Christ and with Christ!

It's time for the big picture to emerge, to really see it in its completeness. Only then when the big picture is clearly set forth can the church rise to her true calling. Only then can she attain to the full knowledge of the Son of God and attain to the full measure of the stature and fullness of Christ (Ephesians 4:11).

The church must get back to Jesus, His finished work and His present and continuing work! She must put her eyes on Jesus! He is the way, the truth and the life! But we must come to the full knowledge of Him! Somehow the way has been obscured and certain truths have been lost so that we aren't experiencing the life of Christ fully. No wonder the church is powerless; she has lost the revelation of the way, the truth and the life of Christ. She is disconnected from her head and dislocated from His heavenly ministry!

The good news is that as we look unto Jesus, and come to the full knowledge of who He is and what He is presently doing, the haze clears and the big picture emerges and becomes so clear that all the pieces of the jigsaw come together in Him. It is my prayer and desire that as you read, your spirit will rise up, your spiritual senses be quickened and that you will receive revelation of the Way, the Truth and the Life!

CHAPTER 1

The Way Defined

The City of God

Let's take a look at the big picture! If we don't see it, we won't seek it. We must understand how the kingdom works so that we can make sense of it and begin to seek it first in our lives and experience it in full. We'll start by putting some pieces together.

Unless God pulls back the curtains and reveals the spiritual realm we are in the dark.

The good news is that He has – He has revealed it in His Word.

The kingdom of God is vast; it incorporates the kingdom of heaven. It also incorporates worlds.

> *"For by Him all things were created that are in heaven and that are on earth, visible and invisible, whether thrones or dominions or principalities or powers. All things were created through Him and for Him."* Colossians 1:16

"God has in these last days spoken to us by His Son, whom He has appointed heir of all things, through whom also He made the worlds." Hebrews 1:2

"By faith we understand that the worlds were framed by the word of God, so that the things which are seen were not made of things which are visible." Hebrews 11:3

The bible reveals that God created the world and all that is in it. In the beginning, heaven and earth were joined together. God brought His heavenly city, Jerusalem, out of heaven and joined it with earth. God's plan was that heaven and earth work together to produce heavenly conditions on the earth (Matthew 6:10).

God made man in His own likeness and image and made him ruler over all the earth (Genesis 1:26-28). Man was God's agent and governor who would establish the government of God in the earth. It was God's plan and intention that mankind had access to God and His holy city, to worship Him, fellowship with Him, seek His knowledge, understanding and wisdom, and access every spiritual source and blessing so that they would establish heavenly government and produce heavenly conditions on earth.

So, in order to produce heaven on earth, mankind had to access God's heavenly city and tap into every resource available. When Adam and Eve sinned against God and heaven, God removed His holy City and it returned to heaven. The end of the bible shows us the Holy City, heavenly Jerusalem coming out of heaven and returning to be joined with the earth. In the end God renews heaven and earth and heavenly Jerusalem is joined once again with earth (Revelation 21).

As we get into our study, we will see how the city was removed and lost to mankind and how God would restore access to it so that we could fellowship with God and activate every spiritual blessing of God's heavenly kingdom in our lives. Let's take a look at God's holy city and learn about it. Although we cannot access it physically, we can access it spiritually and access and activate every spiritual source and blessing.

The Patriarch Abraham saw it, sought it and desired it. **You cannot seek and desire what you don't see!** So, it's obvious that God gave the patriarchs a vision of heaven and the city of God. They saw it as a heavenly country, and a city with foundations whose builder and maker is God.

> *"By faith (Abraham) dwelt in the land of promise as in a foreign country, dwelling in tents with Isaac and Jacob, the heirs with him of the same promise; for he waited for the city which has foundations, whose builder and maker is God."* Hebrews 11:9-10

Moses forsook the treasures of Egypt because he saw Him who is invisible. Wow! Moses saw the invisible. How do you see the invisible? Through spiritual senses and faith! Moses saw the riches of Christ and His kingdom and so forsook the treasures of Egypt and pursued the call of God.

"But now they desire a better, that is, a heavenly country. Therefore, God is not ashamed to be called their God, for He has prepared a city for them." Hebrews 11:16

> *"By faith Moses, when he became of age, refused to be called the son of Pharaoh's daughter, choosing rather to suffer affliction with the people of God than to enjoy the passing pleasures of sin, esteeming the reproach of Christ greater riches than the treasures in Egypt; for he looked to the reward. By faith he forsook Egypt, not fearing the wrath of the king; for he endured as seeing Him who is invisible."* Hebrews 11:24-28

God showed them heaven, and the city of God, Zion, the heavenly Jerusalem above. They saw it and so with all their heart desired and sought it. **You cannot seek what you cannot see!** Remember the parable of the hidden treasure (Matthew 13:44); the treasure was in the field all the time. But it was hidden from sight. It was only through digging that it came to light! However, you need revelation on *where* to dig. Revelation comes from God in the spirit by the Spirit!

When it comes to heaven most believers have a vague idea of it but it's very hazy and wishy washy. It's a place we go to *when we die*. It's spiritual and we can't fully experience it right now. Some think it will be some kind of Casper the ghost experience floating around in the spiritual realm and others think it's going to be an eternal church service of praise and worship! The reason believers aren't more excited about heaven is that they haven't seen it nor have they understood it!

God wants to confer upon us His kingdom. It's His good pleasure to give us the kingdom (Luke 12:32). However, because of ignorance and a lack of understanding the church has conferred upon us a religious way, truth and life. This leads to all kinds of problems and issues.

When you see heaven and the city of God and how it works, you'll desire it and seek it!

The bible encourages us to set our mind on things above and not on the things on the earth.

> *"If then you were raised with Christ, seek those things which are above, where Christ is, sitting at the right hand of God. Set your mind on things above, not on things on the earth."* Colossians 3:1-2

It tells us to look at the things that are unseen and eternal.

> *"While we do not look at the things which are seen, but at the things which are not seen. For the things which are seen are temporary, but the things which are not seen are eternal."* 2 Corinthians 4:18

Clearly, we are told to seek the 'things' above and the 'eternal' things. So, we must ask, 'What are *these* things?' Also, the bible speaks about heavenly 'places' plural, meaning there's more than just heaven! As I began to seek God about the things above the Lord directed me to His word. Remember, you cannot seek what you cannot see!

Zion

"But you have come to Mount Zion and to the city of the living God, the heavenly Jerusalem." Hebrews 12:22

Heaven is a country and its capital city is Zion, heavenly Jerusalem. This is clearly laid out in the bible for us. Zion is known as the Father's house. Jesus said, 'In My Father's house are many mansions' or rooms/dwellings helps us better understand (John 14:2). A house has rooms! And rooms have different functions. There is the throne room, the records room that contains the book of life and books, a dining room where we will sit and eat at the marriage supper of the Lamb. Jesus told the disciples that they would eat and drink at His table in His kingdom (Luke 22:30). It stands to reason that there must be a room like a kitchen for food preparation. I would imagine there would be a design and editing room, as God loves to create and design things. There's probably a room of science too, for God is the Father of science. I'm convinced there's a healing room where we can learn about healing and how to minister it. My wife, Christine in a vision saw a meeting room, where loved ones were being greeted as they arrived in heaven. She saw young children who had died at birth ready to meet parents who had lost those children. The room was filled with tears of joy! There must be rooms/ stables for animals as Jesus rides a white horse (Revelation 19:11). We could go on. One thing is clear: there are *many* rooms in the Father's house!

A country has many cities not just one! Is this what Jesus meant when rewarding his servants; 'Have authority over ten cities!' (Luke 19:17). Citizens and people make up a city and a kingdom, and heaven has no shortage of citizens. Angels as well as the saints make up the population of heaven. In heaven, there are rivers, streets, trees, mountains, hills, ('who will ascend Your holy hill', David asked in Psalm 15:1).

There are also gardens, parks, grass, flowers, animals, birds, fish and in fact, everything that we are accustomed to on earth! I believe that earth was created based upon the heavenly pattern. This is why Jesus taught us to pray; 'On earth as it is in heaven' (Matt 6:10). What I'm trying to do here is broaden your understanding of heaven. If you haven't read, Randy Alcorn's book on Heaven, it will truly enlighten you, plus he does a far better job at it than me.

However, what *I'm* going to reveal is how the kingdom of God and heaven works! As I sought the Lord, I came to a fuller understanding about heaven and Zion, the city of God, and the Lord began to show me how the kingdom works. Let's add a few more pieces to the picture.

Heaven and in particular Zion, is where God dwells. Zion is where the Lord has established His throne, His name and His salvation. God reigns from Zion. This is where His government is established. It is where He is worshipped, served, obeyed and His Word and will goes forth from. Zion is where the glory of God is. It is the place of every spiritual blessing.

All revelation, inspiration and power come from Zion. Zion is also where the Lord Jesus has been established in His *present and continuing ministry.* In 1 Peter 2:6 we read, '*Behold, I lay in Zion A chief cornerstone, elect, precious, And he who believes on Him will by no means be put to shame.*' Zion is the control centre of everything that God has created. All of it under the banner of the Kingdom of God and of Heaven!

Most of what we know about heaven and Zion came from King David who also received revelation about Zion, the heavenly city, and spoke so much about Zion. In fact, all of David's prophetic writings came to Him from His time worshiping in the Spirit, in Zion! The apostle John also gives profound information about Zion, the city of God and of its sanctuary in the book of Revelation.

Let's put some more pieces together.

The Revelation of Revelation

"Blessed is he who reads and those who hear the words of this prophecy, and keep those things which are written in it; for the time is near." Revelation 1:3

The book of Revelation is an important book in the NT. Unfortunately, like so much more of the NT the devil has hijacked its truth and revelation and added his own comments and emphasis. Instead of being blessed by what we read, many believers are afraid of the book and so neglect it and push it aside. You see the devil wants us to see the beast, and the antichrist and the tribulation and wars etc. But the book reveals how God destroys the devil's kingdom. He does it from the throne and the altar! When you see this, it will change your walk of faith and bring you into a fuller truth and a greater desire and confidence to live and walk in the Spirit.

The Gates

"The Lord loves the gates of Zion More than all the dwellings of Jacob. Glorious things are spoken of you, O city of God!" Psalm 87:2-3

A city has gates, and Zion has no shortage of gates; three on the North, three on the South, three on the East and three on the West. The Lord loves the gates of Zion more than all the dwellings of Jacob. The dwellings of Jacob are the private dwellings of all of Israel in the Promised Land. **The blessing of our dwelling is because of Zion.** Thank God for our dwellings and the source of blessings that are found there; love, joy, peace, rest, food, fellowship and so on. But the gates of Zion give entrance to our Father and All of our spiritual sources (Vs 7).

Now, the reason the Lord loves the gates of Zion more is that heavens' gates do three things. Firstly, they give us access into the Father's house, the Father's presence and every spiritual blessing. Secondly, they protect every resource inside the city, Thirdly, they allow every spiritual blessing to go fourth out of those holy gates and touch our earthly lives.

> *"Blessed be the God and Father of our Lord Jesus Christ, who has blessed us with every spiritual blessing in the heavenly places in Christ."* Ephesians 1:3

Every spiritual blessing is to be found in the heavenly places In Christ! God wants us to access every spiritual blessing so that we can establish heaven on earth. We have access through Christ's blood and God's Spirit into Zions' gates as all our sources are there.

> *"All my springs (sources) are in you."* Psalm 87:7

The sources of all our blessings are in Zion, heaven and we draw from them through faith

> *"Therefore, with joy you will draw water from the wells of salvation."* Isaiah 12:3.

> *"Every good gift and every perfect gift is from above, and comes down from the Father of lights, with whom there is no variation or shadow of turning. Of His own will He brought us forth by the word of truth, that we might be a kind of first-fruits of His creatures."* James 1:17–18

We were born in Zion

> *"The Lord will record, When He registers the peoples: "This one was born there."* Psalm 87:6

We were designed and created by God in Zion and we were put on record and registered before being planted and formed in our mother's womb. You see God is the Father of spirits (Hebrews 12:9).

> *"...but the Jerusalem above is free, which is the mother of us all."* Galatians 4:26

Every human being is a gift from heaven and has access to heaven before returning when physical life ends. **We are born with dual capability**. With our spiritual senses we have access to Zion, heaven, to worship the Father and experience spiritual life and blessing. So with our five natural senses of sight, sound, touch, taste and smell we experience the physical world around us.

Adam and Eve lived abundant life in that they had access to both the spiritual realm and the natural realm. They had access to Zion to worship and fellowship with the Father and hear his voice bringing them heavenly knowledge, understanding, wisdom and counsel. All they had to do was be obedient to the Father's direction and earth would reflect heaven's righteousness, peace and joy.

The Throne (*Revelation 4*)

Zion is where God's throne is. The throne of God is majestic and glorious.

> *"Righteousness and justice are the foundation of Your throne; Mercy and truth go before Your face."* Psalm 89:14

Every case and situation we experience can be taken to the throne of grace, where we can appeal to the Father's righteousness and mercy and receive justice according to His truth. The apostle John in Revelation four writes down what he saw. The throne is encompassed with an emerald rainbow which points to the New Covenant of life (Vs 2, 3). God is a covenant keeping God. In the New Covenant, God has made provision for all to come to Him personally, so that he puts His Laws/Word in our mind and our heart. This is where you 'hear' the voice of God, in the spirit of your mind.

The New Covenant has allowed God to be merciful to our unrighteousness, forget our sins and iniquities, be our God and we His people, that all would know Him from the least to the greatest, and to hear the voice of God so that we can bring heaven to earth (Hebrews 8). A bright and glorious display of light and colour is emitting from God's throne as well as lightnings, thundering's and voices (Vs 3-5).

Around God's throne are twenty-four thrones with twenty-four elders clothed in white with crowns of gold on their heads. Before the throne, are four living creatures crying out *'Holy, holy, holy. Lord God Almighty, who was and is and is to come!'* Seven lamps of fire burn before the throne of God, which are the seven Spirits of God (Rev 4:8). Isaiah gives insight into the seven Spirits of God.

> *"The Spirit of the Lord shall rest upon Him, The Spirit of wisdom and understanding, The Spirit of counsel and might, The Spirit of knowledge and of the fear of the Lord."* Isaiah 11:1

In Revelation 5:6, John then sees in the midst of the throne the four living creatures and the elders, a lamb. The lamb is the Lord Jesus. Jesus is positioned at the throne and as we have seen so is the Holy Spirit, the Spirit of the Lord. The river of life proceeds from the throne which speaks of spiritual life and power in the Spirit (Revelation 22:1).

God's throne is described as a throne of everlasting, of glory, of power, of authority, of justice, of judgement, of grace and mercy, of agreement and of blessing. Salvation through Jesus Christ has restored us to the enthroned Life. Every believer in Christ has been called, justified and glorified (Romans 8:30).

> *"But God, who is rich in mercy, because of His great love with which He loved us, even when we were dead in trespasses, made us alive together with Christ (by grace you have been saved), and raised us up together, and made us sit together in the heavenly places in Christ Jesus."* Ephesians 2:4-6

Salvation allows God to fulfil His desire and restore us to the enthroned life.

> *"He raises the poor from the dust and lifts the beggar from the ash heap, To set them among princes*
>
> *And make them inherit the throne of glory."* 1 Samuel 2:8

Although Throne Life is the right of every believer, only those who rise to be overcomers of the world, the flesh and the devil share the privileges and responsibilities of Throne Life (Revelation 3:21).

> *"Let us therefore come boldly to the throne of grace, that we may obtain mercy and find grace to help in time of need."*
> Hebrews 4:16

The throne of God is where we come under the inspiration, revelation and power of the Holy Spirit.

The Holy Spirit reveals the deep things of God and the mind of Christ. He communicates and teaches these to us freely (1 Corinthians 2:9-16).

Angels

Next, we see innumerable angels around the throne.

> *"Then I looked, and I heard the voice of many angels around the throne, the living creatures, and the elders; and the number of them was ten thousand times ten thousand, and thousands of thousands."* Revelation 5:11

God is the Lord of Hosts. He has at His disposal innumerable angels who surround His throne with worship and serve Him and who stand ready to heed and perform the word of God.

> *"Bless the Lord, you His angels, who excel in strength, who do His word, Heeding the voice of His word. Bless the Lord, all you His hosts, you ministers of His, who do His pleasure."* Psalm 103:20–21

Angels respond to the word of God when it is agreed and spoken by faith. The Ark of the Covenant has two Cherubim with wings outstretched and touching in agreement built in to the Mercy seat. Inside the Ark was the 10 commandments (the word), a potful of manna or heavenly bread (the word), and Aarons rod that budded. It all points to the word of God. You see when we come into agreement with God and the word of God, angelic ministry is released to perform God's will. Hallelujah!

Two thirds of the angels remained faithful to God and His kingdom! The devil has only one third (Revelation 12:4). All Angels are ministers and aside from ministering to the Lord, they minister to us the heirs of salvation (Hebrews 1:14). In prayer, the Lord told me that they were created with us in mind. He went on to say that the reason there is joy in the presence of the angels of God over one sinner that repents, is that they then have opportunity to minister to another heir (Luke 15:10). Praise God! Angelic ministry is coming back to the forefront of the ministry of the church!

Angels minister in different ways. Some wage war, others bring messages and direction. Others bring about deliverance and others protect. There are also angels that are associated with healing, like the angel who came to stir the water at Bethesda, where the first one in was healed of whatever disease he had (John 5:3,4). We also know that angels are involved in presenting prayers and bringing the answers to our prayers to us from the Lord (Read Daniel 10).

Angelic ministry is seen clearly throughout the bible in both Old and New Testaments.

Angels ministered with and to Jesus. He said at the cross he could have asked the Father for more than twelve legions of angels to help Him (Matthew 26:53). Jesus clearly had the ministry and helps of angels.

The apostles and early church welcomed the ministry of angels and they are seen many times at their work. In Acts 5, when the apostles were arrested, it was an angel who opened the prison doors and released them. An angel of the Lord spoke to Philip and directed him to witness to an Ethiopian in the desert (Acts 8:26). An angel of the Lord came to Cornelius and was divinely instructed for him and his family to hear and believe the gospel (Acts10).

In Acts 12:7-8 Peter was delivered from prison by an angel. King Herod was struck down to death by an angel who executed the Lord's judgment on him for being proud and arrogant and not giving glory to God (12:23)! Paul was divinely encouraged and directed by an angel during his shipwreck experience (Acts 27:23). The apostle John had an angel speak to him many things concerning the kingdom of God and God's judgment and when he fell down to worship him, he was corrected and directed to worship the Lord (Revelation 19:10).

We don't worship angels but we do work with angels!

The Golden Altar

In the book of Revelation Chapter 8:3-5 we are introduced to the Golden Altar. It is described as before the throne of God. Laying aside the prophetic side to this passage we want to discover the underlying, eternal principle of what happens at the golden altar. As we do, this should encourage us to come humbly, but boldly, with faith and expectancy with our prayers because of what they achieve.

Notice that the prayers of the saints are mingled with much incense and then presented on the golden altar. As the smoke of the incense and the prayers of the saints ascend before God. It causes a stirring of angelic ministry. The angel took the censor fills it with fire from the altar and hurls it to the earth.

This is showing us how prayers are received and answered in heaven. When we speak the word of God at this golden altar it is received before God, who in agreement with His will presented, commands angels to carry out his word, his will and his purpose.

In Revelation 9:13, we see another glimpse of the power of the golden altar. A voice is heard speaking at the golden altar and in response four angels are released! Wow! This is why believers and churches must pray. They must rise in the spirit and pursue their heavenly calling because this is where the kingdom of God is experienced and manifested.

The book of Revelation shows us clearly the dynamic and powerful ministry of angels performing the word of God and accomplishing his will. The word of God says that we believers will judge angels (1 Corinthians 6:3). As we'll see later, Jesus is the High Priest of our confession Hebrews 3:1–2 (and He is the word of God), and what's agreed at the throne and the altar is sent forth to accomplish the Father's will and purpose.

One last thing to mention here. In Revelation 4:5, it says, *"And from the throne proceeded lightnings, thundering's, and voices."* The voices mentioned here include the voices of the saints speaking forth the word of God. When God's word is presented in faith, agreed upon and confessed before Heaven's High Priest, angels are sent forth like lightnings and thundering's to perform God's word.

Look what we *have* come to and not are *coming* to!

> *"But you have come to Mount Zion and to the city of the living God, the heavenly Jerusalem, to an innumerable company of angels, to the general assembly and church of the firstborn who are registered in heaven, to God the Judge of all, to the spirits of just men made perfect, to Jesus the Mediator of the new covenant, and to the blood of sprinkling that speaks better things than that of Abel."* Hebrews 12:22–24

For the moment we want to look at Mount Zion, the city of God, the heavenly Jerusalem, and in particular the throne and the golden altar. We'll be looking at the church of the firstborn, Jesus the Mediator of the new covenant and blood of sprinkling later on.

We want to establish how God gets His will and purposes done. The throne of God and the Golden Altar are where the Word of God is agreed upon and spoken forth for the Spirit of God, the angelic hosts and the saints to perform and accomplish the Father's perfect will. Once it is agreed and released it will not return void but shall surely come to pass. It's all about the Word of God. Everything owes its existence to the Word of God and everything is upheld by the Word of God.

The worlds were designed and framed by the Word of God. In Genesis we are told that in the beginning God created the heavens and the earth. It goes on to reveal how God did it. He spoke the Word, 'Let there be light, day, night, water, land, seas, grass, trees, stars, Sun, Moon, birds, fish, cattle, creepy crawlies, and beasts!' The Word of God is living and powerful (Hebrews 4:12). The creation of man also was by the Word of God.

Then God said, "Let Us make man in Our image, according to Our likeness; let them have dominion over the fish of the sea, over the birds of the air, and over the cattle, over all the earth and over every creeping thing that creeps on the earth." Genesis 1:26

The apostle John states,

> *"In the beginning was the Word, and the Word was with God, and the Word was God. He was in the beginning with God. All things were made through Him, and without Him nothing was made that was made. In Him was life, and the life was the light of men. And the light shines in the darkness, and the darkness did not comprehend it." John 1:1-5*

We know that Jesus is the Word. The Word created everything! All of creation and life exists and is upheld by the Word of God. God's Word is settled in the 'heavens' and when it is believed on and confessed and spoken it accomplishes the Father's will. The Word of God has creative power, sanctifying power, destructive power, binding power, releasing power, healing power and upholding power. **The power of the Word to accomplish the Father's will is in** *agreement.*

> *"For there are three that bear witness in heaven: the Father, the Word, and the Holy Spirit; and these three are one. And there are three that bear witness on earth: the Spirit, the water, and the blood; and these three agree as one." 1 John 5:7-8*

The Word of God is the ultimate power and authority, and when it is believed, agreed and confessed it accomplishes the Father's will and purpose. But how does it get done? Let's see.

In prayer one day as I lay on my bed, I was talking to the Lord about hearing His voice. I was really excited and felt that I was on to something. I told the Lord, 'I know what you're up to! You're teaching me to hear your voice so that I'll recognise it and obey it when I'm prompted.' I went on, 'Oh Lord I need to hear and know your voice.' As clear as day, the Lord told me, 'Dennis, read Psalm 29 and I'm going to show you some things!' I quickly turned to Psalm 29 for a jaw dropping experience with the Lord. Verse 3 is when my jaw dropped open!

1 Give unto the Lord, O you mighty ones, Give unto the Lord glory and strength.

2 Give unto the Lord the glory due to His name; Worship the Lord in the beauty of holiness.

3 The voice of the Lord is over the waters; The God of glory thunders; The Lord is over many waters.

4 The voice of the Lord is powerful; The voice of the Lord is full of majesty. 5 The voice of the Lord breaks the cedars, Yes, the Lord splinters the cedars of Lebanon. 6 He makes them also skip like a calf, Lebanon and Sirion like a young wild ox. 7 The voice of the Lord divides the flames of fire.

8 The voice of the Lord shakes the wilderness; The Lord shakes the Wilderness of Kadesh.

9 The voice of the Lord makes the deer give birth, and strips the forests bare; And in His temple everyone says, "Glory!"

10 The Lord sat enthroned at the Flood, And the Lord sits as King forever.

11 The Lord will give strength to His people; The Lord will bless His people with peace. Psalm 29

I was amazed at how powerful the voice of the Lord is and all that it does. It is over everything, it breaks, it divides, it shakes, it gives birth, and it strips! I thanked the Lord and worshipped Him for responding to me so quickly. And then, the Lord told me to read verse 10 again. 'The Lord sat enthroned at the Flood, And the Lord sits as King forever.' The Lord asked me 'What Flood?' I said, 'Well I'm thinking right now of the great flood of Noah.' The Lord told me to read

Genesis 6. So off I went to Genesis 6 and began to read it. I discovered that everything that happened was commanded by God; the building of the ark, the saving of Noah's family, the saving of the animals, the birds and creeping things and that Noah did according to all that God commanded him (Genesis 6:13-22).

I looked again at verse 10, the Lord '*sat enthroned*' at the Flood. I saw it! The Lord sat enthroned and commanded. The Lord reminded me that he sat enthroned at creation and commanded and it was done. Then the Lord said to me, '*Dennis, you are seated with Christ in heavenly places. I'm going to teach you the voice of command!*' I said to the Lord, 'I see it but how did the commanded word get done?' The Lord told me to read verses 1 and 2. He told me that the 'Mighty Ones' are his angels and that when He commands, angels perform His word.

> "*Bless the Lord, you His angels, who excel in strength, who do His word, Heeding the voice of His word. Bless the Lord, all you His hosts, you ministers of His, who do His pleasure.*" Psalm 103:20-21

Wow! What a revelation. We are enthroned with Christ to give the voice of command and release angelic ministry to release kingdom authority and power and accomplish the Father's will. In that moment the voice of command was rolling off my lips with great authority as I commanded victories for the kingdom of God.

You see angels are constantly tuned in to heed the Word of God. They are eager and keen to perform His Word. Here's how it works. When a believer stands in faith, and in agreement with the word of God, believing and confessing and giving voice to the Word, angels heed, hearken and perform the Word of God accomplishing the Father's will.

Where does this happen? At the throne and the golden altar of the heavenly sanctuary. Our prayers are received as incense and ascend before the Father who stirred by faith, confidence and obedience, commands His angels to perform the Word in the spirit! Take note! It is us the people of God who come into agreement with what God tells us and perform it in obedience on earth.

The altar is all about agreement! When we come into alignment and agreement with the Word of God, kingdom inspiration, revelation, power and authority will be released.

Now that we have established how the kingdom operates let's take a look at the *Way defiled* and the rebellion in heaven.

CHAPTER 2

The Way Defiled

The Fall of Lucifer

And He said to them, "I saw Satan fall like lightning from heaven." Luke 10:18

Before his fall Satan was named Lucifer, meaning 'Bright morning star' or 'Light bearer'.

The books of Isaiah and Ezekiel share insight about Satan. Many bible teachers and commentators believe these passages have a dual meaning and are speaking about Satan.

"You were the seal of perfection, Full of wisdom and perfect in beauty. You were in Eden, the garden of God; Every precious stone was your covering. The workmanship of your timbrels and pipes Was prepared for you on the day you were created." Ezekiel 28:12-13

Lucifer was perfect in beauty and full of wisdom. He was in Eden, the garden of God, meaning he had access and was involved with all that God was pioneering. He was created with a talent musically and it is believed that he was director of worship around God's throne and altar.

It is believed that he was an archangel of the highest order and he was an attendant to the throne and the altar in heaven.

> "You were the anointed cherub who covers; I established you; You were on the holy mountain of God;

> You walked back and forth in the midst of fiery stones. You were perfect in your ways from the day you were created, till iniquity was found in you." Ezekiel 28:14-15

Lucifer was anointed by the Spirit of God in his heavenly calling. He was on Mount Zion and had first-hand information and experience of the workings of God's throne and golden altar. He was perfect in his ways until iniquity was found in him. Iniquity means 'crookedness and perversion.' He lost his way!

> "By the abundance of your trading You became filled with violence within, and you sinned; Therefore, I cast you as a profane thing Out of the mountain of God; And I destroyed you, O covering cherub, From the midst of the fiery stones." Ezekiel 28:16

Lucifer was cast out of the mountain of God, Zion because he sinned. Sin defiled him and controlled him. Therefore, he was removed from his heavenly calling and no longer had access to the throne of God and the golden altar.

> "Your heart was lifted up because of your beauty; You corrupted your wisdom for the sake of your splendour; I cast you to the ground, I laid you before kings, that they might gaze at you." Ezekiel 28:17

Lucifer became proud because of his beauty and ministry and so corrupted his wisdom. In his heart and mind, he thought himself to be wiser than God his creator and Lord. Therefore, God cast him down to the ground.

> "You defiled your sanctuaries by the multitude of your iniquities, By the iniquity of your trading;

Therefore, I brought fire from your midst; It devoured you, And I turned you to ashes upon the earth

In the sight of all who saw you. All who knew you among the peoples are astonished at you;

You have become a horror, and shall be no more forever."
Ezekiel 28:18-19

Lucifer defiled his way and defiled his sanctuaries by the multitude of his iniquities. He went from bad to worse quickly. He became a horror among the peoples and his doom is to be no more when he is cast into the Lake of Fire (Revelation 20:10).

Lucifer defiled the way!

Isaiah also gives insights into the fall of Lucifer.

"How you are fallen from heaven, O Lucifer, son of the morning! How you are cut down to the ground, you who weakened the nations! For you have said in your heart: 'I will ascend into heaven, I will exalt my throne above the stars of God; I will also sit on the mount of the congregation on the farthest sides of the north; I will ascend above the heights of the clouds, I will be like the Most High.' Yet you shall be brought down to Sheol, To the lowest depths of the Pit." Isaiah 14:12-15

Lucifer set and asserted his own will above God's will. He became proud and haughty in his heart and was determined to exalt *his* throne above all other thrones and be like the Most High! He became self-absorbed and filled with self-importance and this led to his downfall.

"Those who see you will gaze at you, and consider you, saying: 'Is this the man who made the earth tremble, who shook kingdoms, Who made the world as a wilderness and destroyed its cities, Who did not open the house of his prisoners?" Isaiah 14:16-17

One day we'll see and gaze upon the fallen Lucifer and Satan and declare, 'Is this him?' 'Is this the one who shook kingdoms and destroyed cities and held prisoners captive?'

Notice that Satan is a defiler of the Way – he defiles kingdoms and cities because they control peoples.

Lucifer fell from heaven. Jesus said that he witnessed and saw Satan fall like lightning, meaning his judgment and casting out were quick like the flash of lightning. His ambition was to ascend into heaven; exalt his throne above God's; sit on the holy mount, Zion; and ascend and take over the position of the Most High! What pride. What treachery. What arrogance and what deception. To think that he could be the Most High above the Lord Himself! And so, he fell!

Someone has rightly said the way to up is down and the way to down is up! The Word of God says it this way:

> *"And whoever exalts himself will be humbled, and he who humbles himself will be exalted."* Matthew 23:12

> *Likewise, you younger people, submit yourselves to your elders. Yes, all of you be submissive to one another, and be clothed with humility, for "God resists the proud, but gives grace to the humble." Therefore, humble yourselves under the mighty hand of God, that He may exalt you in due time.* 1 Peter 5:5–7

The fall of Satan didn't just leave him alone, defeated and deflated. No, his persuasive power led to deceiving a third of heavens angels and bringing about their fall as well (Revelation 12:4).

We must understand what happened next, because it puts the pieces of so many Scriptures, doctrines and teachings together and gives insight into the big picture. When we see and understand what Satan has done, we'll understand both the finished work of Christ and the present and continuing work of Christ as heaven's High Priest and mediator of the New Covenant.

A Rival Kingdom and City

> *"Every kingdom divided against itself is brought to desolation, and every city or house divided against itself will not stand. If*

Satan casts out Satan, he is divided against himself. How then will his kingdom stand?" Matthew 12:25-26

Finding himself fallen and cast out of heaven and Zion, Satan set up his own rival kingdom and city against heaven and Zion, the city of God. It is a kingdom in direct opposition to God's kingdom. It is a kingdom of darkness, sin, rebellion and evil. Whereas God's kingdom is a kingdom of light, righteousness, peace and joy. Remember, Satan has first-hand experience of Zion, its throne and altar and so he has set up his own rival city along with its own throne and altar.

Babylon

Satan's city is Babylon. It is a spiritual city that rivals Zion. There are all kinds of conjecture about Babylon being Rome or America or Iran but Babylon is not a worldly city it is a spiritual city that Satan has set up in order to rule the world. From this evil city the nation and cities of the world are ruled and brought under Satan's wicked and evil influences.

> *"And another angel followed, saying, "Babylon is fallen, is fallen, that great city, because she has made all nations drink of the wine of the wrath of her fornication."* Revelation 14:8

> *MYSTERY, BABYLON THE GREAT, THE MOTHER OF HARLOTS AND OF THE ABOMINATIONS OF THE EARTH.* Revelation 17:5

> *"Babylon the great is fallen, is fallen, and has become a dwelling place of demons, a prison for every foul spirit, and a cage for every unclean and hated bird! For all the nations have drunk of the wine of the wrath of her fornication, the kings of the earth have committed fornication with her, and the merchants of the earth have become rich through the abundance of her luxury."* Revelation 18:2-3

This evil city is responsible for the wickedness and evil played out through the nations and cities of the world. Satan has set up his own throne (Revelation 2:13). He is enthroned in Babylon. This is where he rules and reigns as god of this world. A throne is of no use without an altar! Satan has his rival altar of agreement. From the throne and the altar his evil schemes, programmes, strategies and will is agreed upon and released through his spiritual hosts of wickedness.

High Places and Altars

As I was seeking the Lord for further insight into the spiritual realm, high places and altars were on my mind for a few days. I didn't know why but I had these two things on my mind – high places and altars. As I went into prayer this particular morning the Lord ministered to me. He told me that he was going to teach me about the high places and the altars and told me to read Ephesians 6 and then Isaiah 36. What I read blew my mind but then the Lord said he wanted to teach me about the unholy trinity and how they work Satan's altars.

> *"For we wrestle not against flesh and blood, but against principalities, against powers, against the rulers of the darkness of this world, against spiritual wickedness in high places."* KJV Ephesians 6:12

As I recalled Ephesians 6:12 in my mind – the Lord spoke to me and said, 'The battle is for the high places and the altars.' 'Whoever is established in the high places rules!'

The high places and altars always go together. Next the Lord told me to read Isaiah 36 and that he was going to teach me about the high places and the altars.

> *"Now it came to pass in the fourteenth year of King Hezekiah that Sennacherib king of Assyria came up against all the fortified cities of Judah and took them. Then the king of Assyria sent the Rabshakeh with a great army from Lachish to King Hezekiah at Jerusalem."* NKJV Isaiah 36:1–2

In this account the king of Assyria, Sennacherib has come up against all the fortified cities of Judah and took them. The next city to take is Jerusalem and so he sends his messenger with a great army to King Hezekiah. Next the messenger of the king of Assyria begins to intimidate them with threats so that their confidence and trust in the Lord and Hezekiah is destroyed (Vs 2-6).

> *"But if you say to me, 'We trust in the Lord our God,' is it not He whose high places and whose altars Hezekiah has taken away, and said to Judah and Jerusalem, 'You shall worship before this altar?'"* Isaiah 36:7-8

King Hezekiah had gone through the land with great reform and he had torn down and destroyed all the high places and altars that had been set up for idol worship. He also established the Temple at Jerusalem as the only high place and altar to worship before and seek the Lord. You see, the high place and the altar rules the kingdom, the cities and the peoples! Sennacherib's messenger is undermining Hezekiah before the people and discrediting him for tearing down the high places and the altars. The people had been long established in worshiping at the high places and altars throughout the land and so now this messenger is blaming Hezekiah for the upcoming defeat of Jerusalem.

> *Then the Rabshakeh stood and called out with a loud voice in Hebrew, and said, "Hear the words of the great king, the king of Assyria! Thus says the king: 'Do not let Hezekiah deceive you, for he will not be able to deliver you; nor let Hezekiah make you trust in the Lord, saying, "The Lord will surely deliver us; this city will not be given into the hand of the king of Assyria." Do not listen to Hezekiah.* Isaiah 36:13-16

> *But they held their peace and answered him not a word; for the king's commandment was, "Do not answer him.* Isaiah 36:10

Notice that King Hezekiah had commanded them not to answer a word. In other words, do not come into agreement with what the enemy is saying.

The Lord began to give me revelation of how the enemy's high places and altars work. He told me of the unholy trinity: principalities, powers and rulers of darkness. They are established in the high places in the heavenly places. They come into agreement at their altars with Satan's will and purposes against the Lord, His people and the world. They are looking for someone to come into agreement with them so that they can release spiritual hosts of wickedness who deliver Satan's will and purpose into lives and circumstances. You see just as the Lord has hosts of angels who heed and perform His word, will and purpose, so Satan has spiritual hosts of wickedness (fallen angels) who heed and perform his word, will and purpose. *It's all about agreement in the high places and at the altars.*

I wonder how many times God's people are empowering Satan's altars by coming into agreement with words that kill, steal and destroy. How many times do God's people come into agreement with fear, doubt, and disbelief! Satan is a murderer and a liar (John 8:44-45), he is also a thief and a destroyer (John 10: 10). Nothing can happen in the spiritual realm until there is agreement by someone on earth!

This is why Satan needs the antichrist!

Destroying Altars

As I was meditating and praying the Lord led me to another passage of Scripture in 1 Kings 13.

> *And behold, a man of God went from Judah to Bethel by the word of the Lord, and Jeroboam stood by the altar to burn incense. Then he cried out against the altar by the word of the Lord, and said, "O altar, altar! Thus says the Lord: 'Behold, a child, Josiah by name, shall be born to the house of David; and on you he shall sacrifice the priests of the high places who burn incense on you, and men's bones shall be burned on you." And he gave a sign the same day, saying, "This is the sign which the Lord has spoken: Surely the altar shall split apart, and the ashes on it shall be poured out." NKJV 1 Kings 13:1-3*

Here we find an anonymous man of God, a prophet who had received the word of the Lord to go and prophesy against Jeroboam's false altar. Jeroboam was an ungodly king who had discouraged the people from worshiping at Jerusalem and had set up high places and altars for the people to worship golden calves there. The man of God agreed with the word of the Lord that it should be split apart and destroyed. He simply speaks the word of the Lord against the altar. *'O altar, altar! Surely the altar shall split apart, and the ashes on it shall be poured out."*

> *The altar also was split apart, and the ashes poured out from the altar, according to the sign which the man of God had given by the word of the Lord.* 1 Kings 13:5

I began to prophesy and speak to the altars of Satan in the high places to be split apart and be destroyed. Understand that the Lord has lifted us to Zion and to the ultimate throne of thrones and Altar of altars. Also, when we come into agreement with the word of the Lord and speak it forth from the Golden altar of heaven, the word of God goes forth, carried out by the faithful hosts of God from Zion and it shall not return void!

Stop agreeing with Satan and empowering his altars to work against you; your family, your church and your community. Instead, come into agreement with the altar of heaven and agree with and speak forth the word of the Lord!

The Gates of Hell

Just as Zion has gates so Satan's city, Babylon also has gates. Jesus spoke of this.

> *"I will build My church, and the gates of Hades shall not prevail against it."* Matthew 16:18-19

Gates give entrance and exit. Just as God releases every spiritual blessing out of the gates of Zion, so Satan releases every spiritual curse out of the gates of hell. All wickedness and evil spew forth from Babylon who is the mother of all abominations on the earth (Revelation 17:5).

We have been under Satan's evil city all our lives until Christ delivered and translated us from the powers of darkness and restored us to God's kingdom and Zion. We are now called to renounce and resist the evil flow of Babylon and begin a brand-new flow from Zion of inspiration, revelation and power through its holy gates. The church has received a heavenly call to join the risen Lord Jesus in His present and continuing ministry from Zion, as priests and kings that will activate and release every spiritual blessing out of the gates of Zion and along with the ministry of the Holy Spirit and angels manifest the kingdom of God on earth.

I was in the Spirit one day, when a vision opened up to me. I saw an angel in front of me and beckoning for me to follow him. As I followed, we were on top of a high mountain precipice walking towards a cliff like edge. As I neared and looked down, I saw glimmers of light breaking through what looked like heavy veils as coverings over the ground. When I asked the angel what it was, He told me that they were stolen blessings, answers, destinies that had been hijacked by the devil and dragged down to these deep gorges and then covered with heavy veils as the devil can't stand the light.

When I asked how the devil had hijacked and stolen these things, the angel said that when God's people stand with unresolved issues in their lives, it gives ground for the devil to seize and steal their blessings. I was livid and asked what could be done. The angel told me to call it in. Immediately I called for angels to recover every stolen blessing, return them to Zion to be sprinkled in the blood and sanctified and then presented to the Father on the Sea of Glass. When I did this, the Lord spoke and told me to read Isaiah 45:1-3

> *"Thus says the Lord to His anointed, To Cyrus, whose right hand I have held — To subdue nations before him And loose the armour of kings, To open before him the double doors, So that the gates will not be shut: 'I will go before you And make the crooked places straight; I will break in pieces the gates of bronze And cut the bars of iron. I will give you the treasures of darkness and hidden riches of secret places, that you may know that I, the Lord, who call you by your name, Am the God of Israel.*

Wow, the Lord was leading me in the Spirit to recover the treasures and hidden riches of secret places. I couldn't have done this if the Lord hadn't changed my walk and brought me into spiritual living, walking and ministry in the Spirit.

In another vision whilst deep in prayer, I saw a huge set of gates before me. I had been praying for my city. In front of and guarding the gates was a huge demon. The Lord was with me at my side. As I stood before the gates, the demon got down into my face and began to call me every foul name under the Sun. He told me that I was going to get nothing from him. Again, he was using the foulest of language. I heard the Lord say, 'Let him finish, then rebuke him and seize the gates.' I simply obeyed. I had no fear as I knew that I was firmly established as an overcomer in Christ. I felt powerful and bold and that if God was for me who could be against me. I knew I was growing spiritually and that I was accomplishing more things in the spirit than I had ever done in my previous decades serving the Lord.

CHAPTER 3

The Way Destroyed

The Call and Fall of Man

The word of God clearly shows that heaven and earth are eternally joined and work together.

It was God Most High, Possessor of heaven and earth that blessed Abraham (Genesis 14:19). Heaven is God's throne and the earth is His footstool (Acts 7:49). In the Lord's Prayer we read these words, *'Your kingdom come. Your will be done on earth as it is in heaven.'* (Matthew 6:10). And Jesus said, that *'whatever you bind on earth will be bound in heaven and whatever you loose on earth will be loosed in heaven.'* (Matthew 18:18).

In Revelation 21 we see in the final consummation of all things that heaven and earth are joined forever in God's new order. So, God's will is clear for all to see. Heaven and earth are eternally connected and affect each other. To understand the calling of God on man we must understand that mankind was given earth as a possession to steward and manage and to see that God's kingdom and will would be done on earth.

> *"The heaven, even the heavens, are the Lord's; But the earth He has given to the children of men."* Psalm 115:16

God gave mankind authority and dominion over the earth.

> *Then God said, "Let Us make man in Our image, according to Our likeness; let them have dominion over the fish of the sea, over the birds of the air, and over the cattle, over all the earth and over every creeping thing that creeps on the earth."* Genesis 1:26

But mankind was to manage it with the knowledge, wisdom and understanding and counsel received by the Spirit of the Lord at the throne of God.

Psalm 8 speaks about the glory of God's fingers and hands in creation and how that he has put all things under man. It says,

> *"You have made him to have dominion over the works of Your hands; You have put all things under his feet, All sheep and oxen — Even the beasts of the field, The birds of the air, And the fish of the sea That pass through the paths of the seas."* Psalm 8:6–8

Then it says, *'What is man that you are mindful of him'* (Vs 4). In other words what is man that you would give him so much power and authority?

> *"For You have made him a little lower than the angels, And You have crowned him with glory and honour."* Psalm 8:5

God has crowned man with glory and honour for the purpose of ruling over the works of His hands and bringing heaven to earth. You see, because of man's dual capability, both natural and spiritual senses, Adam had access to the throne and the glory of God. As he came under the inspiration of the Spirit he was endowed with authority and power to bring about God's will.

God's will is heaven on earth and to bring this about man was created with a dual capability. He could access the natural world through his five natural senses; sight, sound, smell, touch and taste, and he could also access the spiritual realm through parallel spiritual senses. It is possible to see, hear, smell, touch and taste in the spiritual realm as we'll see in a later chapter.

Mankind have a huge responsibility to steward and manage the earth and to faithfully execute that responsibility they must be in fellowship with God, and under the inspiration of the Spirit of God. Adam and Eve were created with such a privilege and honour. Through their spirit they could access Zion and the throne of God and tap into the divine knowledge, understanding, and wisdom and then simply walk-in obedience to the word of God.

The big question was 'would mankind walk in obedience to the Father's word and will?' This is why Adam was put on probation and tested in the area of obedience to the word of God. Could he pass the test? Would he remain true to the wisdom of the Father? Or would he fail and flunk the test? Genesis chapters two and three record the test and fall of man.

> *Then the Lord God took the man and put him in the garden of Eden to tend and keep it. And the Lord God commanded the man, saying, "Of every tree of the garden you may freely eat; but of the tree of the knowledge of good and evil you shall not eat, for in the day that you eat of it you shall surely die."*
> Genesis 2:15-17

Adam and Eve were placed in the Garden of Eden and given clear instruction not to eat of the tree of the knowledge of good and evil and were even warned that the day they ate of it they would surely die.

The Tempter to Sin

It was a bad day and a huge mistake the day they began communicating with the devil. Jesus witnessed the fall of Satan like lightning from heaven, and he said of him, *"He was a murderer from the beginning, and does not stand in the truth, because there is no truth in him. When he speaks a lie, he speaks from his own resources, for he is a liar and the father of it."* John 8:44

Once the devil's lies go to work, he has lying spirits that continue to play havoc in the human mind tempting and enticing and persuading them to sin. The devil is a master deceiver and so it didn't take long before he had twisted the truth and deceived Eve's mind to act upon the temptation and disobey the word of God. She was obviously under demonic persuasion and so persuaded her husband to eat too. Adam's decision to sin was wilful and maybe it was seeing that his wife hadn't died, that helped him make the choice to disobey God's word and eat the fruit (Genesis 3:6).

Once they came into agreement with the devil, the power of sin brought about their separation from God and Zion and all of their spiritual sources. Cut off they fell short of the glory of God and became earth bound. The devil became the ruler of this world (John 12:31) and quickly took advantage of his new position. He enslaved mankind and brought them under the rule and influence of his rival city Babylon. He had taken them captive to do his will (2 Timothy 2:26) and now he would use the world and their fallen state and nature to fuel evil across the earth.

What a terrible plight. Cut off from Zion, the Father who loves them and all their spiritual sources and power with which they were to rule the world. Mankind are now enslaved to the world, their sinful flesh and the devil. These three forces would now rule and reign over mankind and be the very things that keep them from their true heavenly inheritance and calling as well as being the sources of evil sinful living. Mankind have no way back to Zion. No way back to the Father by their own merits or efforts. What a quandary. Unless they can overcome the world, the sinful nature and the devil there's no way back. Unless the Father reaches out, they are lost forever. The way and the glory have been lost.

The Power of Sin

In Genesis 3:14-19 the curse of sin entered the world. Not only has mankind come under the curse of sin but the creation itself has been cursed by sin too. Paul tells us in the book of Romans chapter 8 that creation is waiting for the revealing of the sons of God (Romans 8:19), because when they are revealed it will itself be gloriously delivered and set free (Vs 21). In the meantime, it is groaning under its burden Vs 22).

The devil is the original sinner which caused him to fall short of the glory of God. It was him who caused Adam and Eve to introduce sin into the world. Once they were infected with the sin virus, they received its wages; death and separation.

> *"For the wages of sin is death, but the gift of God is eternal life in Christ Jesus our Lord."* Romans 6:23

Death in the bible means 'separation' not annihilation. Death separates the spirit from the body (James 2:26) and it separates the spirit from God. Eternal death is eternal separation from God. Spiritual death is being in a state of separation to God. Spiritual death does not mean that the human spirit is lifeless and cannot function. No, it means that it is separated from God and Zion and cannot therefore come under the influences of the Spirit of God until it has been reconciled through Christ and his finished work on the cross. This helps explain why some people can tap into the spiritual realm and become a vessel for demons, such as spiritualists and mediums etc. It is because their spirit is very much alive and has the ability to function under the darkness of the devil's city and system, but it cannot be a vessel for the Holy Spirit until salvation has been acquired.

The Pull of the World

> *"Do not love the world or the things in the world. If anyone loves the world, the love of the Father is not in him. For all that is in the world — the lust of the flesh, the lust of the eyes,*

and the pride of life — is not of the Father but is of the world. And the world is passing away, and the lust of it; but he who does the will of God abides forever." 1 John 2:15-17

When Adam and Eve sinned, the world fell under the evil one and his evil city Babylon. The devil has created an evil system that rules the world from the lower heavenly places and has designed this system to cater to mankind's fallen sinful nature; the lust of the flesh, the lust of the eyes, and the pride of life. These are very powerful forces that make the world turn around and grip the hearts and minds of men and women. The book of Revelation makes it clear that Babylon is the cause of all the abominations and fornications among the nations.

The devil uses the world to entice us to sin so that we remain under the bondage of the elements and our fallen and sinful nature. Thus, he creates a never-ending cycle of ongoing besetting sins that continually keep people in a state of weakness, guilt and condemnation.

God told Cain concerning sin that it lies at the door with a desire to rule over you (Genesis 4:7).

Jesus said that he who sins is a slave to sin. Sin has an enslaving power and has the ability to grip and hold a person (Proverbs 5:22).

This devil's city thrives on sin, ignorance, darkness and deception. As the god of this age, he continually blinds the minds of both believers and unbelievers to keep them from seeing the truth.

"But even if our gospel is veiled, it is veiled to those who are perishing, whose minds the god of this age has blinded, who do not believe, lest the light of the gospel of the glory of Christ, who is the image of God, should shine on them." 2 Corinthians 4:3-5

Sin gives place to the devil to develop strongholds in the lives of people that become impossible to break with human effort alone. The devil not only tempts a person to sin by showing them the pleasures of sin, but once they take the bait, he quickly turns on them with guilt and condemnation to keep them under his power.

Sin in the life of a believer has a crippling effect as it keeps the believer in carnality and defeat.

You see the believer attempts in their own strength to over-come sin and attain to holiness through self-effort and making vows and promises to God of not doing it or saying it again. The problem here is that it leads to a very serious and devastating 'sin, confess, sin confess cycle.' This compounds the problem and is usually enough to keep the believer from becoming an overcomer and rising up to the 'enthroned life' to join the risen Saviour Jesus in His present and continuing ministry. A topic we will look at in a later chapter.

The curse of sin was introduced to the world and mankind through disobeying God and His word.

Sin has led to the fall of man and continues to pay out its wages of sin and death. It wreaks havoc both in the believer and the unbeliever and continues to keep mankind from the glorious inheritance they have in Zion as royal children in the family of God.

God cannot simply overlook sin nor can he turn a blind eye to it. Sin must be judged.

Sin has been the cause of every evil in heaven and in earth. It separates, it spoils, it mars, it defiles, it enslaves, deceives, it destroys, and it leads to death and destruction.

Sin puts mankind at enmity or war with a holy God.

> *"Because the carnal mind is enmity against God; for it is not subject to the law of God, nor indeed can be."* Romans 8:7

> *"Adulterers and adulteresses! Do you not know that friendship with the world is enmity with God? Whoever therefore wants to be a friend of the world makes himself an enemy of God."* James 4:4

The world, the flesh and the devil keep mankind at enmity with God so that they cannot fulfil the heavenly calling that is upon their lives. Separated from Zion, the Father, the throne and the altar, the Son of God and the Spirit of God and all the hosts of heaven, man exists in the world without god and without hope (Ephesians 2:12).

Sin has caused them to lose the way, turn from the truth and lose spiritual life! Because of this there's no way that people can fulfil the heavenly call to produce heaven on earth as sin has cut them off.

The devil is the tempter to sin, the world is the object of sin, the flesh is the weakness of sin and the law is the reminder of sin.

A terrible plight indeed but in Genesis 3:15 God introduces His redemptive plan. A saviour would come into the world and would defeat the devil and deliver the children of men. This Saviour would be the Way, the Truth and the Life! He would provide the Truth that would provide the Way to bring us back to abundant Life.

CHAPTER 4

The Way in Type and Shadow

The Tabernacle of Moses

The throne and the altar must be restored to man and so God calls Moses to be the vessel by which He would reintroduce in type and shadow the throne and the altar into the earth.

Moses Call

Moses birth, upbringing and call to leadership were filled with the miraculous. Born a Hebrew he was supernaturally protected and brought up in Pharaoh's court and reared and educated as a prince of Egypt. In His early years Moses was nursed by his own mother before being handed over to Pharaoh's daughter to become her son. So, his mother would have instilled Hebrew belief and faith in him. When Moses was forty years old, he saw an Egyptian taskmaster beating a

Hebrew slave. In his anger, he killed the Egyptian and buried him in the sand (Exodus 2:12). After it became known, Moses fled for his life and headed to Midian where he remained for forty years.

Moses had a very dramatic encounter and call from God in Exodus 3. God got his attention with a burning bush and then spoke clearly and called him to his life's mission. God's will for him was to see the Israelites delivered, and formed into a new nation and possess a land of Promise, good and large and flowing with milk and honey (Exodus 3:8). Moses would be God's chosen vessel to bring about their deliverance and lead them in the will of God. Moses was told to return to Egypt and confront Pharaoh commanding him to let God's people go. By the way many who preach and teach in the church today have Pharaoh ministries – they won't let God's people go either!

After a long battle against the stubborn Pharaoh and ten plagues ending with the Passover event, Moses led them out of Egypt. Once again Pharaoh changed his mind and pursued Moses and the people to the Red sea to destroy them. This time God intervened and supernaturally protected Moses and the Israelites through a Pillar of Cloud and Fire. Miraculously, Moses stretched his hand over the sea and divided the waters. The Israelites passed through to the other side and escaped. When the Egyptians followed the waters came together again and they were all drowned.

Mount Sinai

Moses led them through the wilderness to Mount Sinai in obedience to God. When they arrived, Moses went up into the mountain for forty days. It was here that Moses received the Ten Commandments and also the detailed plan for the Tabernacle (Exodus 25-40) which would house the throne (the Ark of the Covenant) and the Golden Altar, as well as details about the priesthood who would minister in the Tabernacle.

God left no room for Moses to have input in anything concerning the divine pattern for the temple or the priesthood. Moses couldn't say, 'But Lord, I prefer yellow for the curtains!' or 'Can we have embroidered butterflies in the fabric?' No, Moses had to build everything according to the divine pattern. What is very powerful and exciting about this is that when Moses obeyed and built it as God directed, the *glory* of God filled the temple.

> *"So, Moses finished the work. Then the cloud covered the tabernacle of meeting, and the glory of the Lord filled the tabernacle."* Exodus 40:33-34

Note: **The GLORY can ONLY fill the Tabernacle when built as directed!**

The Tabernacle was 45 feet by 15 feet and it was housed in a large court area that was 150 feet by 75 feet. Both the outer door and the door to the Tabernacle were on the East side. In the next chapter we will focus our attention on the Ark of the Covenant and the Golden Altar of Incense. These two items are of the utmost importance when it comes to the Tabernacle. In fact, all the other items; the Brazen altar, the Brazen Lava, the Bread of Presence and the Golden Lampstand were to ready the priests and the High Priest to minister at the Golden Altar and the Ark of the Covenant.

It was God Himself who laid down the approach to minister at both the Altar and the Ark and it was through blood sacrifice, ceremonial washings and services in the Holy place. A worshipper could not skip the order or come in their own preferred way. Worship had to be in accordance with the truth of God's Word that had been established.

Everything about the Tabernacle points to the life and ministry of the Lord Jesus Christ, who alone can perfect the worshipper and enable them to come before the throne of God and the altar. Something the Old Testament priests, law and sacrifices could not do (Hebrews 10:1). Listen to the Lord's words, *"I am the way, the truth, and the life. No one comes to the Father (the throne and the altar) except through me."* John 14:6

Jesus said, 'I am the door.' Access to the presence of God is only through Christ. Calvary, and Jesus' final, once for all sacrifice as the lamb of God is the ultimate brazen altar that redeems and renews the worshipper. The Word of God is the Brazen Lavar that washes and cleanses the believer. The word of God cleanses and purifies the worshipper. Christ has provided us with His own righteousness which must be put on as a priestly garment of salvation and righteousness.

Again, Jesus is the door into the Holy Place where we draw near to the Father. Jesus is the bread of life and offers spiritual nourishment and revelation to the worshipper. Jesus is the Light of the world and illuminates the soul and spirit of the believer and readies us to worship and pray. Jesus is the Golden altar and all worship and prayer offered in His Name is received and presented to the Father.

Jesus is the Ark of the Covenant and as such activates all kingdom power and resources in response to living faith and agreement with the word of God from the lips and mouths of priestly believers.

You see from start to finish the Tabernacle is a type and shadow of the ministry of Jesus Christ, the Son of God and Saviour of the world.

We can only come to God through Jesus' sacrifice, sanctifying and cleansing power, the gift of righteousness by faith, and being clothed with Christ. This prepares us for fellowship with the bread of Life and to come under the illuminating light of both Christ and the Holy Spirit. Only then are we readied to minister at the throne and the altar.

When the Tabernacle was erected it was built in the midst of the camp of the Israelites, with the tribes encamped on all sides. An Ariel view gives a clear image of the cross. The Tabernacle of Moses brought the presence of God into the midst of His people, Israel. It restored fellowship with God and established a way of approach to the throne and the altar.

In the book of Hebrews, it clearly tells us that Moses' tabernacle was a type and shadow of the heavenly tabernacle (Hebrews 8:5; 9:11). So, Moses tabernacle is meant to teach us and instruct us as to the ministry and functions of the priesthood and to point us to the greater heavenly tabernacle in heaven where Christ ministers in the office of High Priest after the order of Melchizedek (Hebrews 7). It's only when we grasp and understand Christ's role as High Priest of heaven that we will understand and enter into our own royal-priestly ministry under and alongside Christ (Revelation 1:5, 6). And so, the tabernacle of Moses is an all-important study.

The ministry of the tabernacle was a huge task that involved both priests and Levites. The priests ministered the holy things of the tabernacle: sacrifices, gifts etc. The Levites were assistants to the priests and were responsible for the transportation and setting up the tabernacle. However, it was the priests that ministered the gifts and sacrifices and carried out the ministries in the holy place. Only the High Priest alone ministered in the Most Holy Place on the Day of Atonement once a year.

But the ministry of the tabernacle involved many functions. There were the preparations of the animal sacrifices; the preparing of the priestly garments, the baking of the showbread, gathering fresh wood for the brazen altar and fresh water for the brazen lava, keeping the courts clean and many other duties. The priests served in shifts and according to lotteries set by the chief priest. The priests would assemble early in the morning and participate in the daily lotteries to find out where they would serve and what duties they would undertake.

The ultimate purpose for the tabernacle of Moses was so that God could dwell with His people (Exodus 25:8). It was so that God could have fellowship with His people to direct them and bless them in the earth. God created the world through His Word and so the only way to redeem the world is by redeeming mankind and restoring fellowship, worship and prayer, so that people can come under the glory of God's presence and be inspired to come in agreement with God's Word, confess it and produce God's will on earth.

The tabernacle of Moses brought God's Word through the ministry of priests to the people so that they could be directed and blessed. Next let's look at the two most important pieces of furniture in Moses' tabernacle.

The Ark of the Covenant *Exodus 25:10-22*

The most important item in the Tabernacle was the Ark of the Covenant. The ark was a chest made of acacia wood covered with gold, nearly four feet long and over two foot in width and height. It had a golden border around its top and had four golden rings on each side for transporting it. The lid of the Ark was called the Mercy Seat. Upon it made of pure gold were two Cherubim facing each other with outstretched wings that touched. Inside the Ark was a copy of the Ten Commandments, a gold pot filled with Manna, and Aaron's rod that budded.

The significance of this is amazing and when understood it transforms worship and prayer and brings them to their highest purpose. The Ten Commandments represent the logos Word and the Manna represents the rhema Word. The logos word is the written word and the rhema word is the spoken word in our spirit. The rod that budded represents the priestly ministry of Aaron which can only receive the aid of angels and bear fruit when in agreement with the word of God (Logos and Rhema). We know that angels heed and perform the word of God (Psalm 103:20) and so when a faithful priest stands at the Ark and worships God, he comes under the Spirit of truth and receives inspiration and revelation. The purpose of the Ark was so that God would speak His word to the priest.

> *"And there I will meet with you, and I will speak with you from above the mercy seat, from between the two cherubim which are on the ark of the Testimony, about everything which I will give you in commandment to the children of Israel."* Exodus 25:22

When he comes into agreement and confesses the Word of God at the Golden Altar, angels are released to perform God's word and bring about the will of the Father. Wow! What a revelation! This should light a fire inside every believer's heart to take their priestly role serious and learn how to serve in the heavenly Tabernacle. When we pray in accordance with God's will, he hears us. And if we know He hears us, then we know we have the things asked for.

> *"Now this is the confidence that we have in Him, that if we ask anything according to His will, He hears us. And if we know that He hears us, whatever we ask, we know that we have the petitions that we have asked of Him."* 1 John 5:14-15

This revelation is going to lift the prayer life of every believer and the church to new heights and cause the kingdom of God to manifest in great glory and victories.

The Golden Altar *Exodus 30: 1-10*

The Golden Altar was made of acacia wood and overlaid with gold. It was square and 18 inches on all sides. It was 3 feet high and four horns at each corner. Incense was burned upon it twice a day morning and evening (vs 7-8). The purpose of the Altar of Incense was to meet with God.

> *"And you shall put it before the veil that is before the ark of the Testimony, before the mercy seat that is over the Testimony, where I will meet with you."* Exodus 30:6

It had golden rings fixed to it for transportation. It was positioned in the holy place directly opposite the Ark of the Covenant which was behind the veil. This was the highlight of all the priestly duties and privileges. All the priestly duties were given by lottery. The priests would gather at various times in the day to participate in the lotteries and then they would be assigned their duties.

Only priests who had never ministered at the golden altar were permitted to be included in this lottery. It was a once in a lifetime opportunity and once a priest had ministered at the golden altar, he couldn't be included in the lottery ever again. The reason was that there was to be equal opportunity for all the many priests to have the privilege to minister the incense. Some priests never had the privilege of ministering at the golden altar throughout their years of service and sadly died never experiencing it.

The golden altar was associated with prayer. When the incense was offered the priest had occasion to pray. Prayer at the golden altar was to subdue all of God's enemies and bring them under his footstool and to release every blessing form heaven on God's people.

Again, the purpose of prayer at the golden altar was

1. To subdue all God's enemies under his footstool.

2. Release every spiritual blessing from heaven.

In Revelation 8:2–5 an angel having a golden censor approaches and stands at the altar. After receiving much incense, he offers it along with the prayers of the saints on the golden altar. When the smoke of the incense and the prayers of the saints are received by God, the angel takes fire from the altar and it is thrown to the earth. This is a powerful insight into prayer offered at heaven's golden altar. **The altar is to *alter* everything that needs to be altered and brought into alignment with the will of the Father.**

Jewish tradition says that the life of the priest that ministered at the golden altar changed the day he ministered incense and prayer. God defeated and subdued all of his enemies and he prospered from that day forward with divine favour and blessing. Wow! Once in a lifetime, no wonder the priests were excited about this particular lottery. And we as New Testament believers have access 24/7. Are you making the most of your throne and altar privileges? Knowing this revelation, every believer should be running to the altar! Nothing and no one will keep me from ministering at the throne and altar anymore!

In Luke 1 we find a priest by the name of Zacharias. His wife was Elizabeth and they were both righteous but had no child as Elizabeth was barren and they were both old.

> *"So it was, that while he was serving as priest before God in the order of his division, according to the custom of the priesthood, his lot fell to burn incense when he went into the temple of the Lord. And the whole multitude of the people was praying outside at the hour of incense. Then an angel of the Lord appeared to him, standing on the right side of the altar of incense. And when Zacharias saw him, he was troubled, and fear fell upon him."* Luke 1:8-12

When we stand at the altar, we are surrounded by innumerable angels waiting with bated breath to hear and perform the agreed word of God from our mouths. Zacharias' life is about to change forever. He saw the angel and was afraid but then he is told,

> *"Do not be afraid, Zacharias, for your prayer is heard; and your wife Elizabeth will bear you a son, and you shall call his name John. And you will have joy and gladness, and many will rejoice at his birth."* Luke 1:13-15

What was his prayer? It was obviously that they would have a child. And the angel announces the answer in his hearing and assures him that not only would he have joy and rejoice but many others too. I hope you're seeing the revelation of the golden altar and are stirred in your heart to go there.

God is lifting His people up in the Spirit (Ephesians 2:21-22). They have been earth bound for way too long. God is raising her up in the Spirit to join in the heavenly calling and ministry alongside her faithful High Priest, Yeshua/Jesus. When the church rises up and becomes what the Lord has already made her, a temple and a priesthood, and when she ministers at the throne and the altar of Zion, there's going to be a glorious display and manifestation of the glory of God. Remember, whenever God's pattern is carefully followed and implemented, the glory of God fills the temple!

Prayer is the most neglected ministry of the church but it is about to become the most important ministry of the church. Before Jesus did anything he ministered at the throne and the altar of heaven.

No wonder he had a fruitful ministry as prophet, priest and king! A revival of prayer is about to break loose for the body of Christ. But this revival of prayer is going to be unlike anything the church has previously prayed because of the revelation of the throne and the altar. Prayer is about to be lifted up to its highest purpose and as leaders and churches pray from this position, every spiritual blessing will manifest including 'All' the gifts of the Spirit.

Jesus is the High Priest of our confession (Hebrews 3:1). He is not just praying and interceding for us alone. No, He is waiting for us to join Him there, agree with Him and confess the Word of God so that He can put the kingdom to work and manifest His glory. Because of this it is essential we learn the art of All prayer; thanksgiving, praise, supplication, intercession, agreement, command of faith, declaration, binding and loosing, and teach and equip every believer to be skilful in prayer. More about this later.

CHAPTER 5

The Temple

History

"But you have come to Mount Zion and to the city of the living God, the heavenly Jerusalem." Hebrews 12:22

The tabernacles and temples of the Old Testament were types and shadows that pointed to Mount Zion, the city of the living God and heavenly Jerusalem. The Old Testament is in type and shadow. A shadow is not the substance. If I was to attack your shadow and kick and punch it, it wouldn't hurt you because the shadow is not the substance.

In the same way, the types and shadows are to point us to the heavenly reality and substance of the kingdom of God and of heaven. All the patterns, functions and ministries of the tabernacles and temples find their ultimate fulfilment in the heavenly city and tabernacle in Zion. Note. Adam didn't lose physical life he lost spiritual life. He didn't lose his ability to live in the physical realm but in the spiritual realm. This is what has been restored to us through Christ as the way, the truth and the life.

Let's look at the rise of Zion in the bible.

All earthly tabernacles and temples were types and shadows of the one true tabernacle in Zion, the city of God and heavenly Jerusalem. God is enthroned in the heavenly Tabernacle. He is surrounded by angelic ministry and is enthroned in the midst of continuous worship, praise and prayer. The Father is the Most-High God and rules over all the works of His hands by a divine and eternal and spiritual order that operates in the spiritual realm in Zion.

Earthly Zion was a hill or mount in Canaan. It was known as Jebus before it was named Jerusalem and the Jebusites had settled there and were well established. When the Israelites went in to conquer the land, they couldn't drive out the Jebusites from their stronghold and in fact they held it until the time of David. Jebus means, 'Elevated' 'Highest'.

In those times the battle was for the high places for they were very difficult to defeat by oncoming enemies. Whoever had the high place had the advantage. The hill was given to the tribe of Benjamin but it was never fully conquered. It was David who took the hill and defeated the Jebusites and laid claim to the site (2 Samuel 5:6-9). It became the City of David and after he took it, David strengthened it and built it up. This is where David settled and set up his rule as king.

It's from here on that Zion rises to become Jerusalem, the City of God and of David. It was the political and ecclesiastical centre of the nation of Israel. It became the capital city of Israel.

Zion was the place where king David ruled and it was also the spiritual capital for worshipping the Lord. It combined the roles of priest and king and David functioned in both roles.

As we read the Psalms, especially the Messianic Psalms, they reveal that David was also a prophet as well as a priest and king unto God. In this David was a type and shadow of the greater Prophet, Priest and King to come from spiritual Zion. So, it was here that David set his kingly and governmental ministry as well as the Tabernacle he set up for worship and ecclesiastical ministry. In all of this, Zion with all of its kingly and priestly functions shadowed the heavenly and spiritual Zion. The tabernacle of Moses, the tabernacle of David, the temple of Solomon and the temple of Zerubbabel all foreshadowed the true spiritual temple, the church, Zion.

The Tabernacle Of David

After he was established, David had received from the Spirit of the Lord, a divine pattern for approaching God in worship and prayer (1 Chronicles 28:11-19). It's very clear from reading Psalms and especially the messianic psalms that David had received revelation by the Spirit of the Lord. Also, the fact that David set up a tabernacle for the Ark of the Covenant in Jerusalem confirms that David had received direction by God to do it.

The order of worship that David set up in this tabernacle was completely revolutionary and new to anything the people of Israel had seen before. David pitched a tent and placed the Ark of the Covenant in the midst. There were no divisions in this tent. No Holy place or holy of holies, just the Ark set in the centre and on open show for all to come before and worship the Lord.

David implemented a pattern of 24/7 worship that included; singing, dancing, praising, shouting, clapping, worshipping and praying before the Ark of the Covenant. Why would David do this? Why would David not put the Ark back in the tabernacle of Moses where it belonged? By the way, the Ark never returned to Moses tabernacle from this point on. It continued in its ministries and functions but without the Ark in the Holy of Holies.

The fact that David had the Ark on his mind and in his heart shows that God was already moving upon David and stirring him to do His will. However, in his zeal, David didn't consult the Lord on how to transport the Ark. He had it put on a brand-new cart and Uzzah, one of David's men drove the cart.

As it neared Jerusalem, the oxen stumbled and Uzzah put his hand on the Ark to steady it and immediately the Lord struck him and he died.

> *And David became angry because of the Lord's outbreak against Uzzah; and he called the name of the place Perez Uzzah to this day. David was afraid of the Lord that day; and he said, "How can the ark of the Lord come to me?" So David would not move the ark of the Lord with him into the City of David; but David took it aside into the house of Obed-Edom the Gittite. The ark of the Lord remained in the house of Obed-Edom the Gittite three months. And the Lord blessed Obed-Edom and all his household."* 2 Samuel 6:8-11

David became very angry before the Lord to the point that he was afraid of the Lord and would not move the Ark further. He left it at the house of Obed-Edom, whose house was blessed because of the presence of the Ark in its midst. Somewhere in between David getting angry and afraid before God and his second attempt at bringing the Ark back to Jerusalem, David experienced spiritual encounters and new revelations. David received a detailed plan and pattern of approaching the Lord under a new spiritual order. David was given access to spiritual Zion where he heard a conversation between the God-Head.

> *The Lord said to my Lord, "Sit at My right hand, Till I make Your enemies Your footstool." The Lord shall send the rod of Your strength out of Zion. Rule in the midst of Your enemies! Your people shall be volunteers In the day of Your power; In the beauties of holiness, from the womb of the morning, You have the dew of Your youth. The Lord has sworn And will not relent, "You are a priest forever According to the order of Melchizedek." The Lord is at Your right hand; He shall execute kings in the day of His wrath. He shall judge among the nations, He shall fill the places with dead bodies, He shall execute*

the heads of many countries. He shall drink of the brook by the wayside; Therefore He shall lift up the head." Psalm 110

On into the New Testament, Jesus was talking to the Pharisees about David and whose son he was, and He said this about David's conversation:

"How then does David in the Spirit call Him 'Lord,' saying: 'The Lord said to my Lord, "Sit at My right hand, Till I make Your enemies Your footstool"'? If David then calls Him 'Lord,' how is He his Son?" Matthew 22:43-45

The point we want to make is that David was 'in the Spirit' when he heard the conversation.

'The LORD said to my LORD,' David said. Who was David's LORD? Yeshua! David was brought into and under the eternal, spiritual order of the Royal Priesthood of Yeshua/Jesus. This changed David's relationship with God and heaven forever! David went on to receive in the Spirit the detailed plan and pattern of worship established in a new tabernacle that was centred around the Ark of the Covenant.

"Then David gave his son Solomon the plans for all that he had by the Spirit." 1 Chronicles 28:11

"All this," said David, "the Lord made me understand in writing, by His hand upon me, all the works of these plans." 1 Chronicles 28:19

'All this', included the design of the new temple as well as the new approach unto the Lord through praise and worship in the Spirit. So, David came into the eternal, spiritual order of Melchizedek, which is the spiritual and eternal priestly order of the Most-High God and His Kingdom. From here on David was brought into the Spirit.

David saw and witnessed 24/7 worship around the Father's throne in spiritual Zion. The tabernacle of David would be patterned after the heavenly tabernacle and under the priestly order of Melchizedek. David set in place a 4000 strong worship team who were to minister in three eight-hour shifts around the clock 24/7. David made and provided all the instruments that were to be played. He had scribes set in place ready to record all that they received from the Lord under inspiration of the Spirit.

This is where David most likely received all of his Messianic revelation that is recorded in Psalms. Under this new order and through this new spiritual approach to heavenly Zion he had access to every spiritual blessing in order to establish God's kingdom and God's will for Israel and cause them to come into a blessed golden age of ecclesiastical and governmental authority and power that no-one could challenge.

David was a great enquirer of the Lord. As he approached the Lord under this new order of worship, he was brought into the Spirit and under the order of Melchizedek where he received inspiration and revelation to subdue Israel's enemies and secure God's blessing on the nation. David passed on this divine order to Solomon his son, who continued in this pattern for many years also enjoying peace and prosperity in the earth. Israel reached its zenith under the early part of Solomon's reign enjoying great prosperity and peace and fame among the nations.

Unfortunately, the tabernacle of David fell down and Solomon's temple replaced it. All the articles from the tabernacle of Moses and the Ark of the Covenant from David's tabernacle were all placed in the new temple of Solomon. When it was built and completed as directed, the glory of the Lord filled the temple (1 Kings 8:10). Sadly, over time and as Solomon's heart was turned away and compromise set in, the spirituality of the nation went downhill. The Davidic pattern of worship under the order of Melchizedek in the Spirit was lost and Israel were given over to false worship and idolatry. In this, the tabernacle of David fell.

Obviously, the Lord hadn't finished with the tabernacle of David and this spiritual order because in the books of Amos and in Acts, the Lord promised to rebuild and repair this tabernacle and its order. It's interesting that the Lord didn't say he would raise up Moses tabernacle or Solomon's temple but the tabernacle of David only.

> "On that day I will raise up The tabernacle of David, which has fallen down, And repair its damages; I will raise up its ruins, And rebuild it as in the days of old; 12 That they may possess the remnant of Edom, And all the Gentiles who are called by My name," Says the Lord who does this thing. Amos 9:11-12

> 'After! this I will return And will rebuild the tabernacle of David, which has fallen down; I will rebuild its ruins, And I will set it up; 17 So that the rest of mankind may seek the Lord, Even all the Gentiles who are called by My name, Says the Lord who does all these things.' Acts 15:16-17

It's very clear what all of this points to. *At a future time, God would raise up the tabernacle of David to fulfil His end time plan for overcoming His enemies and harvesting the souls of the earth.* It would be a spiritual temple with a spiritual approach under a spiritual order exactly as David had operated in.

If you can receive it, David was in the New Covenant before there was a New Covenant in the earth. This is why David could be in spiritual Zion and worship the Lord.

Today, the church is the spiritual temple and royal priesthood of God, called to live and walk in the Spirit and bring about the restoration of all things under the order of Melchizedek. It's the tabernacle of David, the spiritual approach that lifts and raises the church up into the order of Melchizedek. It's under this eternal, spiritual order that the church can fulfil her heavenly calling which is to usher in the return of Christ for the restoration of all things, bringing all God's enemies under His footstool and then gathering all things together, both in heaven and earth unto Christ.

We'll look more at the specifics of this heavenly calling on the church in later chapters.

The Tabernacle to the Spiritual Temple

Taking a brief tour of the tabernacles and temples that were established can help us to understand the spiritual temple the church and what God's plan and purpose for her in the heavens and in the earth.

Exodus 25–40 records the setting up of Moses tabernacle. Moses received all the plans and details up on Mount Sinai as he spent time with God in the glory of His presence. When it was built according to the divine pattern the glory of God filled the tabernacle.

> *"So Moses finished the work. Then the cloud covered the tabernacle of meeting, and the glory of the Lord filled the tabernacle."* Exodus 40:33–34

The glory of God was the indicator for when the tabernacle was to move on and when it was to be re-erected (Exodus 40:36-38). The tabernacle journeyed through the wilderness as Israel headed towards the Promised Land. All the tribes had various duties and responsibilities to care for and manage the tabernacle as it journeyed. When Israel finally crossed the Jordan and entered into the Promised Land the tabernacle found a home at Gilgal and remained there. The Ark was transported into battle as the armies of Israel went out to conquer the land. After the conquest the tabernacle was set up at Shiloh (John 18:1).

After suffering a defeat by the Philistines, Israel brought the ark of the covenant from Shiloh into the battle play. They trusted in it more as a lucky charm than putting their faith in God and suffered another crushing defeat but this time losing the ark to the Philistines who captured it (1 Samuel 4:11). It was during this time that Israel was declared 'Ichabod' meaning the glory has departed. The thought around capturing the ark would have been to stop the victory and blessing of the ark and altar.

With the ark in their midst the Philistines came under severe judgment by God and after realising the cause they returned the ark to Israel. Although the ark came back into Israel's' possession it never returned to the tabernacle of Moses. It remained in transit until David came to the throne.

As David was establishing his reign in Jerusalem and building houses for himself, he also pitched a tent or tabernacle in which to place the ark of the covenant (1 Chronicles 15:1). The fact that David did this leads us to believe that David had heard from the Lord and had received revelation on establishing the tabernacle with the ark present for a new order of approach very different to that of the prescribed order established in Moses tabernacle.

Apart from the initial animal sacrifices at the dedication of David's tabernacle there were no other animal sacrifices involved. The sacrifices offered were the sacrifices of joy, praise and thanksgiving, worship and gifts, as well as prayers. There was singing, dancing, clapping, shouting and instrumentation all directed towards the Lord. It's interesting that Moses' tabernacle continued with its approach and sacrifices but the worship under David was in the Spirit.

The ark and the altar joined together with no division and all enjoyed the presence of God under this new spiritual order. It must have been a real difficulty for many who were so used to worship under Moses tabernacle. It would have taken a real shift in thinking and faith. The tabernacle of David brought David and Israel under the order of Melchizedek (Ps 110), this is why they had such confidence to worship so freely before the ark of the Lord without fear or dread.

The order of Melchizedek is the royal priesthood of heaven. It brings the offices of priest and king together. Under the law it was illegal for kings to assume priestly ministry and for those that did they paid a high price for doing so. King Saul and king Uzziah were dealt with very harshly. So, it would have been extremely dangerous for David to assume both priestly and kingly ministry if he hadn't first of all heard from God. After David had set up the tabernacle for the ark, he appointed continual music ministry to the Lord and also extended it into Moses tabernacle (1 Chronicles 16:37-43).

During the reign of David, the ark remained in the tabernacle David had erected to the Lord. But during the end of David's life and reign, the tabernacle David built and the tabernacle of Moses gave way for the rise of the temple of Solomon. Solomon's temple included animal sacrifices and the pattern of worship that David had established. Solomon's temple was a wonder of the world in its day.

It was so elaborate its estimated cost was somewhere in the region of £100 billion in value. It was made of the costliest of materials. Sadly, over time as Solomon and those who followed turned away from the Lord and fell into idol worship, the spiritual life of Israel deteriorated. The Lord warned them time after time through the mouths of the prophets but they persecuted and killed them leaving God no choice but to bring judgment on them.

It was the Babylonians who went up against Israel and ransacked and destroyed the temple of Solomon. The ark was most likely stolen along with the other articles and once again Israel was 'Ichabod' the glory had departed. Israel went into captivity for seventy years as the Lord had said and the temple lay in ruins along with the spiritual life of the priests and the people.

The second temple was built by Zerubbabel and both Ezra and Nehemiah had a part in the restoration of the project. This second temple was no match for that of Solomon's great temple as the nation was coming out of captivity and could not match the great wealth that Solomon had. In fact, as they laid the foundation of the temple, those who remembered Solomon's temple wept as they knew it couldn't match its former glory (Ezra 3:12). The temple after completion functioned without the ark in the Most Holy Place.

The second temple was further enlarged and beautified by Herod during his reign in a move to win over the Jewish people. Herod invested heavily and added all kinds of other courts and buildings to the temple. The ark was absent in this beautified temple also. This was the temple that Jesus visited during His earthly ministry. He taught in its courts many times. He called it His Father's house and reinforced that it was a house of prayer for all nations (Mark 11:15-17). In His zeal he purged it from the money changers and called them to return to its original purpose, prayer and worship. Jesus also prophesied an end to the temple and spoke of its destruction. He said that he would rebuild it in three days referring to His spiritual body, the church (John 2:19). He also spoke of its complete destruction by the Romans in A.D. 70 (Matthew 24:1-2).

At his death, the veil was torn from top to bottom (Matthew 27:51) signifying that the way into the holiest was now open by a new living way that Jesus had secured by His atoning work. God put an end to sacrifices once and for all. The old order was finished with and the new order had replaced it. The man-made tabernacles and temples had now given way to God's spiritual temple, the church. Now, all worship would be to the Father, in spirit and in truth (John 4:21-24).

The new temple was now firmly established and would grow into a dwelling place for God in the Spirit (Ephesians 2:21-22).

CHAPTER 6

The Way Modelled

Christ's Example

Jesus was manifested for a number of reasons. He came to manifest the Name of the Father (John 17:6). He came to manifest eternal life (1 John 1:2). He was manifested to take away sins (1 John 3:5). He came to destroy the works of the devil (1 John 3:8). But he came to manifest the glory of God (John 2:11). This means that Jesus came to lay down an example of how to live and walk in the Spirit as to manifest the glory of God. Jesus came then for two great big purposes:

Firstly, He came to model the Way.

Secondly, He came to recover the Way to enable His followers to do the same.

Wow! Did you catch that? The gospels are a revelation of the Way, the Truth and the Life modelled by Jesus. They also are a revelation of how He recovered and opened up the Way for us!

What the first Adam lost the Last Adam restored.

Christlikeness

Christlikeness is the ultimate goal for every believer.

> *"He who says he abides in Him ought himself also to walk just as He walked."* 1 John 2:6

> *"For whom He foreknew, He also predestined to be conformed to the image of His Son, that He might be the firstborn among many brethren."* Romans 8:29

Christlikeness should be the ultimate aspiration and ambition for every believer. But what does this mean? Is it simply displaying more of the qualities of the *nature* of Christ, such as unconditional love, being more merciful and gracious and kind? It must certainly involves displaying the nature of Christ but it also must mean displaying the ministry, authority and power of Christ too. We are called to walk as He walked – in the power and demonstration of the Holy Spirit.

> *"Most assuredly, I say to you, he who believes in Me, the works that I do he will do also; and greater works than these he will do, because I go to My Father. And whatever you ask in My name, that I will do, that the Father may be glorified in the Son. If you ask anything in My name, I will do it."* John 14:12-14

We are called to do greater works than Jesus performed. How is that possible? If we compare ourselves with Jesus, we don't even come close and so, many believers dismiss this promise. But we must understand that Jesus was completely righteous in Himself. He also did everything by living and walking in the Spirit. Once we understand how to do this, then this promise can become a reality in our lives too.

At Jesus' baptism in John 3:21-22, the Holy Spirit descended upon Him in bodily form like a dove. Then the Father spoke of how pleased He was with His Son.

> *"Then Jesus, being filled with the Holy Spirit, returned from the Jordan and was led by the Spirit into the wilderness, being tempted for forty days by the devil."* Luke 4:1-2

Jesus was led into the wilderness by the Holy Spirit for a battle with the devil. Jesus became an overcomer of the world, sin and the devil. The devil threw everything at Him but had nothing in Him that he could use against Him. He overcame the temptation of the world and its glory; he overcame sinning against the Father and he overcame the temptation to bow down and worship the devil.

These same three enemies are what the devil uses to overcome believers and stop them from operating in the power of the Spirit. Jesus overcame and moved from being filled with the Spirit to operating in the power of the Spirit.

> *"Then Jesus returned in the power of the Spirit to Galilee, and news of Him went out through all the surrounding region."* Luke 4:14

> *"The Spirit of the Lord is upon Me, Because He has anointed Me To preach the gospel to the poor; He has sent Me to heal the broken-hearted, To proclaim liberty to the captives And recovery of sight to the blind, To set at liberty those who are oppressed; To proclaim the acceptable year of the Lord."* Luke 4:18-19

From here on Jesus was anointed and lived and walked in the power of the Spirit.

The Devotional Life of Yeshua/Jesus

How did Jesus operate with such favour and power? He invested blocks of quality time in the spiritual realm as well as in the natural realm. *Everything Jesus taught was not just telling us what to do but it was sharing what He did.* Jesus lived by His own teaching. He walked the talk. He modelled His teaching. Let's take a look at Jesus' devotional life.

Jesus devotional life included singing praises, thanksgiving and worship, as well as fasting and praying. This is how the tabernacle of David functioned. David was a worshipper and pray-er.

It was Jesus who taught that the Father is Spirit and those who worship Him must worship Him in spirit and truth (John 4:23-24). Jesus knew the spiritual approach to Zion, heaven and the Father.

Jesus knew the power of praise and worship – he knew from experience how praise, thanksgiving and worship lifts the worshipper into the presence of God. At the Last Supper Jesus sang a Hymn (the Hymns of Psalms) with the disciples (Matthew 26:30). The Jews sang many of the Hymns and Psalms as they celebrated the feasts of the Lord. They also sang them in their personal devotional lives. This was not an isolated case. Jesus would have sung many songs of the book of psalms and would have incorporated them into His devotional life. Jesus operated in thanksgiving. On many occasions he gave thanks to the Father before teaching, eating or performing acts of kindness, miracles and healing.

Jesus fasted. It was a spiritual discipline. He fasted forty days and forty nights while in the wilderness being tempted of the devil (Matthew 4:2). When the devil tempted him to turn stones to bread, Jesus answered, *'It is written: Man shall not live by bread alone but by every word that proceeds from the mouth of God.'* (Matthew 4:4). In this statement Jesus revealed the real purpose of fasting. 'To hear the Word of God that is proceeding from the mouth of God more clearly.' In other words, fasting helps us to tune in and hear the 'Rhema' word that proceeds from God's mouth.

This is really important to understand. When we need much needed guidance, the 'Logos' word will help, however, it's the 'Rhema' word that will make the difference. Jesus came into a situation in the gospel of Matthew where the disciples couldn't minister healing to a young boy. Jesus called for the young boy to be brought unto Him and then cast a demon out of him and set him free. When the disciples questioned Him as to why they failed, he answered, 'Because of their unbelief, and their lack of fasting.' You see, to operate in the discerning of spirits, one must hear the 'rhema' word revealing the identity of the spirit involved. Fasting helps us hear the proceeding word of God.

In the early church, when they ministered to the Lord and fasted, the Holy Spirit brought a 'now' word (Acts 13:2). Fasting helps sharpen our spirit and spiritual senses. When we hear we can confidently walk in obedience to God and the result will be spiritual power and authority. The disciples didn't fast while ministering with Jesus but after His departure they fasted (Matthew 9:15). It's interesting that the men that wrote the majority of the New Testament (Peter, John and Paul) were holy men that fasted and most definitely heard the word of God that proceeded from the mouth of God. They also moved in spiritual power and authority under the Holy Spirit.

Jesus Prayed. The prayer life of Jesus was exemplary. He spent huge amounts of time in prayer. Jesus had access to Zion, heaven. Prayer to Jesus was not a list of needs but it was a rich spiritual experience. Worship and prayer are to lift us into the spirit, through the heavens and into the third heaven, God's Holy City, Zion, heavenly Jerusalem. They bring us into heaven's sanctuary and before the throne of God and the golden altar.

Jesus operated under the royal priestly order of Melchizedek, which is the eternal, spiritual order of the Most-High God in heaven. It has no limitations or restrictions and is based upon the eternal and spiritual sacrifice of Christ. In fact, Christ was slain from the foundation of the world (Revelation 13:8). This explains why Jesus could offer forgiveness of sins and healing based upon his eternal sacrifice and priesthood. You see, there's no forgiveness without the shedding of blood (Hebrews 9:22). Healing too, is based on the stripes that Christ received at the whipping post (John 19:1). Jesus was able to draw on His own shed blood because it was an eternal and spiritual fact that was already in play.

Prayer for Jesus was a dialogue and not a monologue. It was two way and Jesus had a personal relationship with His Father in heaven. The prayer life of Jesus produced great rewards and blessings. In fact, prayer is how Jesus received from the Father and from heaven. He told the disciples he had meat to eat that they knew not of (John 4:32-34). The word of God and will of God was His food. He fed on them.

Like David and many of the prophets before Him Jesus ascended spiritually and came under the inspiration, revelation and power of the Father. After experiencing the glory, he manifested it on earth through faith and obedience. Jesus was so connected to heaven and the Father that His greatest suffering was not the cross but being cut off from heaven and the Father (Matthew 27:46). Jesus is the ark and the altar so he most definitely took advantage of his throne and altar privileges.

Let's Look at His Prayer Life

"And in the morning, rising up a great while before day, he went out, and departed into a solitary place, and there prayed." Mark 1:35

"So He Himself often withdrew into the wilderness and prayed." Luke 5:16

"And when He had sent the multitudes away, He went up on the mountain by Himself to pray. Now when evening came, He was alone there." Matthew 14:23

"Now it came to pass in those days that He went out to the mountain to pray, and continued all night in prayer to God." Luke 6:12-13

The first thing Jesus did in the morning was invest in prayer. He often withdrew for prayer. Sometimes he spent all night in prayer. What was he doing? He was in the spirit getting His daily downloads. He was asking, seeking and knocking. He was enquiring as to the Father's will. He was spending time with the Father. What he received from the Father through the Spirit, he obeyed and ministered on the earth. Jesus only did and said what the Father showed Him and Told Him.

Then Jesus answered and said to them, "Most assuredly, I say to you, the Son can do nothing of Himself, but what He sees the Father do; for whatever He does, the Son also does in like manner." John 5:19

"For I have not spoken of myself; but the Father which sent me, he gave me a commandment, what I should say, and what I should speak. And I know that his commandment is life everlasting: whatsoever I speak therefore, even as the Father said unto me, so I speak." John 12:49-50

How did Jesus receive from the Father? He operated in the spiritual realm. He activated His Spirit and exercised His faith and spiritual senses. The result was a dynamic and fruitful ministry. The disciples were amazed at Jesus' devotional life – this is what led them to ask Him to teach them to pray (Luke 11).

The first priority for disciples and followers of Jesus is develop a strong and disciplined devotional life. There's no substitute for this. Our missional and ministerial life should stem from our devotional life. If we get this wrong, then we'll never be led of the Spirit. The voice of God and the leading of the Spirit come out of spending time in the spirit with the Father showing us and sharing with us His Word through His Spirit (1 Corinthians 2:9-16).

When we follow Jesus, it should lead to a supernatural life and ministry. The apostle Paul encouraged believers to follow Him as He followed Christ (1 Corinthians 11:1). If our following Christ doesn't lead us into the Spirit so that we come under the Father's glory and the Spirit's ministry, we can never do the greater works of Christ, nor manifest the kingdom of God through spiritual gifts! We should examine ourselves and our following!

CHAPTER 7

The Missional

and Ministerial Life of Jesus

Jesus missional and ministerial life was operated under the eternal and spiritual order of Melchizedek.

As such, Jesus ministered under the divine Royal Priestly order of the Most-High God, He did it in the roles of Prophet, Priest and King. This order operates on the highest level of spiritual authority and power by the Spirit of the Lord, as well as activating the ministry of angelic hosts. It allows the ministerial offices to operate under divine inspiration, revelation and power.

When Jesus ministered under this eternal and spiritual order, He manifested Kingdom knowledge and authority through teaching, preaching, subduing evil and healing the sick. Everything Jesus did was by the anointing and direction of the Holy Spirit. Angels ministered with Christ throughout His life and ministry. He could have asked the Father for 12 legions while on the cross (Matthew 26:53). We know that angels are involved in heeding the word of God and performing Gods will, so there's no doubt that Christ who is the Word, had angelic ministry aiding Him.

Jesus came to model the original call and commission given to Adam, which was to subdue evil and establish the kingdom of God on earth. Adam failed and so Jesus, the Last Adam came to restore mankind so they could rise up and fulfil their original heavenly calling (1 Corinthians 15:45-49).

The first thing we notice about Jesus is His dedicated and disciplined devotional life. He prayed before he did anything. He prayed before ministering, teaching, casting out demons and healing the sick. He prayed before performing miracles which showed His strong reliance on His Father, the Holy Spirit and angels. His prayer life produced powerful ministry.

Jesus ministry was powerful, anointed by the Spirit and full of supernatural works as well as good works. Jesus ministered powerfully in the natural and the supernatural.

> *"God anointed Jesus of Nazareth with the Holy Spirit and with power, who went about doing good and healing all who were oppressed by the devil, for God was with Him."* Acts 10:38

One of the first things that Jesus did as he began His earthly ministry was to call disciples to Himself. He knew that His mission was to not only model the Way so that it was clearly seen, but that the Way was opened up for mankind to be restored to spiritual life, power and authority. And so, Jesus prayed and then chose His disciples. He would train them and turn them into apostles who would in turn establish His temple and royal priesthood and join Him in the restoration of all things (Acts 3:21) including: Ministering the New Covenant (Hebrews 8), manifesting the manifold wisdom of God (Ephesians 3:10), bringing all His enemies under the footstool of God (Hebrews 1:13), and gathering in all things both in heaven and in earth into Christ (Ephesians 1:10).

The kingdom of God was Jesus' priority. He must be about His Father's business which was to restore the kingdom of God on earth. Take note that Jesus came to model the Way and then open up and restore the Way to mankind so that THEY could rise up and FULFILL the heavenly call. There are so many believers who are stuck in their spiritual walk as spiritual infants calling on the Lord to do it all. The reason He returned to heaven was to take up His present and continuing ministry so that we could follow His model and manifest the kingdom as He did.

"...because as He is, so are we in this world." 1 John 4:17

"He who believes in Me, the works that I do he will do also; and greater works than these he will do, because I go to My Father." John 14:12

Let's look at His works.

And when John had heard in prison about the works of Christ, he sent two of his disciples and said to Him, "Are You the Coming One, or do we look for another?" Jesus answered and said to them, "Go and tell John the things which you hear and see: The blind see and the lame walk; the lepers are cleansed and the deaf hear; the dead are raised up and the poor have the gospel preached to them. And blessed is he who is not offended because of Me." Matthew 11:2-6

"Then His fame went throughout all Syria; and they brought to Him all sick people who were afflicted with various diseases and torments, and those who were demon-possessed, epileptics, and paralytics; and He healed them." Matthew 4:24

"Then He healed many who were sick with various diseases, and cast out many demons; and He did not allow the demons to speak, because they knew Him." Mark 1:34

Jesus functioned as Prophet, Priest and King. These three roles minister the kingdom of God and heaven. The anointing of the Spirit and the ministry of angels service these roles and manifest the kingdom of God. Jesus operated in all the gifts of the Spirit except tongues and interpretation of tongues, as they were given for the church to fulfil her ministry. There are a number of manifestations and gifts of the Spirit.

Revelation gifts. Word of knowledge – Word of wisdom – Discerning of spirits

Power gifts. Gifts of healing, working of miracles and faith.

Inspiration gifts. Prophecy – Tongues and Interpretation of tongues

As you read the gospels, you can discover many of the gifts of the Spirit in the gospel accounts. All of these manifestations of the Spirit are received by faith as we come under the Father's glory through worship and prayer. Because Jesus was connected to heaven, to the Father and Spirit, He was able to come under the divine inspiration, revelation and power as well as working with the ministry of angels. Jesus was under the royal priesthood of heaven and so He had all of the resources of the kingdom working with Him, in Him and through Him.

Prophet

When Jesus ministered prophecy, He ministered in the office of a Prophet. Every believer can prophesy under divine inspiration according to their faith but those who hold the office of prophet operate at a different level of anointing. Prophets were God's mouthpiece and as such spoke forth the word of God to their generation. They communicated the thoughts and will of God for their time. Prophets were also 'seers' and had the ability to see into past, present and future situations. They were also able to foretell events before they occurred. In the book of Hebrews, we are told this,

> *"God, who at various times and in various ways spoke in time past to the fathers by the prophets, has in these last days spoken to us by His Son, whom He has appointed heir of all things."* Hebrews 1:1-2

When God wanted to communicate His thoughts and His will, he called prophets to be His mouthpiece. God used prophets to reveal His unfolding revelation throughout the generations and had them recorded in the Scriptures. However, what the

Father would reveal through His Son in the final days would reveal His ultimate will and purpose.

As the ultimate prophet, Jesus spoke many things to communicate the Father's will. He prophesied into people's lives and circumstances on many occasions with exact precision. However, His amazing prophecy concerning the destruction of the temple and the rebuilding of it is so powerful because he wasn't just speaking to His own generation but on into every proceeding generation to come, through to His second coming and even beyond. This prophecy had relevance for what God would do in the 'Last days.' Let's look at it.

> *"Then Jesus went out and departed from the temple, and His disciples came up to show Him the buildings of the temple. And Jesus said to them, 'Do you not see all these things? Assuredly, I say to you, not one stone shall be left here upon another, that shall not be thrown down.'"* Matthew 24:1-2

In this Scripture Jesus predicts the destruction of the temple which came to pass forty years later in A.D.70 at the hand of the Romans. The temple was taken out of the way to make way for the Lord's spiritual temple and priesthood. Remember, Jesus had spoken this word earlier:

> *Jesus answered and said to them, "Destroy this temple, and in three days I will raise it up."* John 2:19

This has to be the most important prophecy Jesus ever gave, as the removal of the old temple and establishing of the new spiritual temple is where He would take up His present and continuing ministry as High Priest and Mediator of the New Covenant. The fact that this is where Jesus operates from now reveals the importance of this prophecy.

Priest

Jesus functioned as a Priest. A priest is a mediator and spiritual negotiator. He represents the interest of both God and the worshipper. According to the book of Hebrews, a priest offers gifts and sacrifices.

In the Old Testament, the priestly duty included ministering everything needed to keep the temple functioning and included the sacrifices, the gifts and the Law, the word of God.

They also had duties of examining the sacrifices, baking the showbread, bringing fresh wood for the brazen altar and fresh water for the brazen lava, as well as laundering the priestly garments and other duties pertaining to the temple and priesthood. The earthly ministry was preparation for Jesus' heavenly role as High Priest.

> *"Therefore, in all things He had to be made like His brethren, that He might be a merciful and faithful High Priest in things pertaining to God, to make propitiation for the sins of the people. For in that He Himself has suffered, being tempted, He is able to aid those who are tempted."* Hebrews 2:17-18

You see, every time Jesus came upon human need in his earthly life, it was an opportunity to enter into the sufferings of people in order to be a merciful and faithful and compassionate High Priest so that he could aid the sufferer. Now, through Christ's High Priestly role we can overcome temptation.

> *"For we do not have a High Priest who cannot sympathize with our weaknesses, but was in all points tempted as we are, yet without sin. "Let us therefore come boldly to the throne of grace, that we may obtain mercy and find grace to help in time of need."* Hebrews 4:15-16

The earthly ministry of Jesus qualified Him to take up His present and continuing ministry. His High Priestly role means that we have also been qualified to become merciful and compassionate priests in ministering alongside Him in Zion. Again, because He is qualified, He qualifies us to come boldly to find mercy and grace that we minister His eternal and royal priesthood. As priests, we can now minister the New Covenant and fulfil our heavenly calling.

King

Jesus is the King of kings (Revelation 17:14; 19:16). The Royal Priesthood brings both roles of King and Priest together. In the Old Testament, the only ones who ministered as Priest/King were Melchizedek and King David. Both of these operated under the Most-High God in this eternal and spiritual order.

Jesus was born King of the Jews and died as King of the Jews. On one occasion the people tried to take him by force and make him king but he wouldn't allow it (John 6:15). The people wanted him to be a political king and ruler and Jesus knew that His kingship had an even higher purpose. Through His redemptive work on the cross, He would not only become King but He would become King of kings. He would conquer every enemy and defeat, disarm and spoil them. He would also open up the kingdom of God and restore his royal family. He would restore us to the throne and invite us to sit in heavenly places far above all principalities and powers and cause us to reign and rule with Him.

As a King, Jesus exercised kingdom authority over the enemy and He conquered, subdued and established the righteous reign of the Father and the kingdom of God. Jesus manifested the glory of God (John 2:11). Mankind were created in God's image and likeness and crowned with glory and honour (Psalm 8). They fell short of the glory of God when they sinned. Unable, to access the Father's house the glory of God evaded them. But Jesus because of His perfection was able to manifest the Father's glory. Jesus spoke about it in John 17. He not only glorified the Father but he passed on His glory to us.

So, the first reason for why Jesus came to earth was fulfilled in Him modelling the Way, the truth and the Life. He showed clearly how to live and walk in the Spirit. His powerful and disciplined devotional life brought Him under the glory and power of the Father through the Holy Spirit. Inspired and powered by the Holy Spirit, Jesus operated under the Royal

Priestly order of the Most-High and manifested the glory of God. His ministry subdued Satan and all demonic powers as well as manifesting every spiritual blessing of the Father in heaven.

Next, Jesus would have to restore and open up the Way for mankind to follow so that they too would be enabled to live and walk in the Spirit and be brought back into heaven's Royal Priesthood. Only then could they subdue evil and establish the kingdom on earth. Now, Jesus must die in order to restore and open up the Way. The powers of Babylon and the world could not defeat Him until He willingly lay His life down as a ransom and a sacrifice. All that Jesus did and accomplished through His finished work was to prepare himself and us to join Him as prophets, priests and kings so that we too could subdue evil and restore heaven to earth!

CHAPTER 8

The Way Recovered

The Saviour from Zion

Satan fell from Zion but Jesus was sent from Zion. Satan's evil city, Babylon and its enterprise to destroy God's plan for heaven on earth came into the world through Adam's sin. Cut off from God and heaven, mankind fell short of the glory of God and were taken captive by Satan to do His will (2 Timothy 2:26; 1 John 5:19). When they disobeyed God and rebelled against His Word, they brought into their soul the knowledge of evil. This knowledge had to do with Satan's sins of pride, rebellion and treachery. God had warned them that they would die (be separated) if they fed on the fruit of the tree of the knowledge of good and evil and that's what happened. They disobeyed and came into agreement with Satan and so the plight of humanity began. **They were banished from Zion, the throne and the altar, from all their sources and the** very power and authority they needed to fulfil their heavenly calling – bring heaven to earth!

The fact that Jesus was *sent* reveals that He existed prior to his life on earth. The apostle John writes, *'In the beginning was the Word, and the Word was with God, and the Word was God. He was in the beginning with God. All things were made through Him, and without Him nothing was made that was made.'* John 1:1-3

He goes on to say, *'And the Word became flesh and dwelt among us, and we beheld His glory, the glory as of the only begotten of the Father, full of grace and truth.'* John 1:14

The bible is the written Word but Jesus is the Living Word.

Crowned With Glory

Adam was made in the image and likeness of God and so he was created to be god of this world.

David wrote this about the call of man in creation.

> *"For You have made him a little lower than the angels, And You have crowned him with glory and honour. You have made him to have dominion over the works of Your hands; You have put all things under his feet."* Psalm 8:5-6

Made a little lower than the angels does not mean inferior or below, for we shall judge angels (1 Corinthians 6:2-3). The word 'angels' in the Hebrew is 'Elohim' which is translated God, as in the supreme God. This should read: *made a little lower than God.*

We have been 'crowned' with glory and honour. This speaks of our royal origin and status. We are kings and priests of the Most-High God and authorised and empowered to produce heaven on earth.

Our spiritual life must be restored in order to access the kingdom!

Our calling and commission also reveal who we are in God's order. We have been given dominion over the earth and all that is in it. Why? For what purpose? To bring heaven and earth together, as one, unified in purpose. This is why in the kingdom prayer of Yeshua/Jesus, the very first thing we are to pray is: 'Thy kingdom come and thy will be done on earth as it is in heaven' (Matthew 6:9-10).

> *"For there is no difference; for all have sinned and fall short of the glory of God."* Romans 3:22-23

'Ichabod' means the glory has departed.

This happened to Israel when the ark was taken from them. Sin, means 'to miss the mark' or 'to fall short.' Death means 'separation.' When Adam sinned, he fell short of the glory of God. He was separated from the very glory he had access to in order to manage earth under the royal priesthood of the Most-High God in heaven. He lost his crown and his spirit was cut off from Eden, heaven and Zion. He lost his access, his spiritual connection, his citizenship and spiritual authority and power. He came under the dominion of Satan, who in turn usurped Adam's position as god of this world. Now, through sin he is spiritually separated and has no way back of his own ability and merit. With man disconnected, dead and defiled, Satan becomes god of this world and now produces a system that is in opposition to God and heaven. Its aim is to keep humanity in darkness and ignorance through materialism.

And so, Jesus was sent into the world from Zion to save, redeem and restore mankind.

> *'But when the fullness of the time had come, God sent forth His Son, born of a woman, born under the law, to redeem those who were under the law, that we might receive the adoption as sons.'* Galatians 4:4-5

The woman was Mary and she was a virgin. The angel Gabriel was sent from God to her to announce how she was highly favoured, blessed and chosen to be the mother of a special child. The child would be born supernaturally by the Holy Spirit and without the help of her betrothed husband, Joseph.

He would be 'Immanuel' translated 'God with us' and He was to be called Jesus, for He will save His people from their sins. The word of God had already been established hundreds of years before by the prophet Isaiah.

> *"Therefore, the Lord Himself will give you a sign: Behold, the virgin shall conceive and bear a Son, and shall call His name Immanuel."* Isaiah 7:14

The reason that Jesus had to be born of a virgin was that His blood was to be unstained from the human condition of sin and death, as it would provide salvation and redemption for mankind and had to be free of corruption. And so, Jesus was born into the world supernaturally to fulfil a great purpose.

> *"For this purpose the Son of God was manifested, that He might destroy the works of the devil."* 1 John 3:8-9

> *"And you know that He was manifested to take away our sins, and in Him there is no sin."* 1 John 3:5-6

Jesus was born to destroy the works of the devil and to put away our sins. He came with the purpose of destroying all that was against us, and all that was keeping us from our heavenly calling and original commission. This means that Jesus' earthly ministry was twofold:

Jesus demonstrated the Way and then died to open up the Way for others to follow!

Jesus was sent to restore us to the kingdom of God and spiritual life. Adam didn't lose religion and he didn't lose physical life, at least not right away. But he did lose spiritual life. He lost his God-given ability and right to access and engage Zion, heaven in the spiritual realm. He lost spiritual power and authority needed to fulfil His heavenly calling. More importantly, he fell short of the glory of God and now could no longer manifest it. Jesus came to open up a new and living way and not just a way by type and shadow that we see in the Old Testament into a copy of the heavenly tabernacle. **Jesus died to open up the heavenly tabernacle.**

"We have such a High Priest, who is seated at the right hand of the throne of the Majesty in the heavens, a Minister of the sanctuary and of the true tabernacle which the Lord erected, and not man." Hebrews 8:1-2

> *"Therefore, brethren, having boldness to enter the Holiest by the blood of Jesus, by a new and living way which He consecrated for us, through the veil."* Hebrews 10:19-20

Jesus came to fulfil the law and then abolish the Old Covenant and system in order to establish a new covenant and order that would restore mankind spiritually to the heavenly tabernacle and the glory of God. This new and living way perfects the worshipper and provides the spiritual approach to heaven, and its true tabernacle (Hebrews 8:2).

The finished work of Yeshua/Jesus has provided in every way for the believer to be completely restored so that we are not only forgiven, but we are raised in perfect righteousness so that we have access by His blood to Zion, the heavenly tabernacle and the glory of God at the throne and the altar. Fully restored, we can now fulfil our heavenly call.

CHAPTER 9

From Type and Shadow

Into Substance Hebrews 8:5

The tabernacle of Moses fully illustrates the perfect redemptive work of Christ and reveals how to function as a prophet, priest and king in the kingdom of God. It clearly shows the Way to living, walking and ministering in the Spirit as Jesus did. Let's see how it works.

The Door/Gate

> *"You shall make a screen for the door of the tabernacle, woven of blue, purple, and scarlet thread, and fine woven linen, made by a weaver."* Exodus 26:36

The only way into the tabernacle of Moses was through the one door situated on the east side. There was no other way to enter the tabernacle. The door was the official and only way to approach the Holy place and experience the presence of God. The door was made of fabric and was a mixture of blue, purple, scarlet and fine/white linen.

> *"I am the door. If anyone enters by Me, he will be saved, and will go in and out and find pasture."* John 10:9

The only way into Zion and to the throne and the altar is through Jesus.

> *Jesus said to him, "I am the way, the truth, and the life. No one comes to the Father except through Me."* John 14:2-6

Each of the colours woven into one to make up the door point to Jesus.

· **Blue is the colour of heaven and Jesus is the man from heaven.**

> *"The second Man is the Lord from heaven."* 1 Corinthians 15:47 (see also John 3:13,31)

· **Purple is the colour of royalty and of Kingship.** Jesus is the King of kings

> *"And He has on His robe and on His thigh a name written: KING OF KINGS AND LORD OF LORDS."* Revelation 19:16

· **Scarlet is the colour of the sacrificial blood**. Jesus is the ultimate once for all, final sacrifice for sins.

> *"Not with the blood of goats and calves, but with His own blood He entered the Most Holy Place once for all, having obtained eternal redemption."* Hebrews 9:12

· **Fine linen points to righteousness**. Jesus is the King of righteousness and the Lord Our righteousness.

> *"Now this is His name by which He will be called: THE LORD OUR RIGHTEOUSNESS."* Jeremiah 23:6

As the door and the only way, Jesus gives us access to the salvation He provided for us.

We cannot come through people, angels or spirits nor can we come through good works and self -effort – ONLY JESUS gives us access to spiritual life and power. He is the way that leads to salvation and He is the way that leads to restored fellowship, inspiration and power to accomplish our heavenly calling.

> *"Nor is there salvation in any other, for there is no other name under heaven given among men by which we must be saved."* Acts 4:12

> *"For there is one God and one Mediator between God and men, the Man Christ Jesus, who gave Himself a ransom for all."* 1 Timothy 2:5-6

There's clearly only one way and one Name that brings people to God – Yeshua/Jesus.

People who are spiritually disconnected from Heaven can access the spiritual realm through their spirit but they cannot enter into the Father's house – spiritual experiences that are had under these circumstances are Satanic and demonic and operate to deceive people. Satan comes as an angel of light (2 Corinthians 11:14). Babylon, and the demonic will gladly entertain enquirers and grant experiences. This explains how spiritualists and mediums do their work. It's a dangerous thing to play around with the spiritual realm and can lead to serious consequences. The following account in the book of Acts illustrates the danger.

> *"Then some of the itinerant Jewish exorcists took it upon themselves to call the name of the Lord Jesus over those who had evil spirits, saying, "We exorcise you by the Jesus whom Paul preaches." Also there were seven sons of Sceva, a Jewish chief priest, who did so. And the evil spirit answered and said, "Jesus I know, and Paul I know; but who are you?" Then the man in whom the evil spirit was leaped on them, overpowered them, and prevailed against them, so that they fled out of that house naked and wounded."* Acts 19:13-16

Divination which covers all false systems of trying to determine the divine will by consulting human or spirit channels is clearly denounced by God. These systems no matter how they are packaged are illegal and unrecognised by God and heaven.

> *"There shall not be found among you anyone who makes his son or his daughter pass through the fire, or one who practices witchcraft, or a soothsayer, or one who interprets omens, or a sorcerer, or one who conjures spells, or a medium, or a spirit-ist, or one who calls up the dead. For all who do these things are an abomination to the Lord, and because of these abominations the Lord your God drives them out from before you."*
> Deuteronomy 18:10-13

People who operate in such practices are vessels for 'Familiar spirits'. Such a person was called by the Hebrews an *'ob'*, which properly means a leathern bottle; for sorcerers were regarded as vessels containing the inspiring demon. The word "familiar" is from the Latin 'familiaris,' meaning a 'household servant' and was intended to express the idea that familiar spirits were associated and attached to family lines and generations.

This allowed them to reveal information about the lives of any family member being enquired of. This explains why mediums and spiritualists can reveal information about deceased family members. Any organisation or movement that encourages people to experience the spiritual realm outside of Jesus are clearly disobeying God's word and command.

Calvary – The Brazen Altar

> *"You shall make an altar of acacia wood, five cubits long and five cubits wide — the altar shall be square — and its height shall be three cubits."* Exodus 27:1

The brazen altar was anointed and set apart for sacrifices. The main purpose for the brazen altar was to offer blood sacrifice for atonement (At-one-ment.)

It was the ONLY place for blood atonement and sacrifice.

"For the life of the flesh is in the blood, and I have given it to you upon the altar to make atonement for your souls; for it is the blood that makes atonement for the soul." Leviticus 17:11

There was no other place recognised by Israel or accepted by God other than the brazen altar. The blood that was sprinkled on everything else in the holy place and most holy place, was first sacrificed on this altar. This altar was a horrid scene – it was a place of judgment, slaughter, death, blood and sacrifice. The cries of the animal sacrifices would have been haunting and chilling to the core of our being. This is the only place that sins could be dealt with. It was here that God judged the sins of the people and extended mercy, forgiveness and fellowship. Day after day, year after year, the daily sacrifices and the blood of bulls and goats, lambs and doves were offered.

All of these sacrifices could not perfect the worshiper. They gave a temporal solution but they couldn't fully redeem the worshipper and bring him before the throne and the altar.

The sacrifices had to be continually offered every day to satisfy God's holiness.

> *"For the law, having a shadow of the good things to come, and not the very image of the things, can never with these same sacrifices, which they offer continually year by year, make those who approach perfect. For then would they not have ceased to be offered? For the worshipers, once purified, would have had no more consciousness of sins. But in those sacrifices, there is a reminder of sins every year. For it is not possible that the blood of bulls and goats could take away sins."* Hebrews 10:1–4

The animal sacrifices could not produce the perfect approach nor could they perfect the worshipper. They were a continual reminder of sins, sinfulness and the inability to obey God. It left them sin conscious. Which produces condemnation in the heart and mind.

*"And every priest stands ministering daily and offering re-
peatedly the same sacrifices, which can never take away sins."*
Hebrews 10:11–14

The animal sacrifices continually offered were unable to take
sins away and offer as permanent solution for the worshipper
to come before God. This system and covenant could not perfect the worshipper and bring him into deep fellowship and
intimacy with God. The brazen altar was used daily throughout Israel's history and pointed to a time when the type and
shadow would give way to the substance. Calvary and the
cross were that substance.

Once For All Sacrifice

Calvary was the ultimate brazen altar. Jesus became the final,
once for all sacrificial lamb of God.

John the Baptist on seeing Jesus approach Jordan said, 'Behold! The Lamb of God who takes away the sin of the world'
(John 1:29). John called Jesus the Lamb of God. As such, the
lamb of God was prepared and given by the Father. Thousands
upon thousands of lambs had been sacrificed since the Jewish
Passover and they all pointed to the one ultimate sacrificial
Lamb of God. They couldn't fully redeem us, couldn't fully
cleanse and renew us, couldn't fully perfect the worshipper
and bring us before our holy and righteous Father in heaven.
Only one lamb could do that: Yeshua/Jesus, the holy, perfect
and spotless Lamb of God.

> *"Knowing that you were not redeemed with corruptible
> things, like silver or gold, from your aimless conduct received
> by tradition from your fathers, but with the precious blood of
> Christ, as of a lamb without blemish and without spot. He in-
> deed was foreordained before the foundation of the world, but
> was manifest in these last times for you."* 1 Peter 1:18–20

Jesus is the Lamb who was slain from the foundation of the
world (Revelation 13:8).

His once for all perfect and final sacrifice alone provides salvation and perfection for worshippers who will fully avail of what He has done and appropriate His finished work on the cross. Yeshua's sacrifice has dealt with everything that was working against us through the power of sin.

In order to open up a new and living way, Jesus had to offer the perfect, once for all sacrifice that would perfect the worshipper forever. This he did when He died on the cross. Jesus' death on the cross was the final, once for all sacrifice, offered on the behalf of every fallen child of Adam and Eve. Jesus' atoning work on the cross would achieve *eternal redemption* for every person throughout time.

> *"But Christ came as High Priest of the good things to come, with the greater and more perfect tabernacle not made with hands, that is, not of this creation. Not with the blood of goats and calves, but with His own blood He entered the Most Holy Place once for all, having obtained eternal redemption."* Hebrews 9:11-13

Jesus knew that He would ultimately die. He spoke of His death many times with His disciples. He also knew His death was *sacrificial and substitutionary*. He said that the Son of man must give His life a ransom for many (Matthew 20:28). He said that He lay down His life for His sheep (John 10:15). He also knew that His death and resurrection was like a seed going into the ground that would sprout and grow and produce a great harvest (John 12:24). Jesus looked beyond the sufferings of the cross to the time that He would sit down at the right hand of the Father and that he would raise up fallen sons to be seated in heavenly places too (Hebrews 12:2; Ephesians 2:6).

In all of this God demonstrated a number of things to us. The cross shows us a demonstration of God's holiness and justice. Sin must be dealt with and so he delivered up His own Son to be the sin bearer. The cross demonstrates God's judgment on sin (Isaiah 53). In that once for all sacrifice, God's holiness, justice and righteousness were completely satisfied.

The cross also demonstrates God's love and compassion (Rom 5:8), as well as His grace and mercy. In the work of the cross, God could judge and punish sin and show his justice, but He could also demonstrate His love, kindness, grace and mercy to sinners and therefore justify them and offer them the gift of righteousness.

When Jesus died on the cross, he dealt with everything that had caused death and separation.

His finished work on the cross would deal with everything once for all (Hebrews 9:12; 10:10).

Now through Christ's perfect work and perfect sacrifice, sinners can be set free and be justified, sanctified and glorified. Spiritual life can be fully restored and the Way is now recovered and accessible. Jesus didn't go to the cross alone. He took a number of things to the cross when He died. In fact, what he brought to the cross and overcame and conquered, makes the believer more than a conqueror too.

The Cross

Firstly, Jesus brought all our sins to the cross, past, present and future.

"Who Himself bore our sins in His own body on the tree, that we, having died to sins, might live for righteousness — by whose stripes you were healed." 1 Peter 2:24

Secondly, Jesus brought our old sin nature to the cross.

> *"Knowing this, that our old man was crucified with Him, that the body of sin might be done away with, that we should no longer be slaves of sin. For he who has died has been freed from sin."* Romans 6:6-7

Praise God. Jesus didn't only die for our sins, he died to put away the very sin nature that produces sin. As believers we can live free from sin.

> *"I have been crucified with Christ; it is no longer I who live, but Christ lives in me; and the life which I now live in the flesh*

I live by faith in the Son of God, who loved me and gave Himself for me." Galatians 2:20-21

Thirdly, Jesus brought the ruler of this world (Satan) to the cross.

"Now is the judgment of this world; now the ruler of this world will be cast out." John 12:31-32

Next, Jesus dealt with the tempter to sin. Satan is called the 'Tempter' and as such he tempts and entices us to sin, promising that it will meet our needs and will have no consequences. Satan was judged, defeated and disarmed at the cross. He was stripped of His authority and cast out. With our sins taken out of the way and the very body of sin crucified the power of the tempter is beaten. Now, we are no longer slaves to sin and have the assurance that if we live and walk in the Spirit, we will NOT fulfil the lusts of the flesh (Galatians 5:16).

Fourthly, Jesus took the world to the cross.

'Now is the judgment of this world.' John 12:31

'In the world you will have tribulation; but be of good cheer, I have overcome the world.' John 16:33

Satan has so influenced the world, that all that is in it; the lust of the eyes, the lust of the flesh and the pride of life are set to work with the body of sin and the power of sin to enslave people and keep them down in spiritual death and defeat. Satan tried to tempt Jesus with the world in the wilderness. He offered him all the kingdoms of the world and their glory if He would bow down and worship him (Matthew 4:8). Jesus couldn't be bought with the world. He didn't allow the world to become an idol above worshipping the Father. He resisted and overcame the rule of this world. When Jesus died, he overcame the world and now through the cross, the world is crucified unto us (1 John 2:16; Galatians 6:14).

"For whatever is born of God overcomes the world. And this is the victory that has overcome the world — our faith. Who is he

who overcomes the world, but he who believes that Jesus is the Son of God?" 1 John 5:4-5

The object of our sin was dealt with at the cross and now we can be free from idolatry. Our faith in Christ's victorious work makes us overcomers.

Fifthly, Jesus took all the Handwriting of requirements to the cross.

"Having wiped out the handwriting of requirements that was against us, which was contrary to us. And He has taken it out of the way, having nailed it to the cross." Colossians 2:14

The very thing that produced sin in us was overcome. This is alluding to the Mosaic law and especially the ceremonial law that was such a burden to keep because of indwelling sin. There were curses associated with not obeying all the requirements of the law. It was a continual losing battle for the worshipper. But, through the cross Jesus has put an end to trying to serve God following rules and regulations that were contrary to us or beyond our ability to keep. He has fulfilled the requirements of the law and now we can enter into His rest (Hebrews 4:1, 9).

Lastly, Jesus took all our infirmities and sicknesses to the cross.

"Surely he took up our pain and bore our suffering, yet we considered him punished by God, stricken by him, and afflicted. But he was pierced for our transgressions, he was crushed for our iniquities; the punishment that brought us peace was on him, and by his wounds we are healed." Isaiah 53:4-5

Forgiveness and healing go together. Through the gospels Jesus both forgave sins and healed diseases. Sometimes Jesus forgave sins and the person was healed.

"Bless the Lord, O my soul, And forget not all His benefits: Who forgives all your iniquities, Who heals all your diseases." Psalm 103:2-3

"When evening had come, they brought to Him many who were demon-possessed. And He cast out the spirits with a word, and healed all who were sick, that it might be fulfilled which was spoken by Isaiah the prophet, saying: "He Himself took our infirmities And bore our sicknesses." Matthew 8:16-17

All of these benefits are ours by grace through faith.

We are told by the apostle Paul to 'reckon' (Romans 6:11). Reckon means to count, to calculate and come to a total and see what it equals. Well, when we reckon all these truths and count them up and total them, they equal complete deliverance and victory over our sinful flesh life.

The truth shall make you free! When Jesus died, we died. Our identification with Christ is very powerful and something that must be grasped and appropriated by faith daily. Jesus told His followers to take up the cross *daily* and deny themselves and follow him (Luke 9:23-25). This means that when we **reckon** and **believe** the word to be true and **confess it**, we enter into the power, salvation and reality of it. Praise God! **Also, following Jesus should lead to where He is TODAY – in ZION!**

Freed From Sin

As believers we can live above sin. All of our hang ups are rooted in the flesh, the old sin nature. There's no hope or therapy for the flesh. Many believers are trying by self-effort to work on areas of their old life in order to overcome. In the flesh is no good thing and no flesh can glory in the Lord's presence, neither can anyone please God in the flesh (Romans 7:18; 1 Corinthians 1:29; Romans 8:8.) Why invest time trying to change something that the Lord crucified? What's the point of weeks and months of therapy, when in one single sweep: crucifixion, you can put to death the flesh and be gloriously liberated? Sound too simple to be true. Test it, it really works! **So, we have access through Jesus, as the door and through**

applying his blood by faith! This finished work brings us into resurrection life – but the journey to intimacy continues....

The Word–The Brazen Laver

> *Then the Lord spoke to Moses, saying: "You shall also make a laver of bronze, with its base also of bronze, for washing. You shall put it between the tabernacle of meeting and the altar. And you shall put water in it, for Aaron and his sons shall wash their hands and their feet in water from it."* Exodus 30:17-20

The brazen laver was anointed and set apart for washing. Its main purpose was to provide cleansing from defilements for the priests so that they could minister in the holy place and before the golden altar. The brazen laver was a large basin set upon a base. It was made of bronze mirrors that the serving women had made (Exodus 38:8). It stood between the altar and the tent of meeting. The priests were to wash their hands and their feet before they served and ministered to the Lord. The mirrors of the brazen laver provided a reflection of their cleansed image.

Later, in Solomon's temple, the laver gave way to the Molten sea. The Molten sea was larger than the original laver and could hold up to 2,000 baths. It was set upon the shoulders of 12 oxen. Oxen represent labour and service, and so the lesson is obvious. Every priest must go through the washing to ready him for labouring and serving in the temple and holy place. The water used was purified.

> *"When they go into the tabernacle of meeting, or when they come near the altar to minister, to burn an offering made by fire to the Lord, they shall wash with water, lest they die. So they shall wash their hands and their feet, lest they die. And it shall be a statute forever to them — to him and his descendants throughout their generations."* Exodus 30:20-21

If a priest didn't apply the laver it meant death to draw near God defiled and stained with sin.

God insisted on purity and holiness in the priesthood. 'Be holy as I am holy' says the Lord.

Resurrection Life

"But now Christ is risen from the dead, and has become the first fruits of those who have fallen asleep." 1 Corinthians 15:20–21

When Jesus rose from the dead in resurrection power, He became the first-fruits of a new creation.

The new creation has replaced the old creation, which is under the curse of sin and will end one day and give way to the new creation.

'But the day of the Lord will come as a thief in the night, in which the heavens will pass away with a great noise, and the elements will melt with fervent heat; both the earth and the works that are in it will be burned up. Therefore, since all these things will be dissolved, what manner of persons ought you to be in holy conduct and godliness, looking for and hastening the coming of the day of God, because of which the heavens will be dissolved, being on fire, and the elements will melt with fervent heat? Nevertheless we, according to His promise, look for new heavens and a new earth in which righteousness dwells.' 2 Peter 3:10–13

So, it is the new creation that God is committed to and it's the new creation that every believer has been birthed into.

'Of His own will He brought us forth by the word of truth, that we might be a kind of first fruits of His creatures.' James 1:18

We are the first fruits of the new creation along with Christ. We are a new breed of creature. Raised up in Christ and glorified in Him so that we can bring about the new creation into the earth.

"'Therefore, if anyone is in Christ, he is a new creation; old things have passed away; behold, all things have become new." 2 Corinthians 5:17-18

Every believer has been resurrected and raised up to new life in Christ. Everything is new about this life. Our new life is nothing at all like our old life. In our old life we were defiled by sin and separated from God and from heaven. We were unrighteous, ungodly and under the curse of sin. We were short of the glory of God and had no way to come before God because we were dead in trespasses and sins.

We had no way of manifesting the glory of God through the Spirit, as we were cut off. *But old things have passed away and died and behold all things have become new.* This is a fact that must be entered into and claimed and confessed as we'll see.

Now, in our new life, we have been raised up into resurrection life and everything is new. In Christ our spiritual life is fully restored. What's more is that our new life in Christ is fully righteous, holy and perfect. We have been justified, sanctified and made righteous by faith in Him.

> *"For whom He foreknew, He also predestined to be conformed to the image of His Son, that He might be the firstborn among many brethren. Moreover, whom He predestined, these He also called; whom He called, these He also justified; and whom He justified, these He also glorified."* Romans 8:29-30

This is really important to know and understand. The finished work of the cross has put to death our old nature and given rise to our new nature. We are new creatures, made new. We are fully forgiven, redeemed, justified and sanctified. We have been set free from the old creation and are fully equipped to walk in the new creation and newness of life. Fully restored we now have access to the Father/glory

Christ Our Laver

When the priests went to the brazen laver, they saw their reflection in the mirror of the basin and it allowed them to cleanse themselves and make sure that they were clean. This they did every time they came to minister in the sanctuary. *Remember, the tabernacle and all of its articles were type and shadow that pointed to the blessed substance and reality in the heavenly tabernacle.* This laver could wash the hands and feet of the priests but it couldn't cleanse and renew them from head to foot and from the inside out. As we come to our brazen laver, Christ we see a reflection of Christ's perfection in us.

> *"But be doers of the word, and not hearers only, deceiving yourselves. For if anyone is a hearer of the word and not a doer, he is like a man observing his natural face in a mirror; for he observes himself, goes away, and immediately forgets what kind of man he was. But he who looks into the perfect law of liberty and continues in it, and is not a forgetful hearer but a doer of the work, this one will be blessed in what he does."* James 1:22-25

The image we see, is who we are in Christ. It's this image that liberates us and must be remembered so that we continue in it and be blessed. We must align to the word and not to our feelings or the lies of the enemy. The purpose of the mirror of God's word is not to show us our shortcomings, but to reveal our perfection in Christ. Too many believers see who they are in Christ and in the word, but very quickly go away and immediately forget what the word revealed. This is further undone through negative confession.

Let's look at our identification with Christ. The new life is hidden in Christ (Colossians 3:3). Christ is the word and therefore is the laver that cleanses and sanctifies the believer/ church. We are clean because of the word (John 15:3). As new creatures raised to life all things have become new. The word of God is likened to water and so it is powerful to cleanse and sanctify believers.

> *"According to His mercy He saved us, through the washing of regeneration and renewing of the Holy Spirit, whom He poured out on us abundantly through Jesus Christ our Saviour."* Ephesians 5:25-27

> *"Just as Christ also loved the church and gave Himself for her, that He might sanctify and cleanse her with the washing of water by the word, that He might present her to Himself a*

glorious church, not having spot or wrinkle or any such thing, but that she should be holy and without blemish." Colossians 2:12

"But you were washed, but you were sanctified, but you were justified in the name of the Lord Jesus and by the Spirit of our God." 1 Corinthians 6:11

Our new life is completely holy and righteous because it's Christ's life and we are placed IN HIM!

The new creation has been washed, cleansed, justified, sanctified and made completely righteous through Jesus. Therefore, the new creation has full right standing with God through the divine exchange. This gives us boldness in our approach to the Father. Here's the divine exchange:

"For He made Him who knew no sin to be sin for us, that we might become the righteousness of God in Him." 2 Corinthians 5:21

Now there's a definite purpose for why we have been raised, justified, sanctified and made righteous.

So many believers confess that they are the righteousness of God without a clear understanding of why the gift of righteousness has been imputed to us.

The door gives access to the altar of sacrifice and atonement, so that sin, the body of sin, Satan and the world might be put away and that we are raised as overcomers. When we apply the work of the cross, we become overcomers of the world, the flesh and the devil. It's overcomers who share Christ's throne (Revelation 3:21).

The gift of salvation includes the gift of righteousness and the abundance of grace so that we reign in life, through Christ. You cannot reign until you've established your righteousness. You must 'put on' the righteousness of Christ. The priests had to wear priestly garments to minister before God and with God.

> *"But put on the Lord Jesus Christ, and make no provision for the flesh, to fulfil its lusts."* Romans 13:14

> *"Put on the new man which was created according to God, in true righteousness and holiness."* Ephesians 4:24

> *"Put on the new man who is renewed in knowledge according to the image of Him who created him."* Colossians 3:10

You must receive the robe of righteousness as a gift and put it on by faith (Isaiah 61:10).

It's this gift of righteousness that makes you an overcomer of the world, the flesh and the devil.

As you accept the crucified life and bury it, you rise an overcomer. As you put on Christ and the new man and establish this position, you'll be an overcomer and begin to reign in life, this life.

> *"For if by the one man's offense death reigned through the one, much more those who receive abundance of grace and of the gift of righteousness will reign in life through the One, Jesus Christ."* Romans 5:17

As we come to the laver, it reveals who we are in Christ in all of its many depictions. In fact, it's a rich and productive study to search out some of the "in Christ," "in Him," "in whom," etc. scriptures in the new testament letters. We are new creatures in Christ, we are righteous in Christ, there's no condemnation in Christ, we have every spiritual blessing in Christ etc.

In the tabernacle, the altar and the brazen laver were to cleanse, prepare and ready the priests to minister in the holy place. *The purpose of renewal and restoration to righteousness was to make us priests and kings, to access the holy place and be restored to the glory that was lost!*

> *"To Him who loved us and washed us from our sins in His own blood, and has made us kings and priests to His God and Father."* Revelation 1:5-6

Calvary and all of the truths around death and resurrection lift us out of defeat and into Christ's victory and triumph. The finished work of Jesus on the cross is to prepare us and ready us to ascend and join Him in the heavenly tabernacle and into His present and continuing work, ministering the new covenant in His blood.

All of these truths must be applied to become an overcomer. Only then can a believer rise to take position in the enthroned life.

The Truth Shall Set You Free

"And you shall know the truth, and the truth shall make you free." John 8:32

Jesus said that it's our 'knowing' the truth in application and experience that sets us free. If we don't know it in the real sense of the word it won't set us free. In chapter 6 of his letter to the Romans, Paul writes, 'do you not know' twice. He also uses the word 'knowing' on two occasions in the same chapter. He wants the believers to know the truth. No knowing, no freedom!

The finished work of Jesus has fully dealt with sin, Satan, the body of sin, the world and the handwritings that were against us. When Jesus died, the believer died with him so that the body of sin was put out of action and the believer is freed from sin (Rom 6:6-7). When we take up the cross and apply it, we enter into the crucified life. This truth will set you free from fleshly and carnal living! Our old life was buried with him through baptism that just as Christ rose from the dead into resurrection life, we also were raised into newness of life (Rom 6:3-5).

"Buried with Him in baptism, in which you also were raised with Him through faith in the working of God." Colossians 2:12

We were made righteous through Christ and must receive it as God's gift through faith.

Our identification with Christ explains who God has recreated us to be – we MUST know it, claim it and confess it. Confession works both negatively and positively. Your confession defines you.

We enter into everything that God has for us through faith and confession.

All we need is a believing heart and a mouth that will confess (agree, say the same as) the word of God.

> But what does it say? "The word is near you, in your mouth and in your heart" (that is, the word of faith which we preach): that if you confess with your mouth the Lord Jesus and believe in your heart that God has raised Him from the dead, you will be saved. For with the heart one believes unto righteousness, and with the mouth confession is made unto salvation." Romans 10:8-10

We must believe in our heart and confess with our mouth to receive the benefits of the promises in the word of God. Look what the word says: *'Confession is made unto'* in other words what you speak you shall have. All these powerful truths will do you no good until they move from your heart to your mouth. It's through confession of faith that these truths become reality in our life. Get rid of all negative thoughts and confessions as you will have what you speak! Align to the word and let the laver reveal who you really are. Work this into your life until you are a prophet, priest and king unto God and have a powerful intimate relationship with the Lord.

> *'For with the heart one believes unto righteousness, and with the mouth confession is made unto salvation.'*

CHAPTER 10

The Heavenly Tabernacle

The Substance

The priests of the Old Covenant were privileged to minister in the tabernacle and the holy place. The ultimate privilege and honour for priests was to minister at the golden altar. However, many lived and died and never got the opportunity. All of this was a type and shadow of the heavenly tabernacle that Christ would open by a new and living way for all of God's people to come into humbly and boldly. The priests were given strict orders on preparing, approaching and ministering to the Lord and had to comply to every directive and command.

Everything that we have looked at so far has been to ready us for our glorified position and privilege.

Jesus is the Way to the heavenly tabernacle, to the throne and the altar. In order to take up our ministry here in the spirit, we must first establish our new identity as 'new creatures' in Christ and in the new creation. As we look at who we have become through the divine exchange at calvary and reinforce this, we become overcomers and enter into the 'enthroned life.' Again, this is accepted by grace through faith and must be believed, claimed and confessed to enter into the reality of heaven's tabernacle, in Zion, the City of God, and heavenly Jerusalem (Hebrews 12:22). **Through Jesus finished work, we are readied and prepared to join Him in His present and continuing work in Zion**. Because of this we must go beyond the cross.

Christ's Ascension

After Jesus conquered Sin, Satan and death on the cross, He rose in resurrection life and power and raised up every believer as an overcomer with Him. Jesus triumphed over Satan's kingdom and spoiled it. Before He ascended, he descended and recovered the keys of death and Hades from the devil (Revelation 1:18), and led captivity captive (Ephesians 4:8). He made a public spectacle of Satan and His kingdom (Colossians 2:15). After His victorious mission, Jesus ascended to Zion, heaven. He passed through the heavens and opened up a new and living way for all of the sons of God to come to where He is.

We've been taught in the church that we go to heaven when we die for our rewards. But this is only partially true. Because of Christ we can go to heaven every day of our lives NOW! It's too late when we're dead and departed. The world needs heaven now. The church needs heaven now. The ascension ministry of the risen and exalted Jesus has been shrouded in mystery for generations. The most believers know of it is that Jesus ever lives to make intercession for us (Hebrews 7:25). There's more to it than we have previously known and been aware of. Jesus defeated and spoiled all of His enemies and then returned to His Father. He brought His own blood because He needed to cleanse heaven's sanctuary of the sin and defilement of Lucifer (Hebrews 9:23).

The blood of Jesus is still active in heaven today and must be ministered by the church, Christ's royal priesthood. He has been highly exalted, far above all principalities and powers and has been given the Name above all names (Philippians 2:9-11; Ephesians 1:21). He has become the head over all things to the church (Ephesians 1:22), and has sat down at the right hand of the Father until all His enemies are under His footstool and all things have been gathered in unto Christ. Christ has been received into heaven until the restoration of all things (Acts 3:21).

Why didn't Christ end it with His work on the cross? The reason is because the church is called to subdue evil and restore the kingdom of God on earth alongside her exalted Royal High Priest. Why is it that the devil is still running rampant through the heavens and the earth continuing to kill, steal and destroy? Because the church is on the ground instead of being in the Spirit.

Everything is about to change for the church. The Lord is lifting her up to her true position in Zion. He is lifting her up to the ascended life and position. From here, in the spirit, the church is going to come into the glory of God and manifest great power and authority in the heavens and in the earth. His work has restored us to the throne, the altar and the glory of God.

Beyond the Cross

Many believers stay at the cross way too long and some believers stay there and never move beyond into the 'enthroned life.' Whilst we must never lose sight of the cross, we must, however, go beyond the cross and rise up to the enthroned life and our heavenly calling. Many believers never experience the enthroned life because they don't appropriate the finished work of Christ and become an overcomer.

Instead, they are continually and daily overcome by the world, the flesh and the devil and find themselves in a vicious cycle of 'sin and confession' and thus end up in guilt, shame and condemnation. Many believers are striving to be holy in their own works and strength only to fail miserably. This is exactly where the devil wants believers to be. The reason is so that they don't rise to the enthroned life – because when they do, they become really dangerous to his kingdom endeavours. Jesus shares his throne (the enthroned life) with overcomers.

> *'To him who overcomes I will grant to sit with Me on My throne, as I also overcame and sat down with My Father on His throne.'* Revelation 3:21

We overcome by entering into the divine exchange wrought by the blood of the Lamb, Jesus.

> *'And they overcame him by the blood of the Lamb and by the word of their testimony, and they did not love their lives to the death.'* Revelation 12:11

We've been redeemed and bought and with the blood of Jesus (1 Corinthians 6:20; 7:23). We are the Lord's possession – He purchased not only our salvation but He purchased *us* also. We must understand the power of Jesus' blood as a sacrifice for sinners and salvation, as well as a weapon against the enemy. We must learn how to minister the blood of Christ. The blood of Jesus not only gives us access to the heavenly tabernacle, but as priests and kings, we minister the power, and authority of the blood of sprinkling (Hebrews 12:24). More on this later.

> *Remember, we enter into everything that God has for us through faith and confession* Romans 10:8-10

Our Ascension

Let's look at our identification with Christ.

When Jesus died, I died. When Jesus rose, I arose and when Jesus ascended, I ascended. Our citizenship has been restored (Philippians 3:21), and so our spiritual life and our access to heaven's tabernacle have also been restored. It's up to us to develop and grow in our spiritual life.

"If we live in the Spirit, let us also walk in the Spirit." Galatians 5:25

Every believer must establish spiritual life and develop it in order to live, walk and minister spiritually. We must exercise our spirit every day, through faith and confession. We are called to walk by faith and not by sight (2 Corinthians 5:7). We are also reminded that the eternal things are in the unseen realm.

"While we do not look at the things which are seen, but at the things which are not seen. For the things which are seen are temporary, but the things which are not seen are eternal." 2 Corinthians 4:18

And again, we are encouraged to seek the things above where Christ is.

"If then you were raised with Christ, seek those things which are above, where Christ is, sitting at the right hand of God. Set your mind on things above, not on things on the earth." Colossians 3:1-2

The believer that doesn't set their mind on the things above, cannot live and walk in the Spirit. The mind is the key to activating your spirit in the same way that it activates the physical body. This is why it's so important to develop a spiritual mind. Being spiritually minded, means that you have your thinking on the truths and realities of the unseen realm, and the word of God and all it has to say about the heavenly places are alive in your mind and thinking. This is the key to living, walking and ministering in the Spirit.

The eighth chapter of Romans states that being spiritually minded leads to life, peace and communion with God (Romans 8:5-8). This means that when we reckon and believe the word to be true and confess it, we enter into the power, salvation and reality of it. Praise God! Also, following Jesus should lead to where He is TODAY – in ZION!

In Christ we have been adopted as sons into the family of God and made joint heirs with Christ in the kingdom of God. This means that we have access as sons and heirs to the kingdom and all of its resources and power. As heirs we have a heavenly inheritance to withdraw from.

> *"For you did not receive the spirit of bondage again to fear, but you received the Spirit of adoption by whom we cry out, 'Abba, Father.' The Spirit Himself bears witness with our spirit that we are children of God, and if children, then heirs — heirs of God and joint heirs with Christ."* Romans 8:15-17

> *"For you are all sons of God through faith in Christ Jesus."* Galatians 3:26

In Christ our spiritual life is fully restored. We have been justified, sanctified and made righteous by faith in Him. We have been raised to where Christ is and have been given access to Zion, spiritually so that we can join Christ in His present and continuing ministry.

> *"For it was fitting for Him, for whom are all things and by whom are all things, in bringing many sons to glory, to make the captain of their salvation perfect through sufferings. For both He who sanctifies and those who are being sanctified are all of one, for which reason He is not ashamed to call them brethren."* Hebrews 2:10-12

> *"For whom He foreknew, He also predestined to be conformed to the image of His Son, that He might be the firstborn among many brethren. Moreover, whom He predestined, these He also called; whom He called, these He also justified; and whom He justified, these He also glorified."* Romans 8:29-30

We have been made sons and we've been brought to glory (Zion) and given access to our heavenly Father and All of His kingdom. It's our Father's good pleasure to give us the kingdom (Luke 12:32). We have been made joint heirs with Christ and brought to glory so that we can fulfil our original calling: **Dominion and authority to produce heaven on earth** – you must be familiar with heaven to produce heaven! **Resurrection power comes out of resurrection life.**

> *"He raises the poor from the dust And lifts the beggar from the ash heap, To set them among princes And make them inherit the throne of glory."* 1 Samuel 2:8

According to Paul in Romans 8:29, we have already been glorified. We share in Christ's ascension and exaltation. We have been raised to where Christ is (Colossians 3:1) and have been made to sit with Him in heavenly places (Ephesians 2:5-6). As believers we are already ascended and glorified spiritually. Positionally, we are already enthroned with Christ.

However, we must appropriate these truths to come into the blessed reality of them. It's such a shame that too many believers are living below their heavenly calling and privileges. You see everything Jesus did for us was to restore us to the heavenly tabernacle. Why? It's all about the glory. No glory, no power. We must spend time in the glory, being transformed by Christ's glory in order to manifest the glory. The whole purpose of the finished work of Christ is to restore us to GLORY and HONOUR. Resurrection life brings us into the spirit. It raises us up to the enthroned life so that we can experience the glory of God and be transformed by it (2 Corinthians 3:18), and manifest it in the heavens and in the earth.

Communion and Fellowship

> *"Let us therefore come boldly to the throne of grace, that we may obtain mercy and find grace to help in time of need."*
> Hebrews 4:16

The finished work of Jesus on the cross is what renews us, restores us and gives us access to the heavenly tabernacle. Through Christ's work, we have been restored to the throne and the altar of heaven. We are therefore, invited to come boldly before the throne of grace, (the throne of divine influence, of divine favour, benefits and gifts) and to obtain, (get hold of, come into possession of), mercy and grace, to help in time of need. This means that in times of personal or public need, we can come boldly and come into possession of divine inspiration, revelation and power to help and make a difference. The purpose of access to the heavenly tabernacle is so that we can be restored to the glory and manifest it and the kingdom through the Holy Spirit. **The key to obtaining all of this is communion and fellowship with God. Communion brings us into union with God and fellowship is where we obtain grace, divine favour, power and blessings.**

This is absolutely essential for being led by the Spirit. Jesus relationship with the Father was daily and very personal. Jesus knew what the Father's will was and performed it with perfect obedience. Jesus lived, walked and ministered in the Spirit. He had a living relationship with the Father. He was committed to the Father's business (Luke 2:49). Doing His Father's will was as essential and needful as eating (John 4:34). He had food to eat that they knew nothing about (John 4:32).

Jesus fed from heaven every day. He fed His spirit. He engaged Zion, the heavenly tabernacle and came under the divine influence and power. He simply obeyed and ministered what He saw and heard from the Father. Jesus came under the divine grace and glory of the Father. He both saw and heard all that the Father was revealing to Him, he discerned evil spirits and engaged them. He was sensitive to the Holy Spirit and ministered the gifts powerfully.

Jesus cast out devils, taught with great wisdom, power and authority and manifested the glory and the kingdom through faith and by the Spirit. Jesus stated that man shall not live by bread alone but by every word of the Father (Matthew 4:4). He also walked in the Father's light and was able to overcome darkness and evil at every side. How was Jesus so powerful in his earthly ministry? His spiritual life was established. He established a strong devotional and spiritual life. He was committed and uncompromising in His devotional life. He lived on both plains: the spiritual realm and the natural realm. He drew from Zion, and heaven's tabernacle daily.

He did it through communion and fellowship with the Father and the Holy Spirit.

The heavenly tabernacle brings us into communion and fellowship with the Father, Son and Spirit. It brings us into union with angelic powers and forces. It brings us before the throne and the altar of God. It's right here that we alter everything that is out of sync with the Father's will and purpose. This is where the kingdom of God is engaged and manifested

Before we can really be effective and powerful for God, we must invest time building our relationship with God. Before the priests would minister at the golden altar, they would first minister the bread of presence and the lampstand. This prepared them to minister powerfully at the golden altar.

Jesus said that he was the bread of life and the light of the world. As such, we are to come under the ministry of the bread and the lampstand.

The lesson is powerful. It's communion that brings us into revelation, inspiration and spiritual power. This is the place that we enquire, ask, seek and knock. It's right here in the heavenly tabernacle that we discover the will of God for our life and ministry.

"And truly our fellowship is with the Father and with His Son Jesus Christ." 1 John 1:3

CHAPTER 11

The Way Renewed

The Two Works of Jesus

The book of Hebrews is probably the most important book of the bible to new testament believers because it tells us what Christ has done in His finished work and what He is doing today in His present and continuing work. When Jesus said, 'It is finished' He was referring to his finished work on the cross. As far as His atoning work on the cross goes it really is finished and it's a done deal. No one can change it or undo it. It simply awaits believers entering into it and applying its benefits by faith. The finished work of Christ on the cross is to renew us, and ready us to join Him in His present and continuing work: TO SUBDUE EVIL AND RESTORE THE KINGDOM OF GOD ON EARTH, THROUGH THE NEW COVENANT! We have covered Jesus' finished work in the previous chapter, so now we want to look at His present and continuing work in the heavenly tabernacle and sanctuary.

Jesus' Present and Continuing Work in Zion is Ministering the New Covenant

"Now this is the main point of the things we are saying: We have such a High Priest, who is seated at the right hand of the throne of the Majesty in the heavens, a Minister of the sanctuary and of the true tabernacle which the Lord erected, and not man." Hebrews 8:1-2

He is the High Priest and mediator of the new covenant. **This is what Christ is doing presently in heaven.** Zion is His spiritual temple, the church. The temple is where the royal priesthood minister's kingdom power and authority under heaven's High priest, Jesus. Notice, that Jesus is a Minister of the sanctuary and true tabernacle that the Lord erected, and not man. He is a minister and as such ministers the royal priestly order of the kingdom of God from this sanctuary. Everything is activated through faith in His Name and His blood of Sprinkling.

The most information we've been taught on Christ's ascension ministry is that '*He ever lives to make intercession*' (Hebrews 7:25), but it goes way beyond this and incorporates so much more. Throughout the book of Hebrews, we are told that Jesus is the High Priest of the eternal, spiritual order of heaven. In Hebrews 12:24, we are told that Jesus is the Mediator of the new covenant.

Because of His faithfulness and sufferings, He has obtained a more excellent ministry, inasmuch as He is also the mediator of a better covenant, which was based on better promises (Hebrews 8:6). All the promises of God are yes and amen in Him (2 Cor 1:20). Jesus is the High Priest of our confession and is waiting to fulfil all the promises of God to the glory of God through us (Hebrews 3:1).

Because of this, knowing God's will and hearing His voice is essential in manifesting the kingdom of God and the will of God. When the word of God is believed, agreed and confessed it releases angelic power to perform the will of God, and the new covenant benefits and blessings.

The New Covenant

In Hebrews chapter eight, we are introduced to the new covenant. Let's take a look at it.

A 'covenant' means an 'agreement'. It is a binding contract and agreement ratified and sealed by blood. A covenant has a mediator who mediates or facilitates the written agreements, terms and promises of the covenant. The new covenant is the new way that the kingdom of God is manifested and ministered in all of its fullness, power and blessing through Jesus Christ and all of heaven.

> *"For this is the covenant that I will make with the house of Israel after those days, says the Lord: I will put My laws in their mind and write them on their hearts; and I will be their God, and they shall be My people. None of them shall teach his neighbour, and none his brother, saying, 'Know the Lord,' for all shall know Me, from the least of them to the greatest of them. For I will be merciful to their unrighteousness, and their sins and their lawless deeds I will remember no more."*
> Hebrews 8:10-12

The main purpose for coming boldly before the throne of God and His presence is so that we hear His voice and receive inspiration, revelation and power. For a person to be intimate with God means that God has to reach out to us and show us the way – remember, Jesus is the way to an intimate relationship with the Father. There is a definite and clear way of approach and it's also revealed in the new covenant. The new covenant here in the book of Hebrews is also found in Jeremiah 31:31-34.

In prayer one day as I was studying the new covenant, the Lord told me to read it back to front. It's interesting that Hebrew is read backwards from right to left. The new covenant makes more sense read backwards and reinforces approaching

God through the mediatorial work of Yeshua/Jesus. Let's see it.

We cannot approach God without first coming through sacrifice.

– Sin and lawlessness are dealt with *'their sins and their lawless deeds I will remember no more.'*

Sin must be dealt with firstly as sin is the cause of the separation.

– Mercy is extended on the basis of blood sacrifice *'For I will be merciful to their unrighteousness'* Because of the once for all sacrifice for sins by Jesus, God can extend mercy and be merciful.

– Next comes the ministry of reconciliation *'None of them shall teach his neighbour, and none his brother, saying, 'Know the Lord,' for all shall know Me, from the least of them to the greatest of them.'*

With sin dealt with, and mercy extended, reconciliation can take place and the relationship can begin and the knowledge of God increase.

– Intimacy is at the heart of the new covenant *'and I will be their God, and they shall be My people.'*

With our relationship with God healed we can now receive the blessings of being the people of God.

– Lastly, hearing the voice of God in our mind and heart is the ultimate purpose of the new covenant – *'For this is the covenant that I will make with the house of Israel after those days, says the Lord: I will put My laws in their mind and write them on their hearts.'*

As we grow in our relationship with God, our spiritual senses sharpen and we can now hear the voice of God in the spirit of our mind and heart.

The new covenant is the means then that we are brought into relationship with God so that we have a deep intimacy and are able to hear His voice in our mind and heart! The finished work of Jesus redeems us and restores us to new covenant status and brings us into the blessings of it. Applying the finished work of Christ readies and prepares us to join Him in ministering the new covenant from heaven's sanctuary as priests and kings. Like Paul we are to be trained and equipped to be able ministers of the new covenant (2 Corinthians 3:6). We have been made ambassadors of the Lord and have been given the ministry of reconciliation.

> *"Now all things are of God, who has reconciled us to Himself through Jesus Christ, and has given us the ministry of recon-ciliation, that is, that God was in Christ reconciling the world to Himself, not imputing their trespasses to them, and has committed to us the word of reconciliation. Now then, we are ambassadors for Christ, as though God were pleading through us: we implore you on Christ's behalf, be reconciled to God."*
> 2 Corinthians 5:18-20

Whilst we have been redeemed on a personal level, we must understand that the high call of the believer is to the corpo-rate identity with Christ's church. The church is the body of Christ and is joined as one body to her head, the Lord Jesus Christ. She is also a spiritual temple being built together as living stones and brought into oneness and the corporate identity of the heavenly calling of God. The church is the family of God and as such, when Christ ascended, he brought many sons to glory. The church is also the Lord's priesthood called to minister the new covenant with Him from heaven's sanctuary. The believer that doesn't own this corporate iden-tity is out of synch with the risen Lord and isn't in alignment with His present and continuing work.

We have both the privilege and responsibility to minister the new covenant with our High Priest, Jesus. We must under-stand it and develop a working knowledge of it so that we can minister the benefits and blessings of it to our generation. The priests of the old testament ministered the old covenant, but it couldn't perfect the worshipper and neither could it fully release the full benefits and blessings of the kingdom. As new testament priests, our heavenly calling is to minister the new covenant from the heavenly sanctuary alongside our risen Priest and King.

Only those who have applied the finished work of Christ and have risen as overcomers can minister in the enthroned life. Fleshly and carnal believers cannot minister at this level. It's overcomers who share Christ's throne. This explains why so many believers don't get answers to their prayers. Their prayers are amiss because of their flesh life. They are literally being undone in the spirit through fleshly living.

For many years I was one of these fleshly believers until the Lord arrested me and broke in and changed my walk. I thought I was walking in the Spirit but now I know I wasn't. The promise over my life and ministry was that God would cause me to walk in the Spirit because then and only then could I really fulfil the Lord's call on my life. I'm so glad he set me free and brought me into the Spirit.

You see, the devil's kingdom operates on two levels: an earthly level and a heavenly level.

Demons, or evil spirits work on an earthly level. They are assigned against people at a personal level. Their work is to keep people trapped in sin patterns, spiritual blindness, offence and condemnation, so that they cannot rise to the victorious, overcoming life. Evil spirits afflict, inflict, oppress, battle, destroy, lie, torment, harass, offend, tempt and condemn. Their aim is to keep people from their spiritual power and authority.

Principalities, Power and Rulers of darkness do their work in the heavenly places. Their work is to strategize and plan evil schemes as to control and manage communities, cities and nations.

We must overcome demons and evil spirits on a personal level through the victory of Christ and the crucified life in order to rise and defeat Principalities, power and rulers of darkness in the heavenlies.

To minister in the enthroned life takes maturity. Maturity is about reaching our fullest potential in order to bear fruit. Christlikeness is our ultimate goal. No believer can attain spiritual maturity without a 'full knowledge of the Son of God' (Ephesians 4:13). If our knowledge is incomplete, we cannot reach maturity. In Hebrews the fifth chapter, the writer is talking about the royal priestly order of Melchizedek and goes on to describe the teaching as 'hard to understand.' He then says that their lack of maturity was because they were 'milk drinkers' and not 'meat eaters' (Hebrews 5:12-14).

This means that without an understanding of Christ's present and continuing as High Priest, no believer can attain to spiritual maturity because their knowledge is incomplete.

There are two keys that open up and manifest the kingdom. Jesus rebuked the Pharisees and Lawyers of the day for withholding the 'key of knowledge' and stopping people from entering the kingdom (Luke 11:52). In other words, specific knowledge opens up doors and opportunities for people to experience the kingdom.

I believe that the *first key* to opening up the kingdom is found in what we call, 'The tabernacle of David.' In Revelation 3:7 it says,

> 'These things says He who is holy, He who is true, "He who has the key of David, He who opens and no one shuts, and shuts and no one opens'.

What is the key of David? It is a particular revelation about David and why He established and erected a tabernacle for the ark of the covenant and then filled it with spiritual sacrifices of thanksgiving, praise, and worship which in turn released the prophetic and the kingdom. The tabernacle of David brought David into the Spirit and into God's glory. David knew about the royal priestly order of Melchizedek which is the *second key* for manifesting the kingdom of God. David wrote of it in Psalm 110 after hearing a conversation between the Godhead.

The tabernacle of David brings us into the spiritual approach into Zion, whilst the knowledge of the Royal priesthood of Melchizedek brings us into the actual ministry of the new covenant. Jesus was the lamb of God who died and shed His blood before the foundation of the world. This means that under the eternal royal priesthood of God, the blood was already in force in the spirit. There is no time or space in the spiritual realm. This explains how come Jesus could forgive sins throughout His ministry even though He hadn't shed His blood at calvary. He was drawing on it from the spiritual realm. We know that without the shedding of blood there is no remission. But the royal priesthood after the order of Melchizedek is eternal and spiritual. David came into the presence of God and Zion and wasn't killed because David was in the Spirit.

> He said to them, "How then does David in the Spirit call Him 'Lord,' saying: 'The Lord said to my Lord, "Sit at My right hand, Till I make Your enemies Your footstool"'? If David then calls Him 'Lord,' how is He his Son?" Matthew 22:43-45

> 'Blessed is he whose transgression is forgiven, Whose sin is covered. Blessed is the man to whom the Lord does not impute iniquity, And in whose spirit there is no deceit.' Psalm 32:1-2

David was a new covenant believer before the new covenant was installed at Jesus' death. David received the revelations in the Spirit as he worshiped God in the tabernacle. David also set in the tabernacle scribes or recorders because as they worshipped in the Spirit, the prophetic broke out. The result of this is the Psalms of David and many of them are Messianic. He received them in the Spirit.

Church leaders must come to these two keys of knowledge otherwise they cannot bring the church to unity and maturity or equip the church for the work of the ministry (Ephesians 4). If leaders are blind then we have the blind leading the blind (Matthew 15:14).

Today, the church is receiving revelation of the mystery of the tabernacle of David and the royal priesthood of Melchizedek.

Why? Because only these two keys can bring the church into her heavenly calling so that she is filled with the glory of God, SUBDUES EVIL POWERS AND PREACHES THE GOSPEL OF THE KINGDOM TO THE NATIONS.

The church must rise in the Spirit through the revelation of the tabernacle of David and the finished work of Christ. She must establish spiritual life in order to walk in the Spirit. **You cannot walk in a place that you don't live in!** The church has been restored to Zion and the throne and the altar. The altar is to alter everything that is out of God's will and order.

The church has received a heavenly calling and only through Christ can she fulfil it. It's time to rise up out of manmade wisdom and programmes to Zion and enter into the work of the ministry with Christ: ministering the new covenant until all God's enemies are under His footstool and all things are gathered together both in heaven and earth unto Christ, and the kingdom is fully restored.

The bible's main theme is 'God's Holy Temple.' God dwells in His heavenly sanctuary in Zion. This is where He has put His throne, His glory, His Name, His salvation and much more. If we lose sight of this, we'll make the bible fit us and our theological message. The danger of doing this is that we miss what God is doing and we confuse the message and frustrate the work. When the message isn't clear, the work is unclear.

In Genesis we see heaven and earth joined together, God tabernacled with man. Adam had access to the presence of God in His holy temple. The fact that the tree of life (that is in heaven Revelation 22) was accessible to Adam and Eve should be plain to see that they had access to both the natural and spiritual realms. The Garden of Eden was joined and had a crossover into Zion, heaven and the spiritual realm.

From the time Adam sinned and was cut off from heaven and barred from accessing it, God implemented another *Way* so that He could be accessible to mankind. The theme of God's holy temple runs through the whole bible, from beginning to end. When we follow the temple theme it pulls the bible together into a powerful united revelation that puts all the books of the bible into context and shows us what God is doing in every generation. **As we'll see in this study, the temple revelation is in its final stage of establishing the kingdom of God and heaven on earth**.

Today, we are a privileged and honoured generation, as God's spiritual temple has replaced and incorporated every previous tabernacle and temple into one final dwelling for God in the spirit and now, and will usher in the final stages of God's redemptive plan to create a new heaven and new earth as well as a new Jerusalem (spiritual temple) that will see heaven and earth joined forever functioning in the eternal state.

The fall of man brought about the spiritual death, separation and banishment of mankind from Zion, heaven and God's temple. In this separated state, people have lost their way and are lost. God in His mercy, put into motion His redemptive plan to make the way back to His holy temple accessible for mankind to be reconciled so that they could once again fulfill their original calling and purpose on earth.

CHAPTER 12

The
Spiritual Temple

The Tabernacle of Moses

"And let them make Me a sanctuary, that I may dwell among them." Exodus 25:8-9

In the process of time the way was brought back to the earth through the tabernacle of Moses. The tabernacle was a true copy of the sanctuary in heaven where God dwells. **It was a material tent, made up of various curtains**. The tabernacle of Moses was God's prescribed way of approaching Him, worshipping Him and seeking and consulting Him in order to subdue evil and establish His kingdom rule in the earth.

Of course, it was a temporary arrangement designed to show forth and lead us to the true sanctuary in the spirit in heaven. Because man was defiled and unclean this was the only way that God could tabernacle with man. It was never God's intention to have man-made temples – His will was for mankind to join Him in His spiritual temple. What folly to think that man-made temples could contain the God who created everything.

> *"God, who made the world and everything in it, since He is Lord of heaven and earth, does not dwell in temples made with hands. Nor is He worshiped with men's hands, as though He needed anything, since He gives to all life, breath, and all things."* Acts 17:24-25

When God called Moses up on the mountain, He gave a detailed plan for the tabernacle to be built and erected including its functions, services and ministries. As we have already seen, Moses' tabernacle served its purpose and it should be studied and grasped because it reveals so much about the spiritual temple and its ministries for the church and new testament priests and kings which we'll see later.

If we don't have a working knowledge of Moses' tabernacle, we won't be able to minister in our roles as priest and kings unto our God. However, Moses' tabernacle was a material temple. It was made up of various curtains and hooks and poles that made it a tent like structure. It was also made by the skilled hands of men and women and because of this it had to be sanctified by blood for service. It was a temporary setup that allowed God to be with His people and His people to come into agreement with His will and purpose but it wasn't meant to be eternal. It was a shadow of the one true heavenly temple.

The Temple of Solomon

> *"So Solomon built the temple and finished it."* 1 Kings 6:14

Solomon built a stone temple that was an amazing structure and a wonder of the world. Although it was an amazing structure, he knew the limitations of the temple he had built.

> *"But will God indeed dwell on the earth? Behold, heaven and the heaven of heavens cannot contain You. How much less this temple which I have built!"* 1 Kings 8:27

Solomon's temple was also a material temple made of costly stone and timber. It was also furnished with pure gold and silver and it is estimated to have cost somewhere in the region of £100 billion. Everything was made bigger in King Solomon's temple. Solomon's temple included more courts as well as the royal buildings.

There were some major differences and inclusions to the holy place and the Most Holy Place. Inside the Most Holy Place, the ark of the covenant was now placed between two Cherubim whose wings spanned from wall to wall. Also, in the holy place instead of one golden lampstand and one table of shewbread, there were now ten of each. In the court of the priests, the Molten sea was placed and also ten smaller brazen lavers around the court for the priests.

Also brought into and included in Solomon's temple was praise and worship. The tabernacle of Moses was a quiet order of worship and prayer undertaken by the Levitical priesthood. But now, the offices of king and priest are brought together in Solomon's temple and the order of worship has included singing praises, the giving of thanks and prayer. It's interesting to note that when both the tabernacle of Moses and the temple of Solomon was built as God directed, without any human input, God's glory came down and rested upon them. They both served a limited purpose in the divine order and plan and pointed to a greater temple to come.

The Tabernacle of David

Somewhere between the tabernacle of Moses and the temple of Solomon, another tabernacle was established, the tabernacle of David.

> *"David built houses for himself in the City of David; and he prepared a place for the ark of God, and pitched a tent for it."*
> 1 Chronicles 15:1

This also was made of material and it was a tent like structure that housed one piece of furniture, the ark of the covenant. **Although it was a material temple, its ministry was spiritual.**

The tabernacle of David was a house of worship and prayer. At its dedication, animal sacrifices were presented to the Lord by David. From then on, it presented spiritual sacrifices of thanksgiving and praise, commemorating and recording what God had done and what He was going to do.

David had been brought into the Spirit on many occasions through worship and prayer and received revelation about how to approach God in and by the Spirit. It was during these times in the Spirit that he learned of the order of Melchizedek (Psalm 110) and heard heavenly conversations about the Messiah and His ministry. Out of all the tabernacles and temples, David's was patterned to a higher degree after God's spiritual temple, Zion. In fact, in our day this is the one tabernacle and temple that the Lord is restoring. **The number one thing that God is doing in our times is found here:**

> *And with this the words of the prophets agree, just as it is written: 'After! this I will return And will rebuild the tabernacle of David, which has fallen down; I will rebuild its ruins, And I will set it up;*

> *So that the rest of mankind may seek the Lord, Even all the Gentiles who are called by My name,*

> *Says the Lord who does all these things.'* Acts 15:15-17

James is quoting the prophet Amos in 9:11-12. He was addressing the early church at a conference about the gentiles coming into the church. James is bringing much needed direction to the church so that the leaders can see that the gentiles coming in was connected to what God had promised long ago through the mouth of the prophets. God is rebuilding and restoring the tabernacle of David, which is His spiritual temple, the church. God is repairing and healing the ruins or breaches and setting up His temple **so that the rest of mankind, the gentiles may seek Him.** Wow! This is why the church exists.

The Church a Spiritual Temple

The church is the spiritual temple of God made without human hands. Initially, the church was Jewish and made up of converted Jewish believers. As the church grew, the Lord began to use His temple to bring the gentiles in to form one, spiritual house or temple of God. The early church had to undergo a massive shift of thought for this to happen and so, we see in Acts 15 a conference of leaders assembling to settle and establish the matter. **They discovered that both Jew and Gentile were called into one faith, and one body and one calling together as a spiritual temple unto God.**

God made the mystery of His will known to the apostle Paul. In his letter to the Ephesians Paul makes the mystery known.

> *"Therefore remember that you, once Gentiles in the flesh — who are called Uncircumcision by what is called the Circumcision made in the flesh by hands — that at that time you were without Christ, being aliens from the commonwealth of Israel and strangers from the covenants of promise, having no hope and without God in the world. But now in Christ Jesus you who once were far off have been brought near by the blood of Christ."* Ephesians 2:11-13

When Jesus died the second temple was still standing but Jesus had foretold that it would be destroyed and levelled (Luke 21:5-38). Jesus said that He would build His church (temple) and that the gates of hell would not prevail. The spiritual temple (the third temple) was established at Pentecost when Jesus' followers had gathered and were waiting for the Promised Holy Spirit. **It was made without human hands by the Lord Himself.**

It was a spiritual temple formed to function both in the spiritual realm and in the natural realm. It took a further forty years for the second temple to be destroyed. The curtain separating the Most Holy Place had been torn from top to bottom at Christ's death. But the fact that it continued to function reveals that they had repaired or renewed the curtain as to continue in their services. The dilemma facing believers in the book of Hebrews was that some were having a difficult time transitioning from the second temple to the third temple, the spiritual temple, the church.

As the church was being established, the Lord made His will known to Peter in a vision that the gentiles were to be brought into His spiritual temple, the church. Up to this point the early church was made up of Jewish believers only. The first gentiles brought in to the church included that of Cornelius and his household in Acts 10. Peter and those with him were astonished as the Holy Spirit was poured out on the gentiles. In chapter 11, Peter went up to Jerusalem and joined his fellow Jewish believers, who heard about what had happened to Cornelius and his household. Peter reported everything that happened on his mission trip.

Up to this point the early church was made up of Jewish believers only.

"When they heard these things they became silent; and they glorified God, saying, "Then God has also granted to the Gentiles repentance to life." Acts 11:18

And so, as God had promised, He was restoring the tabernacle of David which saw both Jewish and Gentile believers worshiping together in the one spiritual temple. Paul in his letter to the Ephesians goes on to explain that God had broken down the middle wall of separation and made one new man from the two (Ephesians 2:14-17). Paul went on to explain that both Jews and gentiles were now being built to form a spiritual temple for God, a spiritual dwelling for God in the spirit (Ephesians 2:19-22). He further explains that the gentiles were to be fellow heirs in the one body along with Jewish believers and partakers of the promises through the gospel (Ephesians 3:6). **God's new temple and new priesthood had now been brought into being together to minister the New Covenant and the glory of God.**

This new temple and priesthood were brought together for the purpose of manifesting the manifold wisdom of God to principalities and powers in the heavenly places (Ephesians

3:10). The apostle Peter grew in his understanding of the new temple and priesthood that were brought together by the will of God through the gospel as he writes in his letters.

> *"Coming to Him as to a living stone, rejected indeed by men, but chosen by God and precious, you also, as living stones, are being built up a spiritual house, a holy priesthood, to offer up spiritual sacrifices acceptable to God through Jesus Christ."* 1 Peter 2:4-5

> *"But you are a chosen generation, a royal priesthood, a holy nation, His own special people, that you may proclaim the praises of Him who called you out of darkness into His marvellous light; who once were not a people but are now the people of God, who had not obtained mercy but now have obtained mercy."* 1 Peter 2:9-10

Peter knew that Lord had brought Jew and Gentile together to form one temple and one priesthood. The Lord Jesus is the chief cornerstone that joins these living stones together.

"Behold, I lay in Zion A chief cornerstone, elect, precious, And he who believes on Him will by no means be put to shame." 1 Peter 2:6. Notice where the cornerstone has been laid, in Zion!

So, the early church made up of Jew and Gentile was built upon the apostles and prophets as a spiritual temple and priesthood to minister God's will. When the church came together and was built according to God's pattern, the glory of God was manifested in spiritual power and authority with signs and wonders through the Spirit.

It didn't take long for the devil to attack this spiritual order and temple and over a few centuries, the temple made up of Jewish and Gentile believers was divided and broken down. From here on the church became predominantly Gentile and was seriously breached. A house divided cannot stand and therefore cannot experience the full glory of God in order to fulfil its mandate: the glory and kingdom of God in all the earth.

The church has over many generations been breached and broken down. The Jewish, Messianic movement and the Gentile church is breached and divided today. As well as this, the church today is so divided through denominationalism that churches are not only separated from one another, but are suspicious and even competitive with one another too. She is anything but one, because there's always someone in the flesh, who sees things differently and sets up a belief system around their thoughts.

This has produced denominationalism and there are that many today it's a sad testimony to the true spiritual temple of the Lord. Denominationalism is an assault of the devil to divide the house of God. Why? Because a house divided against itself cannot stand. **If it cannot stand, it cannot perform its duties and responsibilities.**

God is moving in our day to repair the breaches. This is what God is doing in our day. God is about to restore His temple in the Spirit repairing the breaches between Jewish and Gentile believers and between denominational division. Hallelujah, we are one body and when God restores His temple, and we come together as one, the glory of God is going to fill the temple. When this happens, there will be a glorious display and manifestation of spiritual power and authority that will exceed and be greater than any previous move of God in the earth. The church is God's holy and spiritual temple formed and brought into the spirit to form a spiritual habitation for God. The church is Zion, the city of God and heavenly Jerusalem.

> *"But you have come to Mount Zion and to the city of the living God, the heavenly Jerusalem, to an innumerable company of angels, to the general assembly and church of the firstborn who are registered in heaven, to God the Judge of all, to the spirits of just men made perfect, to Jesus the Mediator of the new covenant, and to the blood of sprinkling that speaks better things than that of Abel."* Hebrews 12:22-24

The writer here is building a train of thought. He isn't describing different places. The church is Zion, the spiritual city and heavenly Jerusalem above. This is a mystery that God is revealing in our generation as He prepares His temple and priesthood for the Grand Finale. One day heavenly Jerusalem will become the New Jerusalem, when God creates all things new. Read Revelation 21 and 22. Why would God create a New Jerusalem? Because the sin of Satan and angels defiled the first one! Praise God, the Lord is lifting His church off the ground into the spirit so that she can be a functioning temple and priesthood.

> *"For the Lord shall build up Zion; He shall appear in His glory."* Psalm 102:14

When the Church aligns to the word of God and is built up a spiritual house and habitation for God in the spirit after the heavenly pattern – the glory of God WILL manifest. Hallelujah!

The Church God's Priesthood

> *"Coming to Him as to a living stone, rejected indeed by men, but chosen by God and precious, you also, as living stones, are being built up a spiritual house, a holy priesthood, to offer up spiritual sacrifices acceptable to God through Jesus Christ."* 1 Peter 2:4-5

> *"But you are a chosen generation, a royal priesthood, a holy nation, His own special people, that you may proclaim the praises of Him who called you out of darkness into His marvellous light; who once were not a people but are now the people of God, who had not obtained mercy but now have obtained mercy."* 1 Peter 2:9-10

From the very beginning, God has always wanted a kingdom of priests to minister His kingdom and will. Adam was the very first priest in the earth. He was created with dual capabilities so that he could experience the spiritual realm as well as the natural realm. Adam was on probation under the word of God to test his obedience and faithfulness to God's word.

He was through his spirit to engage with the Father and come under divine inspiration, revelation and power that he might produce heaven on earth and see the kingdom and will of God done. **It was Adam and Eve's responsibility to subdue evil powers and exercise godly influence and dominion in the earth.** This is the duty of a priest of the Most -High God. **Only priests can legally function and minister the things of the Kingdom of God.**

So, Adam being the first priest was to spearhead the priesthood in this new creation, a kingdom of priests that would rule over the earth. What went wrong? *Adam and Eve compromised the word of God.* They listened to the devil's reasonings and lies and disobeyed the word of the Father, thus disqualifying themselves from the priesthood. God the Father, clothed Adam and Eve with the skin of the first earthly sacrifice, a priestly act that covered them with the Father's mercy.

To restore the priesthood, God called Abraham by whom he would bless all the families of the earth and through whom, the Father's eternal and spiritual priesthood would come through His holy nation, Israel, and ultimately, heaven's Messiah. God formed Israel and brought them out of bondage to the Egyptians and called them to Himself. After God delivered them from Egypt and gathered them together at Mount Sinai under Moses' ministry, He made known His will and purpose for them as a nation. God gave Moses His plans to establish them as a nation and dwell with them and bless them through the priesthood about to be established. It was God's intention to have a kingdom of priests who would know Him and His word that His purposes might be established in the earth but as we'll see, once again God's purpose was thwarted.

> *"Now therefore, if you will indeed obey My voice and keep My covenant, then you shall be a special treasure to Me above all people; for all the earth is Mine. And you shall be to Me a kingdom of priests and a holy nation. These are the words which you shall speak to the children of Israel."* Exodus 19:5-6

Israel was to be a kingdom of priests and a holy nation but what happened? Why was it reduced from the nation to a tribe? Well, remember it's all about agreement with and ministering the word of God. Right there at the mountain Israel refused the word of God, it was too much for them and they happily gave the position to Moses (Exodus 20:18-19). Because Moses delayed on the mountain (Exodus 32), they went on to build a golden calf and sinned before the Lord right there at Sinai. God's plan was thwarted again through disobedience to the word of God.

Moses and Aaron were called up to the top of the mountain to hear the voice of God. The reason Aaron was brought up was that he had become Moses' spokesman when Moses made excuses about delivering the word of God to Pharaoh. It was through Aaron that the priesthood was established because of how he handled the word of God. The priesthood was set within the tribe of Levi, from which Aaron was descended. It was the tribe of Levi that stood with Moses and the word of God when Israel sinned with the golden calf. The priesthood is all about ministering the government of God. The government and will of God are based upon the word of God.

CHAPTER 13

Two Priesthoods

Aaron and Melchizedek

There are only two priesthoods in the bible. The Aaronic or Levitical priesthood and the Royal priesthood after the order of Melchizedek. The Aaronic or Levitical priesthood was a copy and a shadow and a temporary priesthood that pointed to and would one day give way to the Royal priesthood after the order of Melchizedek.

The purpose of the tabernacle/temple was for a ministering priesthood. The priesthood was anointed to minister spiritually before the throne and the golden altar. In the OT the ark of the covenant and the golden altar were separated by a heavy veil. Only the High Priest went into minister before the ark of the covenant once a year on the day of atonement. All other regular priests were allowed to minister before the golden altar. This was the ultimate privilege of the priest.

All other duties and ministrations were for the purpose of preparing the priest to minister before the golden altar. Blood sacrifices, the washings, the wearing of priestly garments, all were to ready the priest for the holy place. The bread of presence and the lampstand were to ready the priest to stand before the golden altar inspired to offer incense and pray!

The Aaronic Priesthood

The Aaronic priesthood was earthly and not heavenly. It was established as a type and a shadow of the heavenly tabernacle. This priesthood was set up under the old covenant received on Mount Sinai to service Israel and secure the presence and blessing of God on obedience to His laws and conditions. If worshipers obeyed God's laws and met all the conditions, the blessing of God would be secured. However, if they disobeyed God, they would be cursed with numerous curses associated with sinful behaviours. There are a number of limitations and restrictions associated with the old covenant and the priesthood.

The Aaronic priesthood was limited and restricted to Israel. The whole setup was to service the children of Israel as a nation. Israel was to be a witness to surrounding nations of living under the divine favour and blessing of God's government in order to bring them to God. The system had further limitations and restrictions too. Only the High Priest could minister in the Most Holy Place and even that was restricted to once a year. The regular priests were also restricted in their ministry.

The opportunity to minister before the golden altar was done by lot and so many priests were restricted by this system and many never got this once in a lifetime opportunity. The priesthood was also restricted to those of the lineage of Aaron and the tribe of Levi. No other tribe was allowed to minister in the tabernacle before the Lord. There were limits to what the system could achieve because of the sinful and carnal nature of God's people. The High Priest and priests were limited because of their own sinfulness and mortality.

The priesthood was ever changing with the various appointments. The blood of bulls and goats was limited and could not perfect the worshipper or the priesthood. All it could do was show the inability of people to be holy and righteous and therefore, it highlighted sin and the carnal nature. The law and the commandments were holy, just and good. But what they did was reveal the law of sin and death at work in the human heart. The purpose of the law was to show human inability to keep the law and therefore reveal the need for a saviour.

So, the system was meant to keep Israel right with God and allow them to live in victory and blessing so that they could be a light and a witness to the gentile world about them. The whole system was meant to keep Israel in fellowship with God so that they walked in righteousness before him not giving place for their enemies to defeat them. However, time and again their sin defeated them and gave their enemies advantage over them. Israel continually fell into sin and idolatry and experienced severe judgment and chastisement from God.

The book of Hebrews clearly shows just how ineffective the Aaronic and Levitical priesthood was and shows the need for a new one (Hebrews 7:11). The system was ministered in a limited and restricted temple, by a limited and restricted priesthood, based upon limited and animal sacrifices that could not perfect the worshiper, and so it became a ministration of death. The whole system could not arrest the sinful, carnal nature at work within God's people. So, these sin cycles continued to work against God's people opening them up to the law of sin and death (Romans 8:2). The apostle Paul calls the old covenant a ministry of death.

> *"But if the ministry of death, written and engraved on stones, was glorious, so that the children of Israel could not look steadily at the face of Moses because of the glory of his countenance, which glory was passing away, how will the ministry of the Spirit not be more glorious? For if the ministry of condemnation had glory, the ministry of righteousness exceeds much more in glory. For even what was made glorious had*

no glory in this respect, because of the glory that excels. For if what is passing away was glorious, what remains is much more glorious." 2 Corinthians 3:7-11

It's not that the old covenant was wrong, it wasn't. Because of *its* perfection and the worshipper's imperfection, it became a ministry that produced death and condemnation in God's people. What was its purpose then? It was to show forth the inability of the worshipper to produce a righteous life and reveal their need for a better salvation built upon a better temple, better sacrifice, a better priesthood and a better covenant.

> *"Therefore the law was our tutor to bring us to Christ, that we might be justified by faith."* Galatians 3:24

The Order of Melchizedek

The second priesthood revealed in the bible is that of the order of Melchizedek. The order of Melchizedek reveals the eternal, spiritual and heavenly royal priesthood of the Most-High God.

This priesthood is the substance of which the old covenant priesthood was a type and shadow of. This priesthood operates from Zion, the city of God and the heavenly Jerusalem. It's this divine order that ministers the kingdom and government of God throughout creation. It ministers God's justice and righteousness, it ministers His creative and sustaining power, His rule and authority, His will and purpose.

The whole government of God is tied to this order. The order is presided over by the Father and Yeshua/Jesus who is the High Priest and the mediator of the new covenant in His blood and the Spirit of the Lord. Yeshua is the king of righteousness and the king of peace. Because of this the order abides in constant state of righteousness, peace and joy in the Holy Spirit (Romans 14:17). It operates on His once for all perfect sacrifice and His exalted Name and has the power to bring the worshipper into righteousness and perfection through faith.

The order is upheld and serviced by the word of God and all of the angelic heavenly hosts of God. The order has complete victory over sin, Satan, death and the sinful world system. It is headed up by the eternal Son of God who is the author of life and can never die. It is this order that must be ministered in the earth. It can however, only be ministered in the earth by Yeshua's royal priesthood whom He has washed in His blood and made priests and kings in this eternal, spiritual order (Revelation 1:5,6). The order of Melchizedek brings together the two offices of priest and king in a combination of spiritual authority and power.

We are first introduced to this Melchizedek in Genesis 14 when He intercepts Abraham on His return from battling a league of kings who had kidnapped his nephew Lot and stole their goods. Abram, as he was named had been called by God and set apart for a great work of God in the earth. God promised him a great name, a great nation and great blessing (Gen 12). God promised that through Abram all the families of the earth would be blessed. When Abraham met Melchizedek, it was revealed that the Most High had blessed Abraham with victory and bounty and that it was because the Most High had brought Abraham into fellowship with Him. Abraham had come under the royal priesthood of heavenly Melchizedek and was blessed and highly favoured.

The next time we hear of Melchizedek is in the life of king David. After David had received revelation of setting up a tabernacle for the ark of the covenant and a divine and spiritual order of approaching God in the spirit with the spiritual sacrifices of thanksgiving and praise, David, in the Spirit, heard a heavenly conversation between the Father and the Son, confirming that the Son, Yeshua/Jesus, was High Priest forever according to the order of Melchizedek Psalm 110. David came into and under this eternal and spiritual order and received inspiration and revelatory truths that brought him into victory over his enemies and the bountiful blessings of God. It was under this spiritual order that David could say, *"Blessed is he whose transgression is forgiven, Whose sin is covered. Blessed is the man to whom the Lord does not impute iniquity, And in whose spirit there is no deceit." Psalm 32:1-2*

It was under this spiritual order that David could function and worship the Lord in his tabernacle. It was this order that allowed him to enter into the presence of God in Zion and hear conversations, receive inspiration and revelation and come under the glory of God. It was under this order that David came into total victory and blessing, and ministered in the offices of prophet, priest and king in order to activate and release governmental authority and power as well as priestly compassion.

This is the spiritual order that is in force today and ministers the government of the kingdom of God including the new covenant. **The eternal emblems of this spiritual order are bread and wine** and its participation in these that bring us into the order and fellowship with the Father, Son and Spirit. The bread and wine are the body and blood of the Son of God, the High Priest who gave His life for us to bring us into His divine order and new covenant so that we could be restored to the Kingdom.

> *And as they were eating, Jesus took bread, blessed and broke it, and gave it to the disciples and said, "Take, eat; this is My body." Then He took the cup, and gave thanks, and gave it to them, saying, "Drink from it, all of you. For this is My blood of the new covenant, which is shed for many for the remission of sins." Matthew 26:26-28*

When Melchizedek met Abraham, they shared bread and wine making it official and celebrating the union between them. Abraham was under the order of Melchizedek and as such could access every spiritual blessing associated with the order. As believers today, when we take of the bread and the wine, we do so with the understanding that our spiritual connection gives us access to every spiritual blessing in the heavenly places (Ephesians 1:3).

One last thing to say here is that this order operates on faith. It is faith that activates this order and puts into action the governmental power and spiritual blessings of the kingdom of God.

> *"But without faith it is impossible to please Him, for he who comes to God must believe that He is, and that He is a rewarder of those who diligently seek Him."* Hebrews 11:6

We must have faith in the promises and word of God. Yeshua/Jesus is the High Priest of our confession.

> *"Therefore, holy brethren, partakers of the heavenly calling, consider the Apostle and High Priest of our confession, Christ Jesus."* Hebrews 3:1

Activating this powerful spiritual order is based on our knowledge of it in the word of God. It is also determined by our level of spiritual maturity produced by the knowledge of this order (Hebrews 5:12).

Our faith must be based upon our knowledge of the word of God.

> *"So then faith comes by hearing, and hearing by the word of God."* Romans 10:17

To operate in this spiritual order requires operating in Zion, and the heavenly tabernacle. To function in this spiritual order requires the righteousness that comes by faith. Functioning in this spiritual order also requires spiritual maturity. Developing spiritual maturity requires a growing knowledge of this spiritual order and our priestly and kingly roles. And lastly, this spiritual order is activated through a daily, committed prayer life.

Priests and Kings

> *"To Him who loved us and washed us from our sins in His own blood, and has made us kings and priests to His God and Father, to Him be glory and dominion forever and ever. Amen."* Revelation 1:5-6

So, we have clearly established that the church is the spiritual temple, built on Christ the foundation and chief cornerstone along with His apostles and prophets. The temple has replaced every previous tabernacle and temple that was established in the bible. Jesus said, "I will build my church' (Matt 16:18). The church is the third temple! The church is also the royal priesthood of the Lord and has replaced the Aaronic and Levitical order. The new testament is clear on this.

> "...having been built on the foundation of the apostles and prophets, Jesus Christ Himself being the chief cornerstone, in whom the whole building, being fitted together, grows into a holy temple in the Lord, in whom you also are being built together for a dwelling place of God in the Spirit." Ephesians 2:20-22

> "Coming to Him as to a living stone, rejected indeed by men, but chosen by God and precious, you also, as living stones, are being built up a spiritual house, a holy priesthood, to offer up spiritual sacrifices acceptable to God through Jesus Christ." 1 Peter 2:4-5

> "Therefore, if perfection were through the Levitical priesthood (for under it the people received the law), what further need was there that another priest should rise according to the order of Melchizedek, and not be called according to the order of Aaron? For the priesthood being changed, of necessity there is also a change of the law." Hebrews 7:11-12

He has abolished and put away the old temple and priesthood along with its sacrificial system and has replaced it with the new order and the new covenant.

> "Now this is the main point of the things we are saying: We have such a High Priest, who is seated at the right hand of the throne of the Majesty in the heavens, a Minister of the sanctuary and of the true tabernacle which the Lord erected, and not man." Hebrews 8:1-2

Now through Christ, we can access and minister as spiritual negotiators through Christ and can minister every spiritual

blessing in the heavenly places. The heavenly tabernacle is officially open and accessible for His royal priesthood. It awaits their ministry. Christ has fulfilled His earthly mission and is now in His present and continuing ministry. It is God's good pleasure to confer upon us the kingdom. Through Christ, He has made all of it accessible and has put all of it at our disposal. The Father, the Son and the Holy Spirit are waiting for the church, the royal priesthood.

We must know and begin to function in our roles. Believers have been made priests and kings by the Lord. It is a heavenly calling. Jesus is both the lion (King) and the Lamb (Priest) and brings both these offices and callings together. Just because we've been washed and made priests and kings doesn't mean that we will automatically function in them, and certainly not if we are ignorant of them.

What is involved? How do we function in them? What are we to do?

Remember, Jesus functioned as heaven's Royal High Priest, which also incorporated the role of prophet. **We must understand how these roles are to work together if we're ever going to make sense of what we are supposed to be doing in them.** Christlikeness is the goal for every believer. This means that we are to be like Jesus in everything; character and ministry. **Jesus said that we would do greater works because He was returning to Zion, heaven, and establishing an open temple and a functioning and anointed priesthood that would allow every believer to function as He did when He lived and ministered on earth.**

Jesus Provides The Way

If we see the way in Jesus, we can follow Him and begin to develop these spiritual roles.

Everyday Jesus operated in these roles. How did He do it and how do these roles work? Well, first of all, through His devotional life, Jesus worshipped and prayed His way into the spirit. He entered into the heavenly tabernacle and came under the Father's inspiration, revelation and power by the Holy Spirit.

In His priestly role, Jesus ministered thanksgiving, praise and worship unto the Father. As priest He received all that the Father showed Him and told Him and came into agreement. Jesus came into the gifts and power of the Spirit. As a faithful and compassionate priest, Jesus prayed with intercessions and supplications. Securing the will of the Father, Jesus entered into His kingly role and subdued Satan, principalities, powers and rulers of darkness in the spirit. He decreed and declared and used spiritual authority and power to subdue the powers of darkness. He put these powers under the footstool of the Kingdom and Majesty of the Father. He then, coming out of devotion and prayer, obeyed the Father's will and functioned as a compassionate and merciful priest, setting the captives free and ministering mercy, forgiveness and healing.

In His Kingly role, Jesus exercised authority over demons and evil spirits at work in people and cast them out with spiritual power and authority. He also preached and proclaimed the kingdom of God. He was an ambassador, sharing the good news of the kingdom. As a prophet and mouthpiece of God, He spoke the word of God, which included preaching the good news and taught with authority the kingdom of God. When people responded, Jesus brought them into discipleship and trained them in the message and mission of the kingdom of God.

Jesus told us to take up our cross and to follow Him (Matthew 16:24). If as believers we truly take up the cross and apply its work, we'll follow Jesus and find Him in heaven's tabernacle as High Priest and mediator of the new covenant. As we get used to worshipping and praying here, we'll come under the same anointing and see and hear the Father – we then simply are to walk in obedience. As we do, we will fulfil our ministry.

Firstly, we have been made priests. In the old testament, priests were called to office.

It wasn't something that they could choose to enter into. It was God's choosing.

> *"And no man takes this honour to himself, but he who is called by God, just as Aaron was."* Hebrews 5:4

It is God who call, anoints and appoints people. We have been chosen by Christ (John 15:16).

Priests were ministers of the sacred things of God. They were mediators between man and God. They were to be consecrated and holy to God and to the services of the temple. The priesthood was responsible for ministering the old covenant. The main priestly duties included ministering the law and the word of God to the people as well as preparing and presenting the sacrifices for sins along with presenting gifts and offerings to the Lord.

The priestly ministry was to keep the people right with God so that they could experience His favour and blessing and live in victory and peace. When Jesus died, He provided the once for all sacrifice needed to not only cover sin but to put it away and perfect the worshipper so that all could come into God's presence. **You see, under the old system, only the priests could draw near to the golden altar and only the High Priest could minister in the direct presence of God in the Most Holy Place.**

The priesthood under the old Aaronic and Levitical priesthood offer great lessons on how to approach the throne and the golden altar. But we have no need to minister animal sacrifices for sins, our priesthood is after the order of Melchizedek. The once for all perfect sacrifice is at work in that eternal and spiritual order. It's this sacrificial offering that has perfected us and brought us into the heavenly tabernacle and before the throne and the golden altar to fulfil our priestly duties.

Our priesthood is in accordance with the tabernacle of David. After David presented the initial animal sacrifices to sanctify the tabernacle, there were no more animal sacrifices used (2 Samuel 6:17).

The sacrifices presented in this tabernacle were sacrifices of thanksgiving, praise, offerings and service. These were spiritual sacrifices offered under the royal priesthood of Melchizedek. This worship brought David and His people into the spirit to come under divine inspiration, revelation and power so that they could operate in spiritual power and authority and defeat their enemies and prosper under the kingdom of God.

Our priestly calling is to minister the kingdom of God. We are called to minister the new covenant with our High Priest. We are also called to bring the good news of the kingdom to the world. The priesthood of the believer has never reached its full meaning and expression in the church until now. Most denominations see the priesthood of the believer as each believer operating in their own individual ministry as they serve the Lord. However, the priesthood of every believer is exactly what it says on the can. Every believer has been washed in the blood of Christ and has been made a priest and king so that they can minister in Zion and the heavenly sanctuary before the throne of God and the golden altar. It is the high and heavenly calling of every believer who must be matured and equipped for it.

As priests we are to offer up spiritual sacrifices.

> *"You also, as living stones, are being built up a spiritual house, a holy priesthood, to offer up spiritual sacrifices acceptable to God through Jesus Christ."* 1 Peter 2:5

What sacrifices are we to offer? Let's see from the word of God, what God is looking for.

Please note, that our spiritual sacrifices are only acceptable to God through Jesus Christ!

1. Praise and thanksgiving.

> *"Therefore I will offer sacrifices of joy in His tabernacle; I will sing, yes, I will sing praises to the Lord."* Psalm 27:5

Because of the revelation David received by the Spirit of God, he knew that God was **not looking for burnt offerings** but the sacrifices he witnessed in heaven, which was the singing of praise and thanksgiving. In heaven God is enthroned and surrounded by praise and thanksgiving.

Psalm 107 offers us insight into our sacrifice of thanksgiving and praise.

> *"Let them sacrifice the sacrifices of thanksgiving, And declare His works with rejoicing."* Psalm 107:22

We are to give thanks to God for his enduring mercy (Vs.1), give thanks for God for His goodness and His wonderful works (Vs. 8), it goes on to speak his provision, deliverance, salvation, healing, protection and blessings. All of which we are to give thanks for.

Praise and thanksgiving release God's blessings. If you're wise, you'll do it.

> *"Whoever is wise will observe these things, And they will understand the lovingkindness of the Lord."* Psalm 107:43

Read king David's song of thanksgiving in 1 Chronicles 16:7-36 for inspiration.

Praise and thanksgiving open up our Father's heart and cause His power and blessing to flow.

> *"Therefore, by Him let us continually offer the sacrifice of praise to God, that is, the fruit of our lips, giving thanks to His name."* Hebrews 13:15

Jesus practiced and gave thanks to the Father on many occasions (Matthew 11:25; 15:36; Luke 10:21; John 11:41).

Our praises are not only for the temple but we are called to shew forth God's praises in the heavenly places to principalities as well as into earth as a witness to God's calling upon us.

"...to the intent that now the manifold wisdom of God might be made known by the church to the principalities and powers in the heavenly places." Ephesians 3:10

"But you are a chosen generation, a royal priesthood, a holy nation, His own special people, that you may proclaim the praises of Him who called you out of darkness into His marvellous light." 1 Peter 2:9

2. Our giving, gifts and alms.

"Now consider how great this man was, to whom even the patriarch Abraham gave a tenth of the spoils. But he whose genealogy is not derived from them received tithes from Abraham and blessed him who had the promises. Now beyond all contradiction the lesser is blessed by the better. Here mortal men receive tithes, but there he receives them, of whom it is witnessed that he lives." Hebrews 7:4, 6-8

Abraham tithed to Melchizedek the priest of the Most-High God. Abraham's tithes were given out of honour not obligation. Abraham knew and realised that He had been blessed by God and the kingdom of God and so he gladly and cheerfully gave tithes to Melchizedek. Under the law, the Levites received tithes from the people for the running and upkeep of the temple and the priesthood. Jesus is Melchizedek and as heaven's High Priest receives tithes, offerings and alms from His royal priesthood.

During His earthly ministry Jesus spoke more about money than any other topic and He encouraged worshippers to store up treasures in heaven by generous giving. Royal priests and kings have no problem giving tithes, offerings and alms to their High Priest as they know that their investment is for a functional temple and priesthood. Also, they know that their investment is in safe keeping and will never be subject to moths, rust or thieves (Matthew 6:19-20).

"I am full, having received from Epaphroditus the things sent from you, a sweet-smelling aroma, an acceptable sacrifice, well pleasing to God." Philippians 4:18

Paul received aid and relief for his wants and needs (Philippians 2:25) from the believers at Philippi at the hands of Epaphroditus and says that it was an acceptable sacrifice well pleasing to God.

A generous spirit and heart go a long way with God. Cornelius' alms and prayers went up before God and brought about salvation and the gift of the Spirit (Acts 10).

3. Our bodies

"I beseech you therefore, brethren, by the mercies of God, that you present your bodies a living sacrifice, holy, acceptable to God, which is your reasonable service." Romans 12:1

To offer the sacrifice of praise and thanksgiving involves our bodies. We are to use our mouths and our lips to give thanks and praise in both speaking and singing. Our bodies, are to be presented to God as a living sacrifice in order to offer service both spiritual and natural. The offering of our bodies involves that sacrifice of our time. Offering spiritual sacrifices to God involves sacrificing and giving time in order to give thanks and offer reasonable service.

King David was a serious seeker of God. His tabernacle operated 24/7 offering continual praise and thanksgiving unto God. The sacrifice of praise and thanksgiving included music, singing, dancing, clapping, shouting and praying, which all demand the use of our bodies. Jesus also presented His body as a living sacrifice that He might serve the Father's will. Every day, morning, noon and night, Jesus disciplined His body and used it to offer spiritual sacrifices and service.

> *Therefore, when He came into the world, He said: "Sacrifice and offering You did not desire, But a body You have prepared for Me. In burnt offerings and sacrifices for sin You had no pleasure. Then I said, 'Behold, I have come — In the volume of the book it is written of Me — To do Your will, O God.'"* Hebrews 10:5-7

The highest aim of spiritual sacrifices is obedience to the will of the Father. Obedience is better than sacrifice.

So Samuel said: "Has the Lord as great delight in burnt offerings and sacrifices, As in obeying the voice of the Lord? Behold, to obey is better than sacrifice, And to heed than the fat of rams. For rebellion is as the sin of witchcraft, And stubbornness is as iniquity and idolatry." 1 Samuel 15:22-23

If all we do is offer the sacrifice of praise and thanksgiving without obedient service then we can never fully please God!

"But do not forget to do good and to share, for with such sacrifices God is well pleased." Hebrews 13:16

Sacrificing and offering our time in obedient service includes ministering:

- Any service rendered for the upkeep and work of the spiritual temple of the Lord. As well as the priests, the Levites, who were the attendants to the priests, served in whatever capacity and duty that was needed. Today, we the royal priests of the Lord serve in the Lord's spiritual temple. For the Lord's spiritual temple to function it involves, leadership, administration, the ministry of helps, teaching, spiritual gifts, ministry, sharing, serving one another, reaching out and evangelising and discipling. All of this ministry is priestly in function. The functioning of the temple and the priesthood is to show forth His praises or virtues in order to glorify God.

As priests we are to minister the new covenant.

As well as offering spiritual sacrifices, we are also to minister the new covenant. The priesthood of the old covenant ministered that covenant to the people. The priests were responsible for not only teaching the law but also enforcing it. God is a covenant keeping God, everything He does is based upon His covenant word and promises.

The highest privilege we have as royal priests is to minister the new covenant with our High Priest, Jesus. All of heaven is at work ministering the new covenant. This is the greatest sacrifice and investment of our time that we can offer our Father in heaven.

How do we minister the new covenant? We minister it through prayer and the ministry of reconciliation. The New Covenant is God's agreement to be merciful to unrighteousness, to forgive sins and iniquities with no recall, reconcile people and be their God, and to allow people to know Him and become intimate with Him (Hebrews 8:7–12). It includes every one of God's promises that are yes and amen in Jesus, to the glory of God (2 Corinthians 1:20).

Ministering the new covenant involves utilizing all that we have come to in Zion, the city of God. We have come to God, the judge so make your appeal to Him. Ask for vengeance on spiritual enemies and justice for those who need it. Make sure you pray for your enemies and ask God to bless them, even when you're in direct conflict with ungodliness. Keeping yourself in the love of God is important and disempowers the enemy. Learn how to minister the blood of sprinkling into lives and situations. It has great power and speaks amazing things we can come into agreement with. Ask the Father for the gifts of the Spirit. They are to help us in our spiritual life and ministry on earth. Ask for the aid of angelic ministry. Ask that they are commissioned to fulfil your prayers of agreement. Ask that they are released into lives and situations to bring about victories and breakthroughs. Come into agreement with the word of God and give it confession. Your High Priest is waiting to agree and endorse your confessions and release kingdom power and authority.

In our whole approach to Zion and the Father, we have been delivered from the fleshly life and have been made Christ-like. We are to be like our High Priest who is holy, merciful, compassionate and self-sacrificing (Luke 6:36; 1 Peter 1:15). Ministering the new covenant also demands the highest level of spiritual maturity and self-sacrifice. The second letter to Corinthians is a new covenant ministers guide that should be read in context.

Paul considered himself to be an able or sufficient minister of the new covenant.

> "Not that we are sufficient of ourselves to think of anything as being from ourselves, but our sufficiency is from God, who also made us sufficient as ministers of the new covenant, not of the letter but of the Spirit; for the letter kills, but the Spirit gives life." 2 Corinthians 3:5-6

Paul was established not in his own sufficiency but God's. Paul was living the crucified life.

He lived his life by faith in the Son of God who loved him and gave himself for him (Galatians 2:20).

Notice that ministering the new covenant is not simply passing on the letter or words alone, which kills, or produces death, but of the Spirit which gives life. The new covenant is about reconciliation with God. Paul was established in the new covenant himself.

To be an *able* minister of the new covenant means that one is established in the new covenant in their own life and able to minister it in the lives of others too.

Again in 2 Corinthians 3, Paul says that the old covenant was a ministry of the letter (Vs 6), written on tablets of stone (Vs 3), a ministry of death (Vs 7), and condemnation (Vs 9). The old covenant, was not able to reconcile us to the glory of God.

A minister of the new covenant is filled and led by the Spirit.

The new covenant is the ministry of the Spirit and the glory of God. It is spiritual and written on tablets of flesh, or that of the heart (Vs 3). An able minister is one that is established in spiritual life and is filled with the Spirit and functioning under the glory of God manifesting spiritual inspiration, revelation and power. The first rule of leadership is: 'Lead yourself first'. You cannot lead others to somewhere that you are not yourself. You can only lead others in the ministry of the Spirit as you yourself are established in living and walking in the Spirit (Galatians 5:25). The new covenant minister has developed an intimate relationship with the Father and has developed his spiritual senses to see and hear from the Father, through the Spirit. Paul lived and walked in the Spirit. He demonstrated life in the Spirit. He had powerful spiritual experiences. He operated in spiritual gifts, power and authority and bore the fruits of the Spirit. He ministered the gospel and the ministry of reconciliation and his aim was to 'win souls' (1 Corinthians 9), and 'present every man perfect' (Colossians 1:28,29). Paul desired to bring all believers into a living, personal and intimate relationship with the Father, His Kingdom and the glory of the new covenant through the Spirit. The need of the church today is for trained Spirit filled, Spirit gifted, Spirit Empowered and Spirit led new covenant priests, able to minister the new covenant. The new covenant minister no longer falls short of the glory of God but is fully restored and living in the Father's glory.

A **minister of the new covenant is an 'intercessor'.**

The new covenant and its work must come through us – God wants to plead through us as we plead and implore for others 'on Christ's behalf' – be reconciled to God.

This means that as royal priests our highest call is to present our bodies a living sacrifice so that we can use it to pray, implore, plead and intercede for those lost in the old corrupt creation. We also use our bodies to carry the gospel of the kingdom as treasure in earthen vessels.

We, as priests, are to plead and release the mercy of God.

We are to release the mercy of God through prayer and practice. We pray and plead that the mercy of God is extended towards unrighteousness. We are also to extend mercy. Be merciful, we are told.

We are to plead the power of the blood of sprinkling and apply it to lives and circumstance as we release forgiveness on sins and iniquities with no recall. As well as praying forgiveness we are to be forgiving, lest our prayers are hindered. Ministering the new covenant in lives includes asking for angelic ministry to be activated around those we are praying for to drive away demons and evil spirits and to restrain their activities. We should pray that minds are released from the blinding effects of the god of this world and demons. We are to pray that the Holy Spirit will awaken them, that He will blow winds of conviction and convince them of the judgment to come and the way of salvation through Jesus Christ. We should ask the Holy Spirit to draw them to the truth and to the kingdom and the Father. We should come in agreement with the High Priest of our confession and agree with and speak out confessing His word that he is not willing for any to perish and for all to be saved and come to the truth and repentance and eternal life (2 Peter 3:9; 1 Timothy 2:4). Jesus ever lives to make intercession; this is part of His present and continuing ministry (Hebrews 7:25). As priest under Him, we have the privilege of joining Him in His intercessory ministry. The Holy Spirit is also involved in intercession. He is the Spirit of intercession. A new covenant minster will be empowered and led of the Spirit in intercession.

> *"Likewise the Spirit also helps in our weaknesses. For we do not know what we should pray for as we ought, but the Spirit Himself makes intercession for us with groanings which cannot be uttered. Now He who searches the hearts knows what the mind of the Spirit is, because He makes intercession for the saints according to the will of God."* Romans 8:26-27

As spiritual negotiators and intercessors, we are to pray for all men.

> *"Therefore I exhort first of all that supplications, prayers, intercessions, and giving of thanks be made for all men, for kings and all who are in authority, that we may lead a quiet and peaceable life in all godliness and reverence."* 1 Timothy 2:1-2

All men are the objects of our intercessions but especially rulers and those in authority. Why? Because they are the decision makers that rule society. We are to intercede and pray that they come into the new covenant so that they can use their influence for the good of God's kingdom in the earth, and that we can live in peace, godliness and reverence.

Secondly, we have been made kings. The minister of the new covenant is a 'king'.

Jesus walked in spiritual power and authority because He took time to secure victory in the spiritual realm through authoritative prayer. He took time to bind principalities, powers and rulers of darkness. He was under the Spirit and was equipped with spiritual gifts and power to deal with any and every eventuality that the demonic manifested. Jesus' ministry involved 'casting out demons' by the finger of God, that is the Spirit of God which He mentions in another place (Matthew 12:28). Jesus operated in the gift of the 'discerning of spirits' and knew what type of demons that needed to be dealt with and cast out; deaf and dumb spirits, unclean spirits, mute spirits, and spirits of infirmity. The bible mentions many other types of evil spirits too, which reinforces the truth that we need the gifts of the Spirit at work in us to deal effectively and triumphantly with them by the Spirit of God.

Through His work on the cross Jesus defeated, disarmed and spoiled Satan and His cohorts for us to bring us into His victory and powerful authority.

> *"Behold, I give you the authority to trample on serpents and scorpions, and over all the power of the enemy, and nothing shall by any means hurt you."* Luke 10:19-20

Jesus trained disciples and sent them out with power and authority to preach the gospel, heal the sick and cast out devils. He delegated His authority to them and empowered them to set captives free.

We must understand that we are *royal* priests, meaning that we are both priests and kings.

As kings we have received great spiritual power and authority. We must understand that power and authority over the enemy is given us through Christ. Our victory is our life In Christ. It is based upon Christ's victory over the world, sin and the devil. Throughout His earthly ministry, Jesus exercised power and authority over Satan and demons. He established His authority over satanic powers through prayer.

> *"No one can enter a strong man's house and plunder his goods, unless he first binds the strong man. And then he will plunder his house."* Mark 3:27

> *"But if I cast out demons with the finger of God, surely the kingdom of God has come upon you. When a strong man, fully armed, guards his own palace, his goods are in peace. But when a stronger than he comes upon him and overcomes him, he takes from him all his armour in which he trusted, and divides his spoils."* Luke 11:20-22

Exercising spiritual power and authority is part of our calling as kings of the King. To minister the new covenant effectively, we must enter into our kingly role and exercise our powers. We have been given authority in the Name of Christ to bind strongmen, which certainly include Principalities and powers and rulers of darkness. We are to bring them under the written judgment of God and under the footstool of God. We do this in prayer. We are authorised to ask the Father for angelic powers to be released against the power, weaponry and strategies of Satan. We have authority to use the Name of Jesus. We overcome the enemy by the blood of the Lamb and the power of the cross and the finished work of Jesus. We are to ask the Father for the gifts of the Spirit. We are to ask, seek and knock as we enquire of the Lord to minister against the enemy and into the lives of those lost, blind and bound. Different lives will have the work of different associations of demons at work against them. Because of this we need the gift of the discerning of spirits. As kings we can use the command of faith as we enforce Christ's victory over the power and assignments of the enemy. We'll look more at this in later chapters. In Christ is hidden all the treasures of knowledge and wisdom and He delights and is willing to share of His knowledge with diligent enquirers. As kings we minister spiritual authority and power and we drive the enemy out. As kings we take enemy territory and claim it for the kingdom of

God. As kings we command victories for the kingdom and the work of God. As kings we decree and declare kingdom rule. As kings we cast out demons and evil spirits. As kings we bring kingdom power into play in order to set the captives free.

The minister of the new covenant is an 'Ambassador' and a 'Prophet'.

We have received the ministry of reconciliation.

> *"Now all things are of God, who has reconciled us to Himself through Jesus Christ, and has given us the ministry of reconciliation, that is, that God was in Christ reconciling the world to Himself, not imputing their trespasses to them, and has committed to us the word of reconciliation."* 2 Corinthians 5:18-19

This is the ministry of the new covenant priest and minister. We have been reconciled to reconcile!

In order to win and reconcile people, we must share the gospel. The gospel is 'good news'.

The good news of the kingdom is a specific message that includes, 'The redemption of creation'. The present earth is reserved for fiery judgment and will be dissolved, burned up, refined and renewed (2 Peter 3). The good news of the kingdom also includes, 'The redemption of the body'. The resurrection of the dead was the gospel the early church preached. This good news message answers the actual problem that came into the world through the curse of sin. What was the problem and what was cursed? Well, **all of creation** was subjected to the bondage of corruption and death, and **our bodies** were subject to corruption and death too.

> *"For the earnest expectation of the creation eagerly waits for the revealing of the sons of God. For the creation was subjected to futility, not willingly, but because of Him who subjected it in hope; because the creation itself also will be delivered from the bondage of corruption into the glorious liberty of the children of God. For we know that the whole creation groans and labours with birth pangs together until now. Not only*

that, but we also who have the first-fruits of the Spirit, even we ourselves groan within ourselves, eagerly waiting for the adoption, the redemption of our body." Romans 8:19-23

This message leads us to the gospel of the glory of Christ.

"*But even if our gospel is veiled, it is veiled to those who are perishing, whose minds the god of this age has blinded, who do not believe, lest the light of the gospel of the glory of Christ, who is the image of God, should shine on them.*" 2 Corinthians 4:3-4

The good news of the glory of Christ now makes sense when presented in the context of the good news of the kingdom. In other words when we share the good news of a 'redeemed creation' and a 'redeemed body', free from the curse of sin, we can then present the way of escape from the old creation and the way into the new one with the message of the 'finished work of Christ'. The message of the cross can now be presented. It all makes perfect sense.

The gospel that church has been sharing falls far short of the gospel of the kingdom. The message has been, 'Give your life to Jesus and receive forgiveness of sins and you'll go to heaven when you die.' That's only partially true and doesn't really convey the full truth and expectation of life after death. We were made for life on earth. There's nothing more that we enjoy than living, breathing, sleeping, eating, singing, dancing, reading, holidaying, sight-seeing, swimming, watching movies, building relationships, and a host of other amazing experiences. We know nothing of an ethereal life, floating around as Casper the ghost, in an out of body experience (that said, it is possible to have spiritual experiences as we engage the spiritual realm and heaven). If God wanted us to live in heaven, He wouldn't have given us physical bodies and He certainly wouldn't resurrect them and redeem them!

Our stay in heaven after we die will be brief. We will be in heaven until the resurrection of the body. The resurrected body will then be lived out on the new earth. What will we do? We will build heaven on earth. We will build what Adam should have built at the beginning when He was commissioned and commanded.

All our investments in this life and this world that we have made for the gospel sake will be added to us and will be rewards in the age and life to come. We will have renewed life and energy as well as all the time we need to build the new world under the kingdom of God. What will the new earth be like? Very much as the one we know but with the curse of sin GONE!! Praise God! The greatest blessing of life in the age to come will be seeing people (family, friends, co-workers and neighbours) that we reconciled to God through the ministry of the new covenant.

> *"Now then, we are ambassadors for Christ, as though God were pleading through us: we implore you on Christ's behalf, be reconciled to God. For He made Him who knew no sin to be sin for us, that we might become the righteousness of God in Him."* 2 Corinthians 5:20-21

As we present our bodies as a living sacrifice, we can use our feet to carry the good news to the world.

> *"How beautiful are the feet of those who preach the gospel of peace, Who bring glad tidings of good things!"* Romans 10:15

We can also use our mouths to preach and proclaim the good news.

> *"And how shall they believe in Him of whom they have not heard? And how shall they hear without a preacher? And how shall they preach unless they are sent?"* Romans 10:14-15

A prophet is a messenger and a spokesman for God. We're not talking here about the office of a prophet but in the wider sense of speaking forth the word of God, namely the good news of the kingdom. Jesus was a prophet and a mouthpiece for the Father. He preached the gospel of the kingdom. He spoke about the future of the kingdom. He warned of a day of judgment and spoke about the resurrection of the dead and the age to come. He encouraged His listeners and followers to seek first the kingdom of God and His righteousness. He told them to store up treasures in heaven and He spoke about the life to come. We too as prophets are to preach the gospel of the kingdom. Prophets speak forth the word of God faithfully. They warn people of impending judgment and declare the way of salvation. As prophets we have a message and a mission. We are ambassadors and have the ministry of reconciliation.

Our message should be clear, 'Be reconciled to God!' 'Receive His mercy, receive his forgiveness of sins and iniquities, receive your pardon and invitation into His kingdom to know the Father and enjoy an ongoing intimate relationship with Him.' Why? Because there's a judgment on this present evil world and God is going to destroy it with fire and refine it so that it is free from the curse of sin and because He is going to raise the dead from their graves and judge them according to their deeds and words. Because He is going to create new heavens and a new earth where righteousness dwells and He loves you and wants you to be part of His kingdom plan.

The ministry of reconciliation is not just declaring the gospel of the kingdom and winning the lost but it also involves making disciples and bringing them into the fullness of the kingdom and new covenant ministry. Prophecy is intended to comfort, exhort and edify believers. The word 'edify' means to build up. As prophets we build up and edify the church and train them in the royal priesthood so that become able and sufficient ministers of the new covenant of God.

> *"But he who prophesies speaks edification and exhortation and comfort to men."* 1 Corinthians 14:3

CHAPTER 14

The Way Revealed

The House of Prayer

As we bring all these studies together and see how they fit together, we begin to see the Way more clearly than ever before. When we see it, we can seek it and then build it. It's like having a blueprint, a set of plans for a new build. As we see the pattern, it becomes clear what we should be building and establishing. **Jesus is the way, the truth and the life. His truth, shows us the way to where and how He is expressing His life right now.**

Who He is and what He is doing is the ultimate pattern for who we are and what we are to be doing. Seeing the big picture puts the bible in context. It gives us a new perspective on the church and what she is called to do. I said earlier, that if you are piecing together a jigsaw puzzle, it helps massively if you have the big picture on the box lid in front of you. I believe that I have brought the big picture into view and focus and that now we can see clearly what the church is called to do.

In the great commission, Jesus charges his church with a clear command:

> *"All authority has been given to Me in heaven and on earth. Go therefore and make disciples of all the nations, baptizing them in the name of the Father and of the Son and of the Holy Spirit, teaching them to observe all things that I have commanded you; and lo, I am with you always, even to the end of the age." Amen.* Matthew 28:18-20

God's will, is that the church fulfils her commission and goes to the nations with the gospel of the kingdom, making disciples of them, baptizing them and then teaching them the way, the truth and the life. For this to happen, the church must rise up and become who the Lord has made her to be. The church is the fulfilment of the tabernacle of David. God had promised that in the last days, that He would restore the tabernacle of David and repair the breaches (Acts 15: 16,17).

Today, this is the number one thing that God is doing. The church is about to come into God's end time plan for reaching and healing the nations. He is restoring the breaches and is about to bring about a true unity across the body of Christ. With so many differing visions of who and what the church is called to be and do, it hasn't helped in healing the big divide and breaches in the first place. **Only a clear vision and blueprint of who the church is and what she is called to do can bring about the unity and oneness that is going to impact the nations (John 17).** The church is God's spiritual temple and royal priesthood, called to function under the order of Melchizedek, bringing the kingdom and glory of God to the kingdoms of this world.

As I was deep in prayer one day, I had a vision. I saw a huge catapult being drawn back with a mighty stretch and then it was released. As it shot, the Lord said that He was catapulting His church into its future. **I knew that the Lord was releasing this revelation because of His calling and purpose for His church.** If we look at the church on the ground, she doesn't look very glorious! Neither is she without spot or wrinkle!

In fact, what we see can lead to discouragement. The Lord sees His church from above, where He has brought her to and there, she is amazingly glorious and most definitely without spot or blemish.

The Lord is lifting His church up into the Spirit! It is time for the restoration of all things. In the book of Acts 13:21, it says that Christ has been received into heaven *until the restoration of all things.* **The church must rise up the glorious church she is, manifest the glory of God and bring in the harvest to usher in the return of Christ for the restoration of all things.** Right now, the Lord is in heaven and has taken up His present and continuing ministry as High Priest after the order of Melchizedek. He is also the mediator of the New Covenant in His blood and stands in the presence of the Father representing us and giving charge over an innumerable company of angels.

After Christ died and rose again, He ascended, passing through the heavens and opened up a new and living way for His church to rise up and join Him in the heavenly sanctuary as priests and kings. **Remember, Jesus is the way! He is the way to heaven right now!** The church has a heavenly calling! She is to rise as living stones forming a spiritual temple and habitation for the Lord. As well as forming a spiritual temple, the church is a royal priesthood to serve under and alongside her High Priest, Jesus.

Remember, Jesus is the High Priest of our confession. As the church catches this and operates as the house of prayer, her confession and agreement with the Word of God, Jesus, is going to release the glory of God across the nations. It is the church in the spirit, in the heavenly place that is glorious, without spot and without blemish, because to rise to this place, believers must become overcomers of the world, the flesh and the devil!

The church has been called, equipped and authorised to join her High Priest and King in the restoration of all things. When the church rises in the Spirit and takes up her heavenly calling, leading to the return of Christ for a glorious church without spot and blemish, then the restoration of all things will begin. Hallelujah!

The Church We See

Learning how the Lord sees the church brought to my attention the church that men see. I can't help but notice on many church websites we find written, 'The church I/we see!' What follows is a description of the church that that leader or church sees! I'm now convinced that the church the Lord sees is very different to the church that we see or have seen!

Many have become disillusioned with church as we know it, because it is filled with so many man-made programmes and ideas that are void of the power of God. I must admit that I have had my share of implementing things that I have copied from other ministries only to experience frustration and failure. The church is so busy with conferences, seminars, missions and programmes that she seems to be overdosing on information and yet still we see no glory in the church. There seems to be no clear 'big picture' to focus on so churches go on juggling the pieces trying to make sense of where they fit.

The church is great with words, she knows how to present sermons and teachings and talks but can't demonstrate power. The apostle Paul told the Corinthians, *"And my speech and my preaching were not with persuasive words of human wisdom, but in demonstration of the Spirit and of power, that your faith should not be in the wisdom of men but in the power of God"* (1 Corinthians 2:4,5). We seem to have it backwards. We have a lot of speech and no power! How many words have we sat under in conference after conference and let's face it, with all the great teaching we have, where is the power of God?

Please understand, I love the church and have given my life, almost forty years in service to her, so I am not coming with a critical spirit or intending just to 'have a dig' at the church. I really believe that when we build with the Lord in this season, **big changes are going to bring about big changes** and the church will be a force to be reckoned with. The sleeping giant will rise and bring about the end time plan of God which will usher in the return of the Saviour, Yeshua/Jesus.

Prayer: The Main Thing

"We have an altar from which those who serve the tabernacle have no right to eat." Hebrews 13:10

The main purpose of all the tabernacles and temples that we have examined has been to restore us to the throne of God and the golden altar so that we can minister the kingdom of God in the earth. All the other ministrations; sacrifices, washings etc. were to bring the priests to the Ark and the golden altar. This was the highest purpose and highest honour of serving as a priest.

In Moses' tabernacle, the brazen altar prepared the priest to minister at the golden altar. We have an altar that far surpasses the altar of the tabernacle of Moses. **The highest purpose for the temple is prayer and the highest ministry of the priest is also prayer.** Before any other purpose, the church, God's spiritual temple is to be a house of prayer.

"Then Jesus went into the temple and began to drive out those who bought and sold in the temple, and overturned the tables of the money changers and the seats of those who sold doves. And He would not allow anyone to carry wares through the temple. Then He taught, saying to them, "Is it not written, 'My house shall be called a house of prayer for all nations'? But you have made it a 'den of thieves.'" Mark 11:15–17

The Lord's anger was because they had made the house of God a place of men's business instead of a place of God's business. In order for the church to fulfil her great commission, she must be established as a house of prayer for all nations. Her commission is to make disciples of all nations. She cannot do it without the house of prayer. The reaching and healing of the nations are depending on the house of prayer.

It's the house of prayer that will bring the church into and under the glory of God and the inspiration, revelation and power of the Spirit. It's the house of prayer that will put the enemy under the written judgment and footstool of God. It's the house of prayer that will see the outpouring of the Spirit and spiritual gifts manifested. It's the house of prayer that will bring about and support a successful gospel mission into the nations.

Leaders today, have made the church the house of the buffet, the house of entertainment, the house of recreation, the house of the coffee morning, the house of merchandise and the house of their business. **It's become everything but the house of prayer.** Put on a night of teaching, or music, or food and congregations come flocking, and yet as soon as the call for a night of prayer goes out, most stay home. The temple of God in the earth has been destroyed and breached by the devil and religion. The priesthood has been hijacked and robbed of its true meaning and ministry.

What is God doing today? He is calling His spiritual temple the church upwards to come as 'living stones' to join the 'chief cornerstone, Jesus, who has been laid in Zion, to form His 'House of Prayer for All Nations.' Why? Because God is about to touch the nations and gather the harvest. Why? Because the 'Day of the Lord' is upon the world and God's offer of salvation is coming to the nations, so that Heaven can release Jesus to close the age and restore all things.

Build My House of Prayer

I was in prayer one day talking to the Lord about His church. 'You can't leave her like this Lord', I said. 'Your word says that you're coming for a glorious church without spot and blemish.' I continued. 'If you're coming for a glorious church she has to change', I said. Immediately, these words from the apostle Peter flooded my mind....

> *'Kept by the power of God through faith for salvation ready to be revealed in the last time.'* (1 Peter 1:5)

Immediately, God gave me revelation and I said to the Lord, 'I know what you're up to!' 'You've got something up your sleeve.' 'You're ready to reveal your salvation in the last time!' 'There's something about your salvation that you have held back until now' 'But you are ready to reveal it now!' The Lord said to me, *'Dennis read Isaiah 56:1'*

> *Thus says the Lord: "Keep justice, and do righteousness, For My salvation is about to come, And My righteousness to be revealed."* Isaiah 56:1

My jaw dropped open. God confirmed my words. He was ready to reveal His salvation and righteousness. I was pumped up with excitement. 'I knew it, I just knew it' I said. The Lord then told me to read on in Isaiah 56. What the Lord revealed to me has lit me up and gripped me and directed me to build what I believe the Lord is doing in this present age.

> *"Also the sons of the foreigner Who join themselves to the Lord, to serve Him, And to love the name of the Lord, to be His servants — Everyone who keeps from defiling the Sabbath, And holds fast My covenant — Even them I will bring to My holy mountain, And make them joyful in My house of prayer. Their burnt offerings and their sacrifices Will be accepted on My altar; For My house shall be called a house of prayer for all nations."* Isaiah 56:6-7

The Lord told me, *'Dennis build my house of prayer.'* As the church functions as the House of Prayer for All nations, she is going to come into divine strategies and plans that will foil the devil's strategies and evil plans and floods of wickedness.

> *"Even to them I will give in My house And within My walls a place and a name Better than that of sons and daughters; I will give them an everlasting name That shall not be cut off."* Isaiah 56:5

'Dennis, what I speak within my walls, the devil doesn't know! I'm going to release devil busting strategies to my people, within my walls!' As we operate within the walls of the temple, we are going to receive revelation, inspiration and power to accomplish God's will and purpose. The strategies, power and resources in God's temple, including every spiritual blessing has to be ministered by God's royal priesthood. The royal priesthood means that every believer is both a priest and a king in God's house.

Before the Lord returns, the church has to fulfil God's plan and purpose, to save souls out of the world. This temple is going to minister the kingdom of God to this generation. The royal priesthood, which includes every believer are about to be brought into a new and living way and form the house of prayer for all nations.

What will happen from this house of prayer?

God's royal priests are going to be supernaturally taught by the Spirit in these 'last times' and they are going to minister the glory of God: The new covenant and the ministry of reconciliation.

There's going to be a revival of prayer – powerful prayer – Spirit led and empowered prayer!

This new house of prayer is going to subdue God's enemies and release God's salvation and blessings.

The highest purpose of prayer is to minister the new covenant from Zion.

The church has been blessed with every spiritual blessing in the heavenly places and these blessings can only be activated by the church from the house of prayer. The new covenant is God's offer to extend mercy, forgiveness and reconciliation so that all people can experience the kingdom of God as well as develop an intimate relationship with their heavenly Father, creator and Redeemer and Saviour. The new emerging church in this season is going to be filled, led and empowered by the Spirit to deal with Satanic and demonic floods of evil.

The Church is God's Government on Earth

"And I also say to you that you are Peter, and on this rock I will build My church, and the gates of Hades shall not prevail against it." Matthew 16:18

The church is the government of God and represents Him on earth. This was God's original intention when He created Adam and Eve. They were the government of God on earth and had access to Zion, heaven to meet with God and consult Him as to His kingdom and will on earth. They were given dominion and authority over everything for the purpose of establishing heaven on earth. What Adam lost, Jesus, the last Adam regained and restored. 'Ekklesia' is the Greek word for 'Church'. It meant an assembly called out by the magistrate to be a ruling body. The assembly was made up of six thousand members and were responsible for selecting officials, decreeing and setting laws, deciding military strategies and declaring war.

Christ the Head of the Church

"He is the image of the invisible God, the firstborn over all creation. For by Him all things were created that are in heaven and that are on earth, visible and invisible, whether thrones or dominions or principalities or powers. All things were created through Him and for Him. And He is before all things, and in Him all things consist. And He is the head of the body, the church, who is the beginning, the firstborn from the dead, that in all things He may have the preeminence." Colossians 1:15–18

There's never been a time when Jesus has lost authority or control of His rule. It was man's authority that was usurped and lost. Christ's mission was to become man to redeem man and restore him and exalt him to his restored position in creation. This is what Jesus came to do. He did everything to defeat the devil along with his principalities and powers that he might lift us up above them and restore our kingdom authority. Jesus has been raised far above all principality and power and might and dominion and every name that is named (Ephesians 1:21). All things have been put under his feet and He is the head over all things.

> *"And He put all things under His feet, and gave Him to be head over all things to the church, which is His body, the fullness of Him who fills all in all."* Ephesians 1:22-23

There is no higher power or authority over our exalted Lord and He is the head of the church. Let all that sink in. Listen to the words of Jesus:

> *"All authority has been given to Me in heaven and on earth."* Matthew 28:18

Jesus has all authority in heaven and in earth. This means that everything in heaven and the heavens and the earth is under Him and we are in Him, who is head over all things. It's time to know our authority and use our authority. The church has been raised and exalted with Him to rule in the heavens and in the earth. The church is the Lord's official representative to act upon God's behalf in the heavens and in the earth. Why did Jesus say that he had authority in heaven and in earth? Because the church has work to do in the heavens and in earth. The church is to use her spiritual authority.

CHAPTER 15

The Early Church and Prayer

Continuing Prayer

The early church started and continued as a house of prayer. After Jesus ascended, they returned at His word to Jerusalem and assembled in the upper room. What were they doing? They were praying.

> *"These all continued with one accord in prayer and supplica-tion."* Acts 1:14

Notice that they continued in prayer with one accord. They were together and they were united.

> *"When the Day of Pentecost had fully come, they were all with one accord in one place. And suddenly there came a sound from heaven, as of a rushing mighty wind, and it filled the whole house where they were sitting. Then there appeared to them divided tongues, as of fire, and one sat upon each of them. And they were all filled with the Holy Spirit and began*

to speak with other tongues, as the Spirit gave them utter-
ance." Acts 2:1-4

The outpouring of the Spirit came as a result of God's timing and their praying. Prayer birthed the church and prayer kept the church in the power of the Spirit.

"And they continued steadfastly in the apostles' doctrine and fellowship, in the breaking of bread, and in prayers." Acts 2:42

Prayer was the main work of the church. They started and continued in prayer.

"Now Peter and John went up together to the temple at the hour of prayer, the ninth hour." Acts 3:1

The early church observed the 'hour of prayer'. There were set times to pray throughout the day. We know that the old testament priests observed the morning and evening sacrifices to the Lord. Daniel prayed three times a day; morning, noon and evening. Jesus also observed the 'hour of prayer' and often withdrew from His ministering to pray. The apostles were set in this powerful discipline too. The apostle Paul prayed day and night for the church.

"And when they had prayed, the place where they were assembled together was shaken; and they were all filled with the Holy Spirit, and they spoke the word of God with boldness." Acts 4:22

Both before and after missions, they came together and they prayed.

It didn't matter what was going on around them, the church prayed continually and saw powerful results. As they prayed, God moved, the Spirit moved and angels moved.

"Peter was therefore kept in prison, but constant prayer was offered to God for him by the church." Acts 12:5

On this occasion it was an angel who released Peter from prison (Acts 12: 5-10).

The early church ministered powerfully because of the house of prayer. The new covenant is ministered by the royal priesthood from and out from the house of prayer.

> *"But you have come to Mount Zion and to the city of the living God, the heavenly Jerusalem, to an innumerable company of angels, to the general assembly and church of the firstborn who are registered in heaven, to God the Judge of all, to the spirits of just men made perfect, to Jesus the Mediator of the new covenant, and to the blood of sprinkling that speaks better things than that of Abel."* Hebrews 12:22–24

Only the church can minister Christ's kingdom authority! It is done through the house of prayer for all nations. Church history has a tale to tell. The early church turned the world in their generation upside down. The gospel of the kingdom went out and was accompanied by miracles, signs, and wonders.

By the end of the first century there were already signs of a waning church as false teachings and deceptions came in.

Soon the church was off the rails and doctrines of demons had taken over. The church had lost its message and mission. For 1400 years the church was around but had become religious and dead. How could the church be so far from its roots to where its selling forgiveness and salvation? Around the year 1517, Martin Luther, a catholic monk, nailed his 95 theses to the doors of the Castle church in Wittenberg, Germany. He was raising issues that he witnessed in the catholic church that he felt needed changing. You could buy indulgences from the Pope and buy forgiveness and salvation. You could even buy your way out of purgatory.

Martin Luther came against this and the main points of his theses were:

- Salvation is by faith alone

- The bible is the only authority

- The priesthood of every believer

  "For by grace you have been saved through faith, and that not of yourselves; it is the gift of God, not of works, lest anyone should boast." Ephesians 2:8-9

The reformation followed this address and the church came into salvation by faith, the bible in the hands of every believer and every believer called to serve as a priest. *Although Luther raised up the priesthood of all believers, he never received the full revelation of it.* So even though it is talked of today in the contemporary church, it still awaits to be fulfilled in the church and in believer's lives.

It has taken over 500 years to come into the revelation of this mystery mentioned in the New Testament until NOW! The church today is not that far from the church Luther rose up and called out. The church today is still attempting to sell the anointing, sell privileges, and sell miracles! **But there's a new reformation that is taking the church into a new season and a new era.** This reformation is going to bring about a fully functional spiritual temple and priesthood. This time, it won't be spiritual celebrities – it will be 'all who want in' – every believer.

We, this generation are in a historic and momentous point in history, where the priesthood of all believers is about to reach those **who see that there's more**, those that are **hungry for more**, and **those that have understanding of the new covenant** and **feel the upward call of God drawing them out of their religiosity and out of the material comfort to a higher place, raising them up as overcomers and into the heavenly calling with Jesus the High Priest and Mediator of the New Covenant.** The royal priesthood has been hijacked by the devil centuries ago and hidden and kept from believers until now. The priesthood in main stream Christendom is out of alignment with the NT priesthood.

The royal priesthood, which includes every believer are about to be brought into a new and living way and form the house of prayer for all nations. What will happen from this house of prayer? God's royal priests are going to be supernaturally brought and taught by the Spirit in these 'last times' and they are going to minister the glory of God: The new covenant and the ministry of reconciliation.

There's going to be a revival of prayer – powerful prayer – Spirit led and empowered prayer! This new house of prayer is going to subdue God's enemies and release God's salvation and blessing. The new covenant is God's offer to extend mercy, forgiveness and reconciliation so that all people can experience the kingdom of God as well as develop an intimate relationship with their heavenly Father, creator and Redeemer and Saviour.

What's stopping this: Spiritual warfare! Satan has led the whole world astray and taken them captive.

As God of this world, He is blinding 'minds' to the glory of Christ and all He has done and offers!

The nations, peoples, cities, communities are under the influence of the Prince of the power of the air.

Floods of Evil

> *"According to their deeds, accordingly He will repay, Fury to His adversaries, Recompense to His enemies; The coastlands He will fully repay. So shall they fear The name of the Lord from the west, And His glory from the rising of the sun; When the enemy comes in like a flood, The Spirit of the Lord will lift up a standard against him."* Isaiah 59:18-19

The new emerging church in this season is going to be filled, led and empowered by the Spirit to deal with Satanic and demonic floods of evil. As the church functions as the House of Prayer for All nations, she is going to come into divine strategies and plans that will foil the devil's strategies and evil plans and floods of wickedness. The strategies, power and resources in God's temple, including every spiritual blessing has to be ministered by God's royal priesthood. The royal priesthood means that every believer is both a priest and a king. In this season, the royal priesthood is going to:

- Bring God's enemies under the footstool of God

- Going to be a light and a witness of victorious and blessed living.

- They're going to gather in the harvest of souls through the ministry of reconciliation, which includes the word of reconciliation, the gospel. It's a new season of training and equipping for the church – it's a new and living way in Jesus. The house of prayer for all nations, which is going to facilitate this, is going to function with great spiritual power and glory. The Gospel of the kingdom is about to go in to the nations as a witness. God is going to heal the nations, those that want it!

The reason that there is so much turmoil in the earth is because of the great upheaval in the heavens.

God is shaking everything.

> But now He has promised, saying, "Yet once more I shake not only the earth, but also heaven." Hebrews 12:26

The shakeup is to wake up!

God is releasing revelation of His age long plan in our day, in our time and on our watch. God is transforming the church – He's lifting her up for her heavenly calling with her High Priest! Together, they are going to minister the new covenant and ministry of reconciliation in kingdom power and glory! **It's this revelation that is causing havoc in the spiritual realm.**

You see, the devil knows a couple of things.

 - He knows that this revelation is coming to the church and is going to hamper his work

> "...to the intent that now the manifold wisdom of God might be made known by the church to the principalities and powers in the heavenly places." Ephesians 3:8

– He knows that his time is short and that his judgment and doom are close to hand.

> *"Woe to the inhabitants of the earth and the sea! For the devil has come down to you, having great wrath, because he knows that he has a short time."* Revelation 12:12

God has His heart on the nations – His original will and purpose was: Heaven on earth. God's purpose was to extend heaven (His spiritual order) to earth – providing the exact conditions on earth (His physical order). Both combined and synchronized in harmony would produce a symphony!

The devil's fall and the rise of his kingdom of darkness upset and frustrated the plan, not because of God's failure but Adam's. Instead of listening to God the Father they listened to the Father of lies.

This is how Satan became the god of this world. He seized his golden opportunity and became ruler!

> *"We know that we are of God, and the whole world lies under the sway of the wicked one."* 1 John 5:19

Satan keeps the world, nations, cities, communities and families under his sway, his influence and his control. He keeps occupied, and distracted with money, sex and power. They live as consumers, consumed by materialistic pursuits, oblivious to reality. The nations of the world are in crisis – but most people have their eyes on themselves. The bible warns us to live soberly and godly!

> *"So the great dragon was cast out, that serpent of old, called the Devil and Satan, who deceives the whole world; he was cast to the earth, and his angels were cast out with him."* Revelation 12:9

Satan blinds the minds of the nations with deception – he blinds them to the truth. He feeds alternatives that have traces of truth – he feeds humanity with lies about their origin, their makeup, about the spiritual realm. He uses philosophies, religion, false teachings etc. His aim and objective are to keep the nations in the dark, in deception, and in ignorance/oblivion. Let's get to the house of prayer for all nations – there's only one answer and it's the house of prayer!

The nations are reeling out of control, oblivious to what is round the corner and upon them.

The world is like a drunken man, staggering, under the influence and oblivious to the dangers.

Science, technology, business, health, law and order, education, media and the arts – all are great until we put fallen mankind into the mix and then.........

Jesus came to the temple and they had made it something it was not – a den of thieves. **When you make the temple/ church something it's not – it cannot release what its got!** The house of prayer for all nations is God's plan to save the nations – it's God's plan to restrain Satan – it's God's plan to roll out His end time agenda and bring in the final harvest.

Only the church operating as God's official temple and priesthood can minister the new covenant in the earth, to the nations! Only the house of prayer can stir the Father, the Son, the Spirit and Angels armies. Only the house of prayer can bring salvation, mercy, forgiveness, renewal, and redemption, and healing to the nations. **Only the house of prayer** can release all of God's kingdom resources, power and blessings into the nations. **Only the house of prayer** can bring the nations out of bondage, out of darkness, out of lostness, out of corruption, out of deception and into true freedom and a living hope.

What is so powerful about the house of prayer – it gives us the true context for prayer. If you don't have the right context for prayer it won't work! YOU CAN PRAY AMISS! When you have context for prayer and when you know how prayer works, you'll pray and get results. We need to see, know and understand what Jesus has restored us to: ZION, HEAVEN! Remember, if you make it something it's not – you cannot release what its got!

There's a revival of prayer about to break loose across the church and it's happening right now – it's going to be different. The church is coming into revelation of the house of prayer for all nations and how God is raising it up. The Spirit of God is going to equip believers with a powerful intercessory anointing to minister the kingdom and glory of God!

> *"And do this, knowing the time, that now it is high time to awake out of sleep; for now our salvation is nearer than when we first believed. The night is far spent, the day is at hand."*
> Romans 13:11–12

CHAPTER 16

Prayer for the Nations

A House of Prayer

When we make the church about man's business over God's business the House of God, the spiritual temple cannot release what it's got. When Jesus came to the temple and found they had replaced God's business with man's business he ran them out and then reminded them of the purpose of the temple – **A house of Prayer for the Nations.**

As church leaders we must build the house of prayer for all nations.

The reason Jesus was so powerful and fruitful in His earthly ministry was because of Prayer.

He was able to completely subdue satanic power, demonic power, and even governmental power.

He was able to minister the gifts and power of the Holy Spirit. He worked in league with angelic ministries. He was able to preach and teach with anointed authority the kingdom of God.

Jesus died on Passover. Pentecost was 50 days later – Jesus spent forty days teaching them the kingdom of God (Acts 1:3). Jesus told His apostles and disciples to wait in Jerusalem for the power of the Holy Spirit. Jesus ascended forty days after Passover and returned to Zion, heaven, to fulfil the promise. This means that the disciples had a 10 day wait for the Spirit to be poured out. They were staying in the upper room – the upper room in those days was a room for devotion!

They came together in prayer and supplication – note: They All started and Continued in prayer.

This was the birth of the spiritual temple and royal priesthood of the new testament. The church had its start and beginning in a prayer meeting and once it started it continued in prayer! What made the difference for this early church? Why were they so powerful and fruitful? Why did they reach cities, and nations? Why did they see mass conversions, miracles, signs and wonders? Why were they so generous and willing to sell all and take care of each other? Why were they so devoted to one another, so hospitable, so committed and devoted? What made the difference? What was it?

The Risen, Ascended and Glorified Christ.

Now when He had spoken these things, while they watched, He was taken up, and a cloud received Him out of their sight. And while they looked steadfastly toward heaven as He went up, behold, two men stood by them in white apparel, who also said, "Men of Galilee, why do you stand gazing up into heaven? This same Jesus, who was taken up from you into heaven, will so come in like manner as you saw Him go into heaven."
Acts 1:9-11

They were so in touch with the **Risen, Ascended and Glorified Lord**. Their eyes had beheld, seen and watched as He ascended to heaven and a cloud received Him out of their sight.

This blessed reality never left them, it was indelibly-marked into their spirit and soul.

They had seen the glorified Christ and it so transformed them that they were changed into His image.

> *"But we all, with unveiled face, beholding as in a mirror the glory of the Lord, are being transformed into the same image from glory to glory, just as by the Spirit of the Lord."* 2 Corinthians 3:18

They knew He had been received into heaven and that He would bring them into His glory by His Spirit. They were so focused on the resurrected and ascended Lord – they knew who He was!

He had all power and authority and would now minister His glory from heaven through them.

They went out bold and confident because of the glorified Jesus.

They prayed in His Name – preached in His Name – cast out devils in His Name – healed in His Name

They drew their power and authority from the Ascended and Glorified Lord of Heaven.

> *Jesus said to him, "Thomas, because you have seen Me, you have believed. Blessed are those who have not seen and yet have believed."* John 20:29

We walk by faith and not by sight!

Zion, Heaven

> *"When the Day of Pentecost had fully come, they were all with one accord in one place. And suddenly there came a sound from heaven, as of a rushing mighty wind, and it filled the whole house where they were sitting. Then there appeared*

to them divided tongues, as of fire, and one sat upon each of them. And they were all filled with the Holy Spirit and began to speak with other tongues, as the Spirit gave them utterance." Acts 2:1-4

They were so in tune with heaven. They were attuned to the sound from heaven. Their very utterance was spiritual, heavenly and governed by the Holy Spirit. They were under His anointing – His gifts – His influence – power – His leading. The early church prayed and the Spirit of God moved mightily. The gifts of the Spirit were demonstrated. They prayed and the ministry of angels was activated – supernatural things happened. There were personal angelic encounters throughout the early church.

When they had important decisions to make, they prayed and heard from heaven.

And they prayed and said, "You, O Lord, who know the hearts of all, show which of these two You have chosen to take part in this ministry and apostleship." Acts 1:24-25

"But you have come to Mount Zion and to the city of the living God, the heavenly Jerusalem, to an innumerable company of angels, to the general assembly and church of the firstborn who are registered in heaven, to God the Judge of all, to the spirits of just men made perfect, to Jesus the Mediator of the new covenant, and to the blood of sprinkling that speaks better things than that of Abel." Hebrews 12:22-24

All of heaven and the ascended glorified Lord was at work in them, with them and through them. Why? Because they were committed to PRAYER. Spiritual power and authority to activate every spiritual blessing is only activated through the house of prayer!

In comparison to the modern, contemporary church, the early church had very little and yet they had greater success – why? The House of Prayer for all nations was up and running. The contemporary church spends more time on planning than it does on praying! Let's reverse that – lets pray more – let's seek to understand the mechanisms of prayer. God and all of heaven are waiting for the house of prayer to form and function so the glory can be released!! Let's do it – let's bring healing to the nations!

Throughout His ministry, Jesus' top priority was PRAYER! He went nowhere without it. He started nothing without it and He accomplished everything through it! When we can get up and go through our day without a quality time of prayer, something is amiss. We are operating in the power of the human strength and resource and cannot manifest God's glory. If we don't establish spiritual life and connection with God the judge of all, Jesus the mediator of the new covenant, with the Spirit of the Lord, we will be unable to release the supernatural power of the word of God, the Spirit of God and angelic ministry.

Jesus said, 'I will build my church.' The word 'church' is translated, 'Eklesia'. The Greek 'Eklesia', was a governmental assembly made up of 6,000 members responsible for executing governmental power, electing officials, setting law, governing, declaring war, developing military strategies etc. The Eklesia was a ruling body. This is the calling of the church. The church is not to be sitting back in defence mode but should be militantly advancing against the gates of hell, subduing the enemy and setting the captives free. The church is to be working together with her Head, Jesus Christ. He is the key to releasing kingdom power, kingdom, growth, kingdom favour, kingdom wealth/resources and kingdom revival.

Pentecost brought the early church into and under the risen, exalted and ascended ministry of Jesus as well as connection to heaven – its sound, resources and ministry. They came into it through prayer and then committed to ongoing prayer.

Let's See it in Operation.

'These all continued in one accord in prayer and supplication.' Once they started. they never stopped.

They continued in prayer and supplication. They prayed continually, continuously ceaselessly.

Supplication is asking for supply or provision. Jesus told them to wait to be endowed with power.

Endowed means supplied or provided with – Pentecost supplied them with spiritual/supernatural power. This is what supplication is all about – what's the point of being supplied with silver and gold but be spiritual impoverished and impotent? They were continually supplied and filled with the Spirit. Why? They prayed...and they prayed...and they...

They were together in one accord – together in devotion, prayer, function, in purpose, in mission, in ministry. They were the temple and priesthood of the Lord and committed to the main purpose PRAYER! They were dwelling and functioning in unity and so the Lord commanded the blessing (Psalm 133:3).

How committed to prayer were they?

The temple prayers were set in hours – the first hour, 6am – the third hour, 9am – the sixth hour, 12pm – the ninth hour, 3pm. The Jewish day runs from 6pm to 6pm – the evening and the morning counts as a day.

> *"Evening and morning and at noon I will pray, and cry aloud, And He shall hear my voice."* Psalm 55:12

> *"Now when Daniel knew that the writing was signed, he went home. And in his upper room, with his windows open toward Jerusalem, he knelt down on his knees three times that day, and prayed and gave thanks before his God, as was his custom since early days."* Daniel 6:10

The early church observed the Jewish hours of prayer. How interesting. It was the third hour of prayer (9am) when the Holy Spirit came (Acts 2:15).

> *"Now Peter and John went up together to the temple at the hour of prayer, the ninth hour (3pm)."* Acts 3:1

> *"The next day, as they went on their journey and drew near the city, Peter went up on the housetop to pray, about the sixth hour (12pm)."* Acts 10:9

> *So Cornelius said, "Four days ago I was fasting until this hour; and at the ninth hour (3pm) I prayed in my house, and behold, a man stood before me in bright clothing, and said, 'Cornelius, your prayer has been heard, and your alms are remembered in the sight of God.'"* Acts 10:30–31

Jesus was committed to the hours of prayer – he observed them and some. He was constantly moving in and out of prayer throughout the day. He was supplied, filled, led and empowered by the Spirit.

The early church was committed to daily continual prayer and so were supplied with the Spirit.

Disconnected from the Head through prayerlessness, the church is nothing but a dead, religious institution powerless and impotent against spiritual powers and enemies and unable to bring liberty, freedom and life to a world of lost people captive and spiritually blind.

Only when the church functions as the house of prayer can she be supplied with the Spirit in supernatural demonstration of power and authority. Peter and the others had been in prayer and at 9.00am on Pentecost the Holy Spirit came in great supply and brought 3,000 souls into the kingdom in one day. They were baptized and committed themselves.

> *"And they continued steadfastly in the apostles' doctrine and fellowship, in the breaking of bread, and in prayers."* Acts 2:42

A house of prayer is going to bring about a revival of prayer like never before – and God is going to release an overflowing abundant supply of the Spirit of God in supernatural power and authority.

When the church prioritises prayer, she's going to manifest the glory of God. Hallelujah!! Are you ready? Are you willing?

God is calling out a people to join Him in the greatest rescue mission the world has ever seen – He's calling men and women, out of every walk of life to make a difference through His House of Prayer for all nations! Make your peace!

The only thing that can minister and release the kingdom, the power and the glory is the House of prayer for all nations. The house of prayer is about a corporate commitment made by believers together in one accord. This is what God is committed to today. It's His number one thing, His top priority. Everything else is second to establishing the house of prayer.

So, the early church was so powerful because they were connected to the risen, exalted and glorified Jesus, as well as connected and supplied with supernatural inspiration, revelation and power by the Spirit of God. All of this through PRAYER! *The early church started and continued in prayer – they never let it go and never stopped praying. It was there number one priority as we've seen – in fact they made sure that every new convert was discipled and trained to continue steadfastly in prayer.*

The early church knew and understood the importance of being established steadfastly in prayer.

Making your peace with God and experiencing the new covenant is done through prayer.

'*Whoever calls on the Name of the Lord shall be saved.*' Prayer produces salvation. **But as new believers we are to** *continue in prayer.* The kingdom of God and the new covenant are ministered through daily devotion and skill in prayer. This is a learned practice and leaders are to model it, teach it and prioritise it!

In our text, we read that the new converts were introduced to prayer and encouraged to continue steadfastly in it. If we get this wrong, it can lead to problems. If we win people with hype, you must keep them with hype. If you win them with entertainment, you'll have to keep them, entertained. If you make them reliant on you, they'll stay immature and won't learn how to exercise their spiritual senses in order to be empowered and directed by God. These new believers were added not only to the church but to the house of prayer! New converts must be added to the house of prayer asap and encouraged and trained to pray.

This is what happened on the Day of Pentecost. Three thousand souls were added to the house of prayer. The apostles were prayer warriors – they were committed to the Jewish temple hours of prayer.

Their spiritual senses were alert and they were seeing heavenly visions, hearing from heaven and having angelic encounters. They were constantly being endowed and supplied by the Spirit with spiritual inspiration, revelation and power.

The early church caught what these mighty apostles had and were modelling. The early believers were moving in heavenly anointing and power also. The gifts of the Spirit were flowing powerfully and cities were experiencing revival. The reason was that they were born into a prayer movement! They had powerful anointed, Spirit filled and Spirit led leaders. The best thing you can do for spiritual growth is find a praying leader and don't let them out of your sight.

The new believers of the NT church were introduced to the apostle's doctrine and teaching, to breaking of bread, to fellowship and MOST importantly, to prayers! Do you have a daily, disciplined prayer life? Do you have leaders that model and lead you in prayer? We do new believers a disservice when we leave them to drift into prayerlessness. The longer it is left, the harder it is for grown believers to begin a powerful and purposeful prayer life.

- Prayer is the only way you can know your Father intimately.

- It's the only way you can receive spiritual inspiration, revelation and power.

- Prayer is the only way that you can minister spiritual power and authority.

- It's the only way that you can defeat Satan, and His co-horts.

The apostle Paul is another great example of being birthed into prayer. He was Saul of Tarsus up to his conversion. He was an enemy of God and the church and had been persecuting believers. But when he had a powerful spiritual encounter with the risen, exalted and glorified Jesus, everything changed! His spiritual senses were awakened and his spiritual eyes and ears were opened. God spoke to a believer called Ananias and told him to go and minister to Saul the new convert.

> So the Lord said to him, "Arise and go to the street called Straight, and inquire at the house of Judas for one called Saul of Tarsus, for behold, he is praying. And in a vision he has seen a man named Ananias coming in and putting his hand on him, so that he might receive his sight." Acts 9:11-12

Notice that Saul was praying! Prayer is supposed to connect us to the spiritual realm, to Zion, heaven, to God the Father, Jesus the Mediator of the new covenant, to innumerable company of angels, so that the kingdom is experienced in powerful, relevant, and supernatural ministry.

When Ananias came to Paul, he was healed of blindness, filled with the Spirit and baptized. Saul became the apostle Paul and continued in steadfast prayer. He entered into a powerful ministry that brought him into amazing spiritual experiences and encounters with the risen Jesus as well as angels and powerful spiritual gifts of the Holy Spirit.

> "I thank God, whom I serve with a pure conscience, as my forefathers did, as without ceasing I remember you in my prayers night and day." 2 Timothy 1:3

Only prayer can bring a believer into this kind of spiritual and supernatural encounters with the risen Jesus, the Spirit of God, spiritual gifts and angelic encounters. If new believers are not introduced to prayer immediately, they will lack the supernatural blessings of the kingdom of God. Let's make sure that we are leading new believers into continued and steadfast prayer.

> *"Train up a child in the way he should go, And when he is old he will not depart from it."* Proverbs 22:6

Today we want to see the importance of the word of God and prayer. In our text, the apostles faced a challenge. As the church was growing, believers were selling properties and bringing the proceeds to the apostles for distribution. The early church saw every member's needs met, no one lacked anything as they shared with one another (Acts 4:34). The proceeds were also used to meet the needs of the poor and widows amongst them. Some of the Greek speaking widows were being neglected in the daily food distributions. The apostles called for a meeting and brought direction to the church. Choose seven men of good reputation, full of the Spirit and wisdom and appoint them to this ministry. **The apostles refused to get side tracked as to their calling to 'wait on tables.'** It wasn't that they were above this task, for spiritual leadership is about servanthood! It was about priorities! If they got this wrong, the church would fall down on this point. So, they said clearly – 'we must give ourselves to the word of God and prayer.'

We must understand the connection between both word life and prayer life.

Our word life will only be as strong as our prayer life – and our prayer life as strong as our word life! In fact, prayer doesn't work without the word and the word is no use without prayer.

Listen to the word....

> *"One who turns away his ear from hearing the law, Even his prayer is an abomination."* Proverbs 28:9

Listen to this, if we have a prayer life with no word life, our praying is more than likely to be off!

"If you abide in Me, and My words abide in you, you will ask what you desire, and it shall be done for you." John 15:7

Again, Jesus connects the importance of the word of God and prayer. The word of God must abide in us in order to have a successful prayer life. The word 'abide' means to 'dwell' or 'live'. We are told to allow the word of God to dwell in us richly! We are encouraged to build both a word life as well as a prayer life! Many believers invest tons of time in developing 'word life' but seriously neglect 'prayer life!' This imbalance is the root cause of powerless and unproductive ministry!

Moses had a ministry of the word of God and prayer – he would go up on the mountain and meet with God, pray, and then come down with the word of God for Israel (Exodus 32–33).

The OT priests had a ministry of the word of God and prayer.

"They shall teach Jacob Your judgments, And Israel Your law. They shall put incense before You, And a whole burnt sacrifice on Your altar." Deuteronomy 33:10

The priests were to teach Israel, God's people the Word, judgments and law. But they were also to put incense before God on the golden altar and offer prayer.

Samuel the prophet was strong in the word of God and prayer.

"Moreover, as for me, far be it from me that I should sin against the Lord in ceasing to pray for you; but I will teach you the good and the right way." 1 Samuel 12:23

And again, in the life of Daniel.

"I, Daniel, understood by the books the number of the years specified by the word of the Lord through Jeremiah the prophet, that He would accomplish seventy years in the desolations of Jerusalem." Daniel 9:2

Daniel learns what God is about to do from the word and what does he do?

> *"Then I set my face toward the Lord God to make request by prayer and supplications, with fasting, sackcloth, and ashes."*
> Daniel 9:3

The word of God produces faith – faith should lead to prayer! When a minister or ministry puts more emphasis on the word to the neglect of prayer it cannot manifest the kingdom and the supernatural power of the Spirit.

The Spirit is big on the word of God and prayer!

> *"...and take the sword of the Spirit, which is the word of God; praying always with all prayer and supplication in the Spirit."*
> Ephesians 6:17–18

Jesus was balanced in both word and prayer and so were the apostles and many others in the Bible.

> *"Now in the morning, having risen a long while before daylight, He went out and departed to a solitary place; and there He prayed. And Simon and those who were with Him searched for Him. When they found Him, they said to Him, "Everyone is looking for You." But He said to them, "Let us go into the next towns, that I may preach there also, because for this purpose I have come forth."* Mark 1:35–38

The word of God enlightens us but prayer enables us – we need to be balanced in both!

This season will see a revival of prayer throughout the church like never before.

It will be praying based upon the new wave of revelation that God is releasing into the church.

In this new balance and harmony of the word of God, the church is going to come under, experience, and manifest the glory of the new covenant through the Spirit of God!

Ministry done without prayer cannot achieve kingdom purposes!

CHAPTER 17

God's Business

For All Nations

Jesus said that the temple, the Fathers House, shall be called a house of prayer for all nations (Mark 11:17). It's interesting that when Jesus came to the temple of His time, it was void of the ark of the covenant. It wasn't there in the holy of holies it had been long gone along with the glory. However, Jesus is the ark and the glory and when He came into the temple, the glory met with the flesh and judgment ensued. He upturned the tables of the money changers and drove out those selling sacrifices and wares. No flesh can glory in His presence and the Lord will not share His glory with those in and driven by the flesh.

The temple is not for man's business but God's business. What is God's business? God's business is reaching and discipling the nations (Matthew 28:20). It's still the business of God and the church.

This means that the church cannot reach and disciple the nations without the house of prayer. Neither can the nations be helped and healed without the house of prayer. **Now we can see why Satan does everything to destroy and stop the house of prayer.** Satan isn't threatened when churches are all wrapped up in ministry and programmes that busy them and distract them from the real message and mission.

God has His heart on the nations – His original will and purpose was: Heaven on earth.

God's purpose was to extend heaven His spiritual order) to earth – providing the exact conditions on earth (His physical order). Both combined and synchronized in harmony would produce a symphony!

The devil's fall, and the rise of his kingdom of darkness upset and frustrated the plan, not because of God's failure but Adam's. Instead of listening to God the Father they listened to the Father of lies.

This is how Satan became the god of this world. He seized his golden opportunity and became ruler!

> *"We know that we are of God, and the whole world lies under the sway of the wicked one."* 1 John 5:19

Satan keeps the world, nations, cities, communities and families under his sway, his influence and his control. He keeps them occupied, and distracted with money, sex and power. They live as consumers, consumed by materialistic pursuits, oblivious to reality. The nations of the world are in crisis – but most people have their eyes on themselves. The bible warns us to live soberly and godly!

> *"So the great dragon was cast out, that serpent of old, called the Devil and Satan, who deceives the whole world; he was cast to the earth, and his angels were cast out with him."* Revelation 12:9

Satan blinds the minds of the nations with deception – he blinds them to the truth. He feeds alternatives that have traces of truth – he feeds humanity with lies about their origin, their makeup, about life and about the spiritual realm. He uses philosophies, religion, false teachings etc. His aim and objective are to keep the nations in the dark, in deception, and in ignorance/oblivion.

Let's get to the house of prayer for all nations – there's only one answer and it's the house of prayer!

The nations are reeling out of control, oblivious to what is round the corner and upon them.

The world is like a drunken man, staggering, under the influence and oblivious to the dangers.

Science and technology, business and commerce, law and order, health and education, media and the arts – all are great until we put fallen mankind into the mix and then they corrupt the systems. Jesus came to the temple and they had corrupted it and made it something it was not – a den of thieves.

When you make the temple/church something it's not – it cannot release what it has got!

> *"Go into all the world and preach the gospel to every creature."* Mark 16:15

The church has a global mission and calling. The house of prayer for all nations is God's plan to save the nations – it's God's plan to restrain Satan – it's God's plan to roll out His end time agenda and bring in the final harvest.

- **Only the church operating as God's official temple and priesthood can minister the new covenant in the earth, to the nations!**

- **Only the house of prayer can stir the Father, the Son, the Spirit and Angel armies.**

- **Only the house of prayer can bring salvation, mercy, forgiveness, renewal, and redemption, and healing to the nations.**

- Only the house of prayer can release all of God's kingdom resources, power and blessings into the nations.

- Only the house of prayer can bring the nations out of bondage, out of darkness, out of lostness, out of corruption, out of deception and into true freedom and a living hope.

The Context for Prayer

What is so powerful about the house of prayer is that it gives us the true context for prayer.

If you don't have the right context for prayer it won't work! YOU CAN PRAY AMISS (James 4:3)!

When you have context for prayer and when you know how prayer works, you'll pray and get results.

We need to see, know and understand what Jesus has restored us to: ZION, HEAVEN!

Remember, if you make it something it's not – you cannot release what it has got!

The true context for prayer is ZION, the heavenly tabernacle and the kingdom of God.

What we have come to is a clue to how and what we should be praying.

Zion, the city of God and heavenly Jerusalem reveals to us what God's throne room is doing.

- God is the ultimate judge ready to pass judgment and give justice and vengeance on all His and our enemies.

- Jesus is the mediator of the new covenant of mercy, forgiveness, reconciliation and intimacy waiting for intercession and confession as High Priest to add His amen and endorse our prayers before the Father.

- The Spirit of the Lord is ready to bring inspiration, revelation and powerful spiritual gifts into play, so that we know the Father's will and purpose.

- Innumerable angels are poised and ready around the golden altar ready to heed and perform the word of God agreed and confessed and given the amen by the Amen.

- The blood of sprinkling that speaks is still in effect and has power to save, deliver, heal, protect, wash, cleanse and bless with victory when believed, and spoken.

Prayer is how we activate the kingdom and will of God. We are blessed in the heavenly places with every spiritual blessing and it's only through prayer that we access and activate them.

Understanding the tabernacle of David brings us into the spirit and into the heavenly tabernacle so that we come under and into the royal priestly order of Melchizedek, so that we can function as priests and kings in our heavenly calling.

Our heavenly calling as royal priests is to minister the new covenant in every detail. It is our duty to become spiritual negotiators and intercessors along with our merciful and faithful High Priest, ministering the new covenant in prayer. This is the highest purpose of prayer.

Prayer brings all of heaven together to this one aim and objective: To minister the ministry of reconciliation to the glory of God.

Prayer is coming into agreement with the word of God and presenting it at the golden altar in praise, thanksgiving, intercession, supplication, binding and loosing, agreement, commands of faith, decrees and proclamations. Prayers that are prayed with faith, and with the right motive and that align to the word and will of God are mingled with holy fire from the golden altar and then presented by angels to the Father who approves and endorses and releases angels on assignment to perform His word.

When we know how prayer works and what happens when we pray it gives us great faith and confidence and should stir us to pray daily without ceasing.

The Kingdom First

Many believers make prayer about their needs, wants and desires, with no thought about the kingdom or will of God, which is totally out of context.

The Lord's prayer also gives us context for prayer. Prayer is about ministering the kingdom of God and its message, mission and agenda.

"Our Father in heaven, Hallowed be Your name. Your kingdom come. Your will be done on earth as it is in heaven." Matthew 6:9-10

Prayer is how we minister the kingdom and will of God. It is our praying in accordance with God's kingdom and will to release the forces of the word and heavenly hosts to bring the Father's will about. Knowing the context of prayer and how prayer works will make us able ministers of the kingdom.

"Give us this day our daily bread." Matthew 6:11

This request is not so much for physical sustenance but for the bread of revelation needed to bring about God's kingdom and will on earth. This is why Jesus said, 'Man shall not live by bread alone, but by every word that proceeds from the Father.' Jesus is the bread of life and in Him is hidden all the treasures of wisdom and knowledge (Colossians 2:3).

"And forgive us our debts, as we forgive our debtors." Matthew 6:12

We cannot minister effectively in the enthroned life if we are walking in sin and unforgiveness and have relational turmoil, as the enemy will shut down our spiritual authority and make our praying ineffective.

"And do not lead us into temptation, But deliver us from the evil one. For Yours is the kingdom and the power and the glory forever. Amen." Matthew 6:13

One reason why many believers cannot minister the kingdom and will of God is that they have never embraced the crucified life and are still getting caught and trapped by the temptations of the evil one.

Notice that this prayer is all about the kingdom, the power and the glory!

Later in the chapter Jesus reinforces the context for prayer.

"But seek first the kingdom of God and His righteousness, and all these things shall be added to you." Matthew 6:33

We are told to seek first the kingdom of God and His righteousness and when we do, we are assured that all these things will be added to you. When believers make their wants, needs and desires the context for prayer with no thought to the kingdom or will of the Father, it's the wrong context.

This is not to say that we shouldn't pray for our needs, wants and desires, as the word of God tells us to let our requests be made known (Philippians 4:6). When we come in the right context it keeps our priorities and our motives right before God. Put the kingdom first and God will see that you don't lack any thing you need. He will even give you the desire of your heart (Psalm 37:4).

Even when we are asking for God's blessings on our health, family, work life and our finances, we should have the new covenant in mind. God blesses us so that we can establish the covenant.

"And you shall remember the Lord your God, for it is He who gives you power to get wealth, that He may establish His covenant." Deuteronomy 8:1

Many in the body of Christ today are asking for prosperity completely out of context. They're asking to prosper so that they may spend it on their own pleasures (James 4:3). When we seek first the kingdom God and keep the covenant of God a priority God will prosper us and we will use our prosperity to establish His covenant. Prayers with the right motive get answered.

Jesus and the Nations

The focus of the house of prayer is all nations. God will have His remnant out of every nation.

The nations will be carried over into the new earth – the nations are the Lord's inheritance. The nations are promised to Jesus.

> "Yet I have set My King On My holy hill of Zion." "I will declare the decree: The Lord has said to Me, 'You are My Son, Today I have begotten You. Ask of Me, and I will give You The nations for Your inheritance, And the ends of the earth for Your possession." Psalm 2:6-8

When Jesus was driven into the wilderness by the Spirit to be tempted of the devil, the devil showed Jesus all the kingdoms of this world and their glory and promised Him them if He would bow down and worship Him (Matthew 4:8-10). Jesus rebuked Him for He knew that the Father would bring about this promise in His life.

> "The kingdoms of this world have become the kingdoms of our Lord and of His Christ, and He shall reign forever and ever!" Revelation 11:15

The house of prayer for all nations gives the church the wonderful privilege and opportunity to co-labour with the Lord in reaching and discipling the nations. This again, lifts prayer to a higher level than that of personal wants, needs and desires. The house of prayer is to fulfil the Lord's desire of the nations redeemed and serving under the umbrella of the kingdom of God. Could there be any higher purpose to prayer than this? For this to happen, the church must rise to her heavenly calling. She must come under the divine inspiration, manifest God's wisdom to principalities and powers in the heavenly places, bring them under His footstool and then preach the gospel of the kingdom and gather in the harvest. Is there a higher calling than this for the church? The house of prayer for all nations will be a great success in reaching, redeeming and healing the nations.

> *"And have redeemed us to God by Your blood Out of every tribe and tongue and people and nation, And have made us kings and priests to our God; And we shall reign on the earth."*
> Revelation 5:9–10

The book of Revelation gives us a sneak preview of the successful mission of Jesus Christ and the house of prayer. John saw and heard the redeemed out of every tribe, and tongue and people and nation, singing a new song before the throne of God.

The house of prayer is going to be instrumental in the last days as she rises to fulfil the great commission and usher in the return of Christ. There's no higher calling on the believer, no high purpose or privilege than functioning in the Lord's spiritual temple and royal priesthood with all prayer.

All prayer reaches the throne and the golden altar. However, not all prayers are endorsed by the High Priest, Jesus/Yeshua. Only those prayers that are aligned to the will of God and have met the right conditions will be endorsed and answered.

There's a revival of prayer about to break loose across the church and it's happening right now – it's going to be different. The church is coming into revelation of the house of prayer for all nations and how God is raising it up. The Spirit of God is going to equip believers with a powerful intercessory anointing to minister the kingdom and glory of God!

Everything that Adam and Eve lost has been regained and restored. Adam and Eve had access to Zion, heaven and to the throne of God as well as the golden altar. The throne and the altar are what the Father, through the work of the Son and the Spirit has restored to us. **Why? Because the altar is where the kingdom and will of God is agreed upon, confessed and** released for fulfilment by both angels and mankind in complete obedience to the Father.

The golden altar is about agreement! When the Father wants His will done it proceeds from the throne and is agreed, sanctioned and endorsed at the golden altar by the Godhead and carried out by angelic hosts who speedily heed and perform the word and will of God. In Genesis 1:26, God said, *'Let us make man in our image, and according to our likeness.'* Here we find the power of agreement. God has chosen that a matter is established by the power of agreement.

> *"...by the mouth of two or three witnesses the matter shall be established."* Deuteronomy 19:15

> *"For there are three that bear witness in heaven: the Father, the Word, and the Holy Spirit; and these three are one. And there are three that bear witness on earth: the Spirit, the water, and the blood; and these three agree as one."* 1 John 5:7-8

Creation and mankind came about through the power of agreement by the Godhead.

We must understand how God's will is done. We must also understand how prayer is received, endorsed and sanctioned. Prayer is coming into agreement with the word of God. Prayer must be filled with the word of God to qualify and be approved. When we understand what happens when we pray, and the process and behind the scenes of prayer, everything changes. Armed with this revelation, our praying will see more answers than ever before.

When the apostle John saw Jesus in his vision, he said that out of His mouth went a 'sharp two-edged sword' (Revelation 1:16). In Revelation 2:16, Jesus warns the church at Pergamos to repent for holding to false doctrines and tells them that He will *'fight them with the sword of His mouth'*. Again, in Revelation 19:15 out of Jesus' mouth goes a sharp sword with which He strikes the nations. In Ephesians 6:12 we are told to take up the sword of the Spirit which is the Word of God. Jesus is the Living Word and provides a sharp edge to the sword of the Spirit. Our agreement and confession make it a two-edged sword. When we speak the word of God it has power to strike in any situation and bring God's judgment against anything that has been raised up against the knowledge and will of God.

I was deep in prayer and in the spirit one day and I was lifting up a family member who was clearly demonized and was being really nasty against my wife and myself. This family member wouldn't talk to us and was not only ignoring us but was making their feelings known to others. On top of this, they were really sick and I was very worried.

As I was praying, I told the Lord that I was really worried and I wanted to help the situation. I asked the Lord to bring me to the person in the spirit and show me what to do. Immediately I saw a huge wall in front of me and the Lord said, 'It's a wall of offence and told me that the person was deeply offended.' I asked what could be done? I became aware that I was dressed for battle in pure white armour and in my right hand, I had the sword of the Spirit.

As I looked to my left and my right I was flanked by angels. Then I heard the Lord say, 'Dennis, take the sword and strike the wall three times in my Name.' The family member had ignored my calls for over twelve months. In the spirit, I obeyed the Lord. I invited the angels to accompany me, went to the wall, lifted up the sword of the Spirit and struck it three times as I was told. Within seconds my phone rang and it was the family member. It wasn't the best initial response but within weeks there was reconciliation and the relationship was healed. The Lord told me, *'Dennis you have just broke this in the spirit!'* Praise God for the two-edged sword. When we learn how to wield it skilfully it will bring about many and great victories.

The law of the golden altar works on agreement of the word of God. When we approach God as royal priests through the mediatorial work of Yeshua, we can come boldly to the throne and the altar. When we bring the word of God in our heart and in our mouth to the golden altar of heaven, and come into agreement with the Living Word and the Spirit of Truth, and when we give faith filled confession, angels lift our prayers on top of the golden altar and mingle them with the fire and coals (Revelation 8:3-5). When the smoke and prayers rise as incense into our Father's nostrils as a sweet-smelling aroma, the High Priest approves and endorses our prayer(s) and gives the 'Amen' (Revelation 3:14). Angels are then released like lightning to carry out the will of God (Revelation 4:5). Yeshua/Jesus is the High Priest of our confession (Hebrews 3:1). Jesus is the High Priest of our confession and not our silence! Our High Priest can do nothing with negative confession. He can do nothing with complaining and moaning about life's trials and hardships. We must agree with His word. But, the word of God is of no use until it is in your heart and your mouth.

> *"But what does it say? "The word is near you, in your mouth and in your heart" (that is, the word of faith which we preach): that if you confess with your mouth the Lord Jesus and believe in your heart that God has raised Him from the dead, you will be saved."* Romans 10:8-10

Notice that salvation is the result of confessing the word with your mouth. There are hundreds of promises and statements of God's will just waiting to be confessed from your mouth! Our task is to get the word of God in our heart to establish a reservoir of truth and then have it in our mouth for confession and fulfilment. Our voice is powerful and is our greatest asset, especially when we use it to confess the word of God. Without our heart involved in faith, our confession will be empty.

When our prayers have been approved and have received the 'Amen', that's not the end of it. We must 'prevail' in prayer as the answers are coming to us from Zion and through the heavenly places. We must 'hold fast' our confession and continue to stay in faith, giving thanks and praise to the Father. We must be aware that Satan and the demonic realm will attempt to ambush and hijack our blessings by withstanding angelic hosts and messengers. The enemy is looking for any failure, unresolved sin, relational upset or anything else that will give him legal ground to hijack and snatch your blessings. Remember, Jesus said he is a thief and that he comes to steal, to kill and to destroy (John 10:10). The apostle Paul encouraged us to walk in forgiveness continually, *'lest Satan should take advantage of us; for we are not ignorant of his devices.'* 2 Corinthians 2:11

If he cannot find something, he will attempt to create issues in order to gain the advantage. It's so important to know how to cover your prayers whilst your answers and blessings are in transit. **Too many believers fall prey and even give up during this crucial time.** I wonder what would have happened if Daniel gave up praying on day five or day ten or even day twenty? Daniel stayed the course through thanksgiving and praise and received the answers to his prayers.

Daniel was told by Gabriel that the Prince of Persia, a powerful principality 'withstood him' in the spiritual realm and that he had to call on the archangel Michael for victory (Daniel 10:13). What was this 'withstanding' about? What was happening in the spiritual realm? The devil is the accuser of the brethren and accuses them day and night. If there's ground and truth in the accusation, our blessings can be hijacked and stolen. There was most likely arguing going on probably around Daniel's life. Maybe a failure, a sin, an attitude, a wrong word, something that was allowing the battle and hindrance to go for twenty-one days.

The fact that the answer came through as Daniel continued in prayer and fasting shows the importance of staying the course. It's usually at this part in the process of prayer that believers fail to press on and prevail in prayer and so lose their blessings. We should commit to persistence and perseverance to the prayer process to secure the answers and blessings are delivered to us successfully.

"Then He spoke a parable to them, that men always ought to pray and not lose heart." Luke 18:1

The enemy is cunning, he looks for issues or creates them to withstand angels carrying our answers and blessing in transit, so that he can weary us to the point of giving up. Again, many believers give up too soon and because they don't understand the spiritual realm and how it works, they think that God didn't hear or answer their prayer.

"And let us not grow weary while doing good, for in due season we shall reap if we do not lose heart." Galatians 6:9

We shall reap answers and blessings when we overcome the enemy's tactic of trying to weary us so that we give up. How can we stop this? How can we overcome it? What can we do whilst we are waiting for our delivery?

Command Victories

"You are my King, O God; Command victories for Jacob. Through You we will push down our enemies; Through Your name we will trample those who rise up against us." Psalm 44:4-5

We must come into agreement with the Lord and command victories into the process. We overcome the accuser of the brethren by the blood of the lamb and by the word of our testimony (Revelation 12:10). We must command the victory of Christ's cross and blood over the enemy. What gives this great power is when we establish the crucified life, as this gives the devil no grounds to steal, kill and destroy.

"...and they did not love their lives to the death." **Revelation 12:11**

The crucified life keeps us out of the flesh and in the Spirit. It also gives no grounds for 'withstanding and opposing'. We are to keep ourselves in the righteousness that comes by faith (Philippians 3:9).

Praying from the enthroned position demands that we live and walk in the Spirit,

> *"If we live in the Spirit, let us also walk in the Spirit."* Galatians 5:25

You cannot walk in somewhere you don't live. As we establish spiritual life and begin to live our spiritual life it leads to walking in the Spirit. We establish our presence in the spiritual realm.

In the account of the seven sons of Sceva in the book of Acts 19, the evil spirit spoke.

> *And the evil spirit answered and said, "Jesus I know, and Paul I know; but who are you?"* Acts 19:15

As believers we need to make our presence known by living and walking in the Spirit. Spiritual authority is used in the spiritual realm. This is where we minister victory over demonic powers.

> *"I say then: Walk in the Spirit, and you shall not fulfil the lust of the flesh."* Galatians 5:16

Paul assures us that when we establish our spiritual life and begin walking in the Spirit, we shall not fulfil the lust of the flesh. This is great news! We shall not fulfil the lust of the flesh means that we won't be living trapped by fleshly and carnal ways that lead to condemnation and defeat. This also means that we can maintain a life of holiness and righteousness 'In Christ' as to keep ourselves unspotted from the world and the flesh and so give no place to the devil.

This assures us of the victory in the prayer process. It means we have confidence before God to approach Him as well as confidence that our prayers will be heard and approved. It also means that we have confidence in overcoming spiritual marauders and hijackers in the spirit. It means we can have confidence and victory from start to finish in the praying process. Wow! This is massive. This is a game changer. This is amazing. All of this because of the finished work of our Saviour and Lord, Yeshua/Jesus. His gift of salvation, redemption, restoration and righteousness makes us more than conquerors and assures us of the victory (Romans 8:37)

We must command victories for angels that they push down our enemies and trample those who rise up against us, and deliver our answers and blessings. David prayed into the spiritual realm.

> *"Let them be like chaff before the wind, And let the angel of the Lord chase them. Let their way be dark and slippery, And let the angel of the Lord pursue them."* Psalm 35:5-6

We can give prayer cover for the ministry of angels and ask for successful mission assignments.

When we pray, we should set a guard over our heart, our mind, our mouth and our members. Don't give the enemy a foothold. Lift up and enforce the victory of Christ, the cross, the blood and His Name over principalities and powers. Lift up and confess the new covenant victory over the enemy and claim the Lord's mercy over unrighteousness, forgiveness of sins and iniquities. Lift up and confess the ministry of reconciliation and remind the enemy that he has no power or authority over you. Let psalm 149 be your guide.

> *"Let the high praises of God be in their mouth, And a two-edged sword in their hand, To execute vengeance on the nations, And punishments on the peoples; To bind their kings with chains, And their nobles with fetters of iron; To execute on them the written judgment — This honour have all His saints."* Ps 149:6-9

- Keep the high praise of God in your mouth

- Keep the twoedged sword in your hand

- Use your spiritual authority to bind the enemy

- Execute the written judgment (of the cross) upon them

I love this last part - This honour have all the saints! This is for every saint, every believer. Every believer can operate in this level of power and authority. Wow, we are called to stand upon serpents and scorpions and triumph over all the power of the enemy (Luke 10:19). We have been given power and authority so use it. If you don't the enemy will run amok.

The church and believers have been reluctant to use this level of authority that they have. Most believers find it easier to ask God to do everything. But what was Jesus' finished work all for if we are still powerless against the enemy. I believe that God is waiting for mature sons and daughters to rise up in the spirit and present themselves as royal priests before the throne and the altar and enter into the enthroned life. Praying in a defensive way doesn't work! The body of Christ has been in defence mode for way too long.

The church is encouraged to trust in the Lord, sit it out and trust that God is on the throne. However, there's never been any question as to God being on the throne. In fact, there's never been a time when He wasn't on the throne. The real question is, 'Is the church on the throne?' More importantly, 'Are you on the throne?' Now that's the question. Until believers rise up as overcomers through the finished work of the cross and then rise to the enthroned life to be royal priests, the devil will continue to create havoc in the church and in the world. It's time for the house of prayer to form and function. It's time for overcomers and royal priests to come to centre stage and act, not in a hypocritical way but in a real, and powerful world changing performance against the powers of darkness. Everything Christ did was for this very purpose. He wants us to mature and minister.

The church is called to minister the new covenant from the throne and the altar. She is called to come under the divine inspiration, revelation and power of the Spirit of God from the temple. As she comes under the ministry of the glory, she is to show forth the praises of God and manifest the manifold wisdom of God to principalities and powers. The church will receive divine strategies for victories and its these that she must minister in the heavenly places.

As she does this, she is going to bring all God's enemies under the footstool and majesty of God. The great and last outpouring of the Spirit will come out of the house of prayer. The gifts of the Spirit will then manifest through these enthroned royal priests and they will preach the gospel of the kingdom with accompanying miracles, signs and wonders to give the most glorious display of the glory of God. This will result in filling the nations with the knowledge of God as the waters cover the see. Then will come the gathering in of the greatest harvest from the nations setting the stage for the second coming of the Lord Jesus from heaven.

We can be successful in prayer if we understand the process from start to finish. When we grasp the revelation of the throne and the altar and obey the law of agreement based upon the word of God, we will see great results. Understanding how the will of God is accomplished and the part that agreement and confession plays will give us greater confidence of knowing that the Father hears us and will answer us when we pray in line with His will.

Understanding that prayer is not finished with simply releasing it before the throne and altar can alter our understanding and arm us with a fuller knowledge of what happens when the prayer is approved and sent forth to be delivered by angels. As we commit to the full process, we can command victories over the enemy and secure our position as Spirit filled and Spirit led and Spirit empowered saints of God. If we stay aware and alert to the fact that the enemy wants to fault find or accuse us before God, we can defeat him by walking in the Spirit. This way we will not fulfil the lust of the flesh and therefore, protect our answers and blessing coming through the heavenly places.

We must exercise spiritual authority over the enemy as he seeks to steal and hijack our answers to prayer. Becoming more aware and committing to the whole process will assure us of victory and encourage us to pray more knowing that the prayer process doesn't fail on God's end but more often than not on our end. Prevailing and persevering through to the finish will definitely yield great rewards.

> *"Now this is the confidence that we have in Him, that if we ask anything according to His will, He hears us. And if we know that He hears us, whatever we ask, we know that we have the petitions that we have asked of Him."* 1 John 5:14-15

CHAPTER 18

Praying with All Prayer

Saviours and Deliverers

One of the reasons God has restored us to Zion is for us to be deliverers and saviours in Zion through prayerfulness. Throughout the bible we see God using saviours and deliverers. Moses was a great deliverer and throughout Judges, God raised up many deliverers to save and deliver His people. As priests, kings and judges, we are called to be deliverers and to be a part of our Saviours work in setting the captives free.

"Then saviours shall come to Mount Zion" Obadiah 21

Of course, these saviours cannot take the work of *the* Saviour, Jesus, but they can act as saviours and deliverers as they minister the new covenant and the ministry and word of reconciliation in prayer from Zion. As the house of prayer is established and gets under way and the royal priesthood begins to come before the throne and the altar with every form of prayer and boldly and confidently prays to the Father, through the Spirit and in Yeshua's Name, heaven's powers, influences, supplies, resources and blessings will be activated and the glory of God will be manifested and demonstrated by a church so in the Spirit and attuned to her God and Saviour.

The mid heavens will be brought under the written judgment and footstool of God, and the manifold wisdom of God manifested to principalities and powers in the heavenly places. The glory will be accessed and manifested and the ministry and good works that go forth will be anointed, powerful and productive. The outpouring will be released, the restorative work will be completed and will usher in the glorious return of the long-awaited Saviour Yeshua/Jesus Christ. All of this will come through the house of prayer in action. Everything the church is called to do should come out of the house of prayer. Ministry and good works that do not come out from and flow out of the house of prayer will lack anointing and blessing! It's time to pray with all prayer and supplication in the Spirit.

> *"Praying always with all prayer and supplication in the Spirit."* Ephesians 6:18

The bible tells us to pray with 'all prayer' or with the different types of prayer. Let's identify some types of prayer. The bible speaks about the prayer of faith, the prayer of thanksgiving, the prayer of agreement, supplication, intercession, petitions, or prayer requests, warfare prayer, praying in the Spirit, praying in tongues, decreeing and declaring or the command of faith, prayer and fasting, and finally meditative prayer, which is probably the most important type of prayer as we'll see.

The house of prayer will use all forms of prayer, so it's important to understand and practice them so that we become skilful in all forms of praying. *The kingdom and will of God are realised, received and released through prayer.* The word of God is the basis for all praying and in order to become effective and powerful in prayer we must have an ongoing developing relationship with the word of God (John 15:7). The Spirit of God is our helper in prayer (Romans 8:26-27). Unless the Spirit of God is leading us into all truth and guiding us, we will have a difficult time praying. It's the Spirit of God that helps us in our weakness. Not that we are meant to be continually weak but we are to grow and develop spiritual knowledge and stamina so that we become powerful prayer warriors. For this to happen we must commit to knowing the Holy Spirit and the Word of God.

If the house of prayer is to impact the nations, then we must know how to pray with all prayer.

Many believers as has already been said, approach prayer on the level of needs, wants and desires and miss the fact that the house of prayer is for the nations. When we pray at this level, the kingdom of God goes into effect and all of our needs, wants and desires get taken care of. Whilst it's not wrong to pray for personal needs, it can lead to a selfishness that blinds us to the wider needs of the world around us. If the church is going to impact the nations on a global level, she must understand the importance of prayer and learn what the different forms of prayer mean in this context. Let's see.

The church is called to access the glory of God in order to manifest it. She is to come under the divine presence and glory so as to come under divine inspiration, revelation and power. She is called and authorised to subdue all God's enemies and bring them under the written judgment as well as showing forth the manifold wisdom of God to principalities and powers in the heavenly places. She is also called to preach the gospel of the kingdom in the demonstration and power of the Holy Spirit. For all of this to happen, the church must be committed to continual prayer.

Let's identify the forms of prayer and see how they work.

The prayer of Faith

"And the prayer of faith will save the sick, and the Lord will raise him up. And if he has committed sins, he will be forgiven." James 5:15

The prayer of faith is powerful because it connects us to Mount Zion, the city of God and heavenly Jerusalem. It connects us to God, the Judge of all, and to Jesus, the mediator of the new covenant and High Priest of our confession. It connects us to the Spirit of God and His ministry and gifts. It connects us to the throne of grace and the altar of incense and to the blood of sprinkling. It also connects us to the government of God and to innumerable company of angels (Hebrews 12:22-24). It connects us to every spiritual blessing. Faith is confident belief. Faith connects us to the invisible, spiritual world and realms.

"But without faith it is impossible to please Him, for he who comes to God must believe that He is, and that He is a rewarder of those who diligently seek Him." Hebrews 11:6

The prayer of faith connects us to the power of God and of heaven, to saving, delivering, healing and prospering power! The prayer of faith not only connects us to the power but it releases the power of God and of glory. Prayer releases the rewards of God. The prayer of faith connects us to what's accessible and available: reward! Rewards are released to diligent seekers! Mature pray-ers. Those who will exert great effort and work at it! The prayer of faith 'knows' what is accessible and available!! Faith is dead without works. Faith helps us to see the invisible realm as well as connect us to all that is available. Faith must lead to confession (Romans 10:10). Prayer is confession, it's confessing the blessed realities and releasing heavenly power and blessings from Zion. The prayer of faith believes the word of God, agrees the word of God and confesses the word of God. All of heaven's power and blessings are released through the prayer of faith.

Praise, thanksgiving and Rejoicing

"Therefore, by Him let us continually offer the sacrifice of praise to God, that is, the fruit of our lips, giving thanks to His name." Hebrews 13:15

Praise, thanksgiving and rejoicing brings us into the presence of God. As we praise God for salvation, and all of its benefits, we are lifted out of the flesh and into the Spirit. As we praise and thank our way through the saving process (forgiveness, cleansing, justification, sanctification, glorification), we are perfected to come before our Father in heaven. Praise, thanksgiving and rejoicing bring us into the victory of God. Praise, thanksgiving and rejoicing release spiritual powers and puts them to work. This is a simple strategy but it has far reaching effects.

When David pitched the tabernacle that housed the ark of the covenant – he set the priests before it 24/7 to give thanks, to praise and rejoice with instruments. This released great spiritual power that subdued his enemies, and blessed and prospered the people and the work of God in the earth. Praise, and thanksgiving also are in order when we are in trials, suffering, blessed, in victory, in hope or whatever else. This form of prayer puts angels to work to perform the word of God!

There were seven kings and leaders in the OT that came into and implemented the Davidic order of worship and every last one of them experienced breakthroughs, victories and blessings supernaturally.

> **Solomon** – 2 Chronicles 5-8 – **Jehoshaphat** – 2 Chronicles 20 – **Joash** – 2 Chronicles 22-24 – **Hezekiah** – 2 Chronicles 29-31 – **Josiah** – 2 Chronicles 34-35 – **Zerubbabel** – Ezra 3 – **Nehemiah** – Nehemiah 11-12

Reading through these godly leaders' experiences is a worthwhile effort and will yield rich rewards.

Meditative Prayer

"It is doubtless not profitable for me to boast. I will come to visions and revelations of the Lord: I know a man in Christ who fourteen years ago — whether in the body I do not know, or whether out of the body I do not know, God knows — such a one was caught up to the third heaven. And I know such a man — whether in the body or out of the body I do not know, God knows — how he was caught up into Paradise and heard inexpressible words, which it is not lawful for a man to utter."
2 Corinthians 12:1-4

Meditative prayer is probably the most important prayer to develop as it brings us into visions and revelations and into seeing the works of God and hearing the words of God. There are many in the bible that discovered this art of meditative prayer and came to both see and hear from God through the Spirit – Moses, Samuel, David, Ezekiel, Daniel and so on. Jesus was skilled in this form of prayer. This is how He was able to see the works of the Father as well as hear the words of the Father. The apostle Peter as well as Paul and John were skilled in this form of prayer and experienced both the ministry of the Holy Spirit and angels through this form of prayer.

This form of prayer is where we experience the ministry and gifts of the Holy Spirit. We must be educated in how to discover and develop and use our spiritual senses. Our spiritual senses must be exercised in order to function. To activate our spiritual senses, we must internalise our praying. We use our spirit. To activate our spirit we simply begin talking, listening and looking within the spirit of our mind. In the new covenant, God says that He will put His law/word in our heart and in our mind (Hebrews 8:10).

God is Spirit and so He communicates with us through His Spirit to our spirit. We all use our spirit every day when we daydream, when we have inward conversations etc. Once this form of prayer is realised and experienced, everything changes. We are more attuned to the Father and become able to see heavenly vision and hear heavenly words. When we master this form of prayer, we will begin to receive the rhema word of God into the spirit of our mind. We will begin to be led of the Spirit in greater ways in both praying and ministering to others. This is vital for knowing the will of God and for releasing and manifesting the glory realm.

Supplication

"These all continued with one accord in prayer and supplication." Acts 1:4

As Jesus' ascension drew near, He told His followers to wait in Jerusalem until they were endued or supplied with power from 'on high' (Luke 24:49). Jesus knew that for His followers to accomplish their mission, they must be endued with spiritual power from Zion, heaven. After he ascended before them, they returned to Jerusalem and gathered in the upper room waiting to be supplied. Supplication is about requesting and asking for spiritual supplies. The 120 were richly supplied when the Spirit of God came upon them. They were certainly endued with spiritual anointing, power and authority and spiritual gifting to go forth and fulfil the heavenly calling.

We cannot fulfil a heavenly calling with earthly power supply! We must be supplied with power from on high, Zion! Our greatest need is heavenly and spiritual supplies. Prayer supplies us and fills us. We should ask to be filled with the Spirit, to be controlled by the Spirit, to be led and guided and instructed by the Spirit. We should ask to be supplied with the gifts of the Spirit and to receive help by the Spirit. We should ask for supplies of spiritual refreshing and living waters to flow into us and out of us. We should ask for rich supplies of angelic ministry, aid and assistance. We can ask for rich supplies of mercy and grace and every spiritual blessing in the heavenly places. Supplication is about being supplied with heavenly power.

Praying in the Spirit/Tongues

"And they were all filled with the Holy Spirit and began to speak with other tongues, as the Spirit gave them utterance." Acts 2:4

John the Baptist spoke of one who baptize in the Holy Ghost and fire (Matthew 3:11). Jesus also promised that as His earthly work was completed and He returned to heaven, that the Father would send the Holy Spirit to help His followers, lead them and guide them. In Mark 16:17, Jesus said these signs; 'casting out demons' and 'speaking with new tongues' would be done in His Name by those who believe. He went on to tell the disciples to wait in Jerusalem for the promise of the Father (Luke 24:49) and promised that they would be baptized with the Holy Spirit (Acts 1:5) and that it would be a baptism of power when the Holy Spirit came upon them (Acts 1:8). When the Holy Spirit was poured out on them, one of the signs was that they spoke with tongues and glorified God. We see from thereon that those who experienced the Holy Spirit spoke with new tongues and glorified God (Acts 10:44-46; 19:5-6).

Praying in the Spirit or in tongues is a powerful form of praying and has a dual purpose.

Firstly, speaking in tongues is for personal use.

"For he who speaks in a tongue does not speak to men but to God, for no one understands him; however, in the spirit he speaks mysteries." 1 Corinthians 14:2

Speaking in tongues is about talking to God. Speaking in tongues is speaking mysteries. Words are powerful and activate blessings and cursings.

Praying in tongues is a beautiful and powerful way of building yourself up spiritually, speaking directly to God, speaking forth mysteries, and worshipping God with your spirit. Tongues can be both spoken and sung. Praying and singing in the Spirit or tongues connects you to the Holy Spirit in the exercise. Even though our natural understanding does not comprehend it, nevertheless it is a powerful mode of prayer.

> *"He who speaks in a tongue edifies himself."* 1 Corinthians 14:4

> *"But you, beloved, building yourselves up on your most holy faith, praying in the Holy Spirit."* Jude 20

> *"For if I pray in a tongue, my spirit prays, but my understanding is unfruitful. What is the conclusion then? I will pray with the spirit, and I will also pray with the understanding. I will sing with the spirit, and I will also sing with the understanding."* 1 Corinthians 14:14-15

Secondly, speaking in tongues is for a powerful witness and corporate edification when accompanied by interpretation of tongues which equals to prophecy.

In 1 Corinthians 12 through 14, Paul is addressing orderly worship as the church gathers and assembles. He encourages them not to be ignorant of spiritual gifts but to desire and seek them so that the church can be edified (1 Corinthians 12:1; 14:1). Spiritual gifts are the manifestations of the Holy Spirit for the profit of all members so that they are built up and encouraged (1 Corinthians 12:7). Every believer is to give honour to each and every member and also pursue love as they minister spiritual gifts (1 Corinthians 13).

In chapter 14, Paul begins to address the use of prophecy and tongues in the corporate gatherings. He says that tongues in the corporate gathering should only be used if there is one who can interpret what has been said, otherwise it leaves the hearers confused (1 Corinthians 14:4-19). Tongues and interpretation of tongues equal prophecy and prophecy speaks edification, comfort and exhortation to men (1 Corinthians 14:3). Believers who speak in tongues should pray that the Holy Spirit would use them in the corporate gathering to speak a tongue and interpret or that another would interpret. The manifestation of spiritual gifts should bring honour and glory to God as well as building up and edifying the church.

We have been restored spiritually and have access to Zion to be saviours along with our Saviour. Jesus ever lives to make intercession and it's to this holy calling and privilege we have been called. God is pleading through us to the world to be reconciled to Himself. There's no higher calling than this. It also means that there is a great responsibility upon every believer to be a royal priest and minister the new covenant and ministry of reconciliation through prayer, all prayer. The house of prayer must be filled with every type of prayer in order to minister the kingdom and power of God. Prayer connects us to God and His kingdom but it also is the means by which spiritual power, authority and blessing and heavenly resources are released. Prayerfulness is going to change the church and change the world. Prayer is going to put the devil in His place and release the glory of God into the earth.

The whole purpose of Jesus dying for us was to offer up the perfect sacrifice that would raise us up out of spiritual death, deliver us from the power of sin, Satan and the world system, renew us spiritually and restore our spiritual life, position and authority so that we could access Zion, heaven in order to be inspired, empowered and led by our heavenly Father.

The finished work of Christ raises us as overcomers and then elevates us to the enthroned life, to take up and pursue our heavenly calling. Our heavenly calling is to join Christ, the mediator of the new covenant and the High Priest of our confession in His holy work of producing heaven on earth, this is done through 'All Prayer.' We must therefore, be trained and equipped in all the types of prayer found in the Bible, God's word. Let's continue to look at other types of prayer and see how they work in the kingdom context.

Asking, seeking and knocking

"Ask, and it will be given to you; seek, and you will find; knock, and it will be opened to you. For everyone who asks receives, and he who seeks finds, and to him who knocks it will be opened." Matthew 7:7–8

This form of prayer is used in conjunction with meditative prayer. This type of prayer is where we are seeking and enquiring of God as to spiritual knowledge, understanding, wisdom and counsel so that we are equipped to know what to do. We are promised answers but we must tune in with our spiritual senses to see and hear by the Spirit. Asking, seeking and knocking is about enquiry!

Without asking, seeking and knocking, we won't **receive** specifics, we won't **find** out key info and **doors won't open**. Meditative prayer is where we receive such information and direction.

It's where we hear the voice of the Father through His Spirit (1 Corinthians 2:10-16). We must learn the art of meditative prayer so that we can ask and receive, seek and find, and knock and have doors open. In this form of prayer, we are enquiring of God. We are asking, seeking and knocking, and looking for direction and strategies for victories. Get ready to encounter the gifts of the Spirit through this form of prayer. God wants to release strategies for victories to us so we should be great seekers and enquirers.

Warfare Prayer

"I will build My church, and the gates of Hades shall not prevail against it. And I will give you the keys of the kingdom of heaven, and whatever you bind on earth will be bound in heaven, and whatever you loose on earth will be loosed in heaven." Matthew 16:18-19

Warfare prayer is a powerful type of praying that hinders and binds the movements, assignments, consignments, strategies, intents and agenda of hell. Jesus says here, and again in Matthew 18:18, that heaven follows earth. Heaven can do nothing in the earth until a legal royal priest enforces the victory of Christ over all his enemies. Binding and losing has to do with allowing and disallowing movement. The church, the Ecclesia, government of heaven on earth has all authority and power to disallow the illegal movements of hell and Satan's forces.

The church also has all power to allow heavenly movement through the Spirit of God and angelic forces to call for and establish the Father's will on earth. However, until YOU enforce it through prayer, the devil goes on free to move against and oppose God's will on earth. The church is to enforce the written judgment on the enemies of God, bringing them under the written judgment as David declared in psalm 149

> *"To bind their kings with chains, And their nobles with fetters of iron; To execute on them the written judgment — This honour have all His saints."* Psalm 149:8-9

Spiritual warfare is raging in our time as the ages come to a close. Things are intensifying as Satan fights to establish his victory over the church. If he can keep them in ignorance, busyness, deception and distraction, then he can prevail against the kingdom of God on earth. Jesus has already defeated him and his forces and has executed judgment on them. However, it's the church and the saints that must enforce the written judgment daily through prayer to ensure that hell is stopped and that heaven prevails. We have powerful spiritual armour as well as spiritual weaponry in our arsenal provided by the Father, Son and Spirit of God. The Father in heaven also has spiritual gifts available and accessible by the Spirit for the church to receive strategies to defeat these wicked powers.

Confession

> *"Therefore, holy brethren, partakers of the heavenly calling, consider the Apostle and High Priest of our confession, Christ Jesus."* Hebrews 3:1

Confession is a powerful type of prayer that has two sides to it.

The word 'confess' means, 'to agree or to speak the same thing.' The prayer of confession is used firstly, to confess any known sin or wrongdoing before the Lord. As we approach God in order to fellowship with Him and join in His holy work and heavenly calling, we should do inventory and examine ourselves allowing the Holy Spirit to reveal areas of our life where we have sinned and fallen short of the glory of God.

We are to be honest before God and confess or admit our wrongdoing (1 John 1:9-10) and put it right, accepting the mercy and forgiveness of God through the blood of Jesus. We don't want to give place to the devil for accusation so that our praying is hindered and amiss. Staying humble and making confession a part of our approach to God is really important for our prayers to be received, heard, amen-ed and endorsed. As believers we are not sinless but as we establish ourselves in the spirit, we most definitely will sin less.

Another important side of confession is acknowledging the truth, the word of God and all of its promises and speaking them in powerful confessions for our High Priest to endorse and commission angels to go forth and perform His word and His will. Prayer should be filled with the word of God in holy confessions. There is great power in the word of God as it is living and active to produce God's will in any and every situation. Remember, Jesus is the Word of God and when we come into agreement and confess His word, as High Priest He adds His amen. Jesus, our High Priest can do nothing with negative confessions so we should be careful to make our confession line up with the word of God, then they will be positive and powerful.

Intercession

"Therefore I exhort first of all that supplications, prayers, intercessions, and giving of thanks be made for all men, for kings and all who are in authority, that we may lead a quiet and peaceable life in all godliness and reverence." 1 Tim 2:1-3

Both Jesus and the Spirit of God are committed to ongoing intercessory prayer (Romans 8:26-27; Hebrews 7:25). Intercession means to intercede, to negotiate or plead on the behalf of another. This type of prayer makes us powerful spiritual negotiators as we use the word of God, Christ's victory, the Spirit's inspiration and revelation to intervene in the life and circumstances of another. The Holy Spirit empowers us to be intercessory prayer agents by leading us in praying in the Spirit with groans (Romans 8:26–27).

We use this type of prayer to intercede firstly for kings or rulers and those in authority, as these are the ones that affect our lives on earth. They have the power to make it quiet and peaceful or harsh and restrictive. We should intercede for them praying that they would be under the divine influences of God and not under the powers of Satan. We should pray that they produce quiet and peaceable life that favours the kingdom of God. We are also to pray for all men, for those lost in darkness and sin and be saviours and redeemers through intercessory prayer. We should especially intercede for the church and for all believers to be strong in the Lord and established in the faith.

The prayer of Agreement

"Again I say to you that if two of you agree on earth concerning anything that they ask, it will be done for them by My Father in heaven. For where two or three are gathered together in My name, I am there in the midst of them." Matthew 18:19–20

Remember, that the law of the throne and the golden altar is agreement. When we come into agreement with the word of God, believe it in our heart and confess it with our mouth, it receives the amen, and sets in motion the heavenly hosts released to perform God's word and will. When we are in agreement with the word of God it will always receive an amen and endorsement, for the word of God produces the will of God. So why do we need others to come in agreement with us when we pray?

Well, there's great power and authority released through agreement. In fact, God commands the blessing when He finds such unity and agreement (Psalm 133). Some situations call for assistance and the help of other faith-filled believers who are seasoned in prayer and can add their authority and amen to the situation. Jesus himself, promises to be in the mix when he finds two believers in agreement ready to enforce kingdom business.

The Voice of Command

> *So Jesus answered and said to them, "Assuredly, I say to you, if you have faith and do not doubt, you will not only do what was done to the fig tree, but also if you say to this mountain, 'Be removed and be cast into the sea,' it will be done. And whatever things you ask in prayer, believing, you will receive."*
> Matthew 21:21-22

As believers we have been washed in Christ's blood and have been made kings and priests unto God (Revelation 1:5-6). We have been raised to newness of life and have been seated together with Christ in heavenly places (Ephesians 2:6). The enthroned life is the special privilege of every believer in Christ. However, only those who rise through the work of the cross as overcomers, will come into this position and function at this level of faith. Enthroned kings command and decree things.

This is what this prayer is all about. Death and life are in the power of the tongue (Proverbs 18:1). As we grow in our faith and our spiritual life, we should be aiming for the enthroned life. When we establish this position, we can use the voice of command, knowing that this is how we use our spiritual authority. We can command obstacles to be removed, demons and evil spirits to flee, we can command doors to open and close, circumstances to change, breakthroughs to come about, and we can command God's will be done. We can command victories in the Name of the Lord and healing into lives. The voice of command is not for the immature but for those who are seasoned and have risen to the enthroned life.

Fasting

"Behold, you fast only to quarrel and to fight and to hit with a wicked fist. Fasting like yours this day

will not make your voice to be heard on high." ESV Isaiah 58:4

Here we find a powerful principle and reason for fasting. Fasting amplifies our voice in heaven. However, we can waste a fast by allowing strife in our life. God refuses to acknowledge our fasting and will not hear our voice when we have strife in relationships. True fasting that is done in the right spirit amplifies our voice and raises our prayers up to the top of the golden altar to receive an amen and be endorsed and answered.

Fasting that pleases God not only amplifies our voice in heaven but it empowers and charges our voice with power and authority. The disciples came across a situation where they were unable to cast a demon out of a young boy (Matthew 17:16). Jesus came and saved the day. When the disciples asked Jesus for the reason, they couldn't cast out the demon, Jesus said that what was needed was prayer and fasting (Vs 21), something the disciples were not doing (Matthew 9:14-15). From the throne of God proceeds lightnings, thundering's and voices (Rev 4:10). Fasting helps our voice be heard, it increases the volume of our prayers and also adds a greater level of power and authority to use in kingdom business.

Petition, prayer of request

"Be anxious for nothing, but in everything by prayer and supplication, with thanksgiving, let your requests be made known to God." Philippians 4:6

As we go about kingdom business, we have the privilege of coming boldly before the throne of grace with our personal petitions and requests in our time of need (Hebrews 4:16). We are assured that as we seek first the kingdom of God and His righteousness, that all things will be added unto us (Matthew 6:33). In this type of prayer, we can make our requests known to God. Whatever needs we have, great or small, we can confidently bring them before our loving Father believing and expecting that He will answer us and meet our needs as requested.

> *"Now this is the confidence that we have in Him, that if we ask anything according to His will, He hears us. And if we know that He hears us, whatever we ask, we know that we have the petitions that we have asked of Him."* 1 John 5:14-15

We can and should also make petition and make requests on the behalf of others too – we are encouraged to not only look out for our own interests but also for the interests of others too (Philippians 2:3-4). Don't miss out, make your requests known unto God, He cares for us.

The local church should above all else be a house of prayer for all nations. It should be ministering the new covenant as well as ministering the ministry of reconciliation. Helping believers develop a prayer life should be the number one priority for leaders and churches. Every type of prayer should be known and included in our prayer life in order to minister and manifest the kingdom of God. The nations are in desperate need of mature believers who will take up their position and begin the spiritual discipline and labour of prayer.

There are seven mountains of culture that must be prayed into using all prayer types available if we are to see positive transformation and change. Only prayer can bring the church into God's glory, only prayer can release the glory and power of God, only prayer can defeat God's enemies, and only prayer can empower us to win lost souls and bring in the end time harvest. Will you take up your position? Will you commit to developing and deploying all types of prayer? Will you commit to prayer? The kingdom of heaven is relying on you. The world is in great need of your praying. What will you do?

CHAPTER 19

Hindrances to Effective Prayer

Do Not be Ignorant

It is in the devil's interest to stop you from praying. It's also his aim to hinder your prayers in every way possible when you decide to develop a prayer life and join your High Priest, Jesus, in His great work of intercession. Satan knows the power of prayer and that its only praying believers who are a serious threat to his kingdom and agenda. As the house of prayer is established the church cannot be ignorant of the devil's devices.

Paul wasn't, he knew that ignorance of them gave Satan advantage over believers (2 Corinthians 2:11). The devil relies on our ignorance and weakness in order to take advantage and hinder prayer. Understanding the *process* of prayer from beginning to end is crucial if we are going to experiencing answered prayer. Being *conscious* and *aware* of the process of prayer is vital. This is why we are exhorted to be watchful in prayer.

"Watch and pray, lest you enter into temptation." Matt 26:41

Why should we be watchful? Because the devil, the tempter is out to catch us out in the process of prayer. He wants us to undo our own prayer confession by tempting us to sin in thought, word, attitude and deed. Why? So that he can hinder our prayers and hijack our answers and blessings. So much is lost in the prayer process because believers don't take heed and stay watchful in prayer.

Prayers can be hindered, let's see how prayer can be hindered and how we can guard and protect ourselves and experience victory.

1. Doubt

"If any of you lacks wisdom, let him ask of God, who gives to all liberally and without reproach, and it will be given to him. But let him ask in faith, with no doubting, for he who doubts is like a wave of the sea driven and tossed by the wind. For let not that man suppose that he will receive anything from the Lord; he is a double-minded man, unstable in all his ways."
James 1:5-8

Doubt is double-mindedness. One part of our mind thinks, 'I need to pray about this' and so speaks out the prayer request before God. However, another part of our mind begins to doubt that God has heard or will respond to our request and so this part of our mind undoes what the other side prayed. We must also guard our mouths as not only is doubt double-mindedness but it also leads to double talk. Doubt causes us to give voice to doublemindedness. The enemy loves to shoot arrows of doubt into our minds. Many believers have no context or setting for coming before God in prayer and so this creates doubt, but when we understand the new and living way and the setting for prayer and how prayers are answered, it leads to single mindedness and a bold confidence that when we come with the right approach, the right knowledge, faith and motive, we are assured that our prayers will be answered.

2. Strained Relationships

> *"Husbands, likewise, dwell with them with understanding, giving honour to the wife, as to the weaker vessel, and as being heirs together of the grace of life, **that your prayers may not be hindered.**"* 1 Peter 3:7

It is very clear then, that our prayers can be hindered as to prevent them from being answered.

It is the prayers of a 'righteous man' that are effective and avail much (James 5:7). We are to seek first the kingdom of God and 'His righteousness' to have the things we need and ask for added to us (Matthew 6:33). Establishing ourselves in God's righteousness keeps us right with God, ourselves and others. This protects our prayer life and makes it effective. Strained relationships at home or in church can hinder our prayers. The devil loves to stir relational trouble and strife as it hinders prayer.

Jude 21 says,

> *"Keep yourselves in the love of God, looking for the mercy of our Lord Jesus Christ unto eternal life."*

Keeping ourselves in the love of God protects our hearts and our spiritual authority and prayer life. Love holds no record of wrongs and never fails. When we keep ourselves in the love of God – we will be merciful and loving and seek reconciliation in all matters. This gives us the advantage over the enemy.

3. Sin and Disobedience

> *"If I regard iniquity in my heart, The Lord will not hear."*
> Psalm 66:18

Sin and disobedience will most certainly hinder our prayers. There are sins of commission and sins of omission, so we should always do some inventory and self-searching when we come before the Lord.

The word 'regard' implies 'esteeming sin and showing affection to it'. When we are comfortable with sin and refuse to confess it and forsake it, the Lord will not hear us. If he won't hear us, He won't answer us.

If we practice the approach correctly as we come before God it deals with sin on every level. It puts the flesh in its place – dead at the cross! This positions us to have a powerful and effective prayer life. Jesus died so that sin shall not have dominion over us. Appropriating the work of the cross makes us overcomers of the world, the flesh and the devil. We should establish this daily. As we do, we'll find ourselves living and walking in the Spirit and not fulfilling the lust of the flesh. Paul admonishes us: *'Therefore, having these promises beloved, let us cleanse ourselves from all filthiness of the flesh and spirit, perfecting holiness in the fear of God.'* 2 Corinthians 7:1

4. Praying Amiss

"You ask and do not receive, because you ask amiss, that you may spend it on your pleasures." James 4:3

We must understand that prayer is first of all for the purpose of bringing about God's kingdom purposes (Matthew 6: 10). Many believers only use prayer for their own needs and desires. There's no mention of the kingdom or the will of God or even others! Praying amiss means praying incorrectly or missing the primary purpose of what prayer is for. James says that we're praying amiss when prayer is all about us and fulfilling our pleasures.

Our own pleasures are the wrong motive for prayer. It's when we seek first the kingdom and make that our priority that God promises to add 'all these things' to us. Don't expect your prayers to be heard and answered if you are not prioritising the kingdom. Many believers have given up on prayer because they prayed amiss, and didn't get answers. They simply conclude that prayer doesn't work and therefore throw in the towel. Prayer works when we approach it properly with the kingdom prioritised.

5. Neglect

> *"Yet you do not have because you do not ask."* James 4:2

This may sound simple but there are many believers who simply don't ask! Jesus is the High Priest of our confession not our silence! Prayer is communication, talking to God. It's talking in the right setting and with the right attitude and the right motive.

> *"Be anxious for nothing, but in everything by prayer and supplication, with thanksgiving, let your requests be made known to God."* Philippians 4:6

You have to speak up and confess the word of God. If you don't make the request you don't get the answer. Jesus assures us that whatever we ask in prayer, believing we shall have them (Mark 11:24). In Luke 11:9, he tells us to ask, and it will be given to us. In John 14:13, Jesus says that whatever we ask in His Name it will be done for us.

6. Busyness, Preoccupation & Distraction

> *"Then He spoke a parable to them, that men always ought to pray and not lose heart"* Luke 18:1

> *"Continuing steadfastly in prayer."* Romans 12:12

> *"Pray without ceasing."* 1 Thessalonians 5:17

Jesus set the example when it comes to prayer. He never allowed busyness to get in the way of prayer. Also, he never was so preoccupied with ministry and service that he had no time left to pray. He rose early in the morning, every morning and he prayed. He was faithful in His prayer habit and would not compromise it for anything, even ministry. Even when he was out and about preaching, teaching and ministering to people, he took time to break away from the crowds and from his schedule in order to pray. He knew that He couldn't perform for the Father and the kingdom without being sourced by prayer. One of the greatest threats to the believer's prayer life is busyness and preoccupation. There will always be a hundred and one things to do in life, so, if we don't make prayer a priority and a habit, it won't happen. One week without prayer makes one weak!

7. Unwholesome Talk

"Do not let any unwholesome talk come out of your mouths, but only what is helpful for building others up according to their needs, that it may benefit those who listen." Ephesians 4:29 NIV

In Ephesians 4:17-31, Paul has been dealing with the believer's walk. He talks about not giving place to the devil. He points out that not only will anger give place to the devil (vs 26-27), but so will unwholesome talk. What constitutes unwholesome talk? Well, lying, swearing and cursing, gossiping, slander and outbursts of anger and wrath.

Nothing will hinder your praying faster than unwholesome talk. Guard your mouth and restrain your tongue. Make sure you bring it under the Spirit of God. Make sure all your words are wholesome, God honouring and edifying to others. James says that blessing and cursing coming out of the same mouth shouldn't happen in the life of a believer (James 3: 10).

If you want to experience answered prayer, control your tongue!

8. Unresolved Issues

"Therefore, if you bring your gift to the altar, and there remember that your brother has something against you, leave your gift there before the altar, and go your way. First be reconciled to your brother, and then come and offer your gift." Matthew 5:23-24

Unresolved issues are probably the biggest hindrances to prayer. Deep in prayer, I had a vision. I saw an angel in front of me who beckoned and called me to follow him. As I followed him the scene changed and I was walking on top of a high precipice. I felt a little fear at how high it was, plus I was a little unsteady due to how narrow and rugged it was. I knew I was in the heavenly places. The angel stopped at a deep chasm ahead and beckoned for me to join him. As I inched closer to the edge, I looked down and saw glimmers of light breaking through what looked like dark, heavy coverings sprawled over the ground. I asked the angel what it was and he told me that underneath the covers were the blessings, answered prayers and destinies of God's people.

I was shocked. I asked him how this could happen and he told me that when God's people have unresolved issues in their lives it gives the devil a license to steal their answered prayers, blessings and destinies. He went on to say that spiritual marauders operate in the heavenly places, looking for, and creating opportunities to hijack and steal blessings that angels are delivering to God's people. When there are unresolved issues, they seize them and drag them down to deep ravines and then cover them with heavy veils because they cannot stand the light. I was livid and felt a holy anger come upon me. 'What can be done?', I asked. He said to me, 'You're going to call it in!'

Immediately, I commanded angels to go and destroy the veils and then to recover everything stolen. I commanded that everything was to be returned to Zion, to be sprinkled with the blood of Christ and then presented on the sea of glass before the Father. I had never prayed that way before, but it just seemed to come natural to me. It's like I knew exactly what to say. I believe I was being led of the Holy Spirit.

I'm convinced that there are spiritual marauders, that hijack what belongs to us and has been endorsed and released in answer to our prayers. The devil is cunning and knows how to set us up with the works of the flesh: anger, wrath, envy, malice, unwholesome talk, contention, strife, unforgiveness and bitterness. When we don't guard our hearts and minds and lips, we can unwittingly and unknowingly give place to the devil. This is why Paul admonishes us

> *"Be angry, and do not sin: do not let the sun go down on your wrath, nor give place to the devil."* Ephesians 4:26

In the book of Daniel chapter ten, we find a very interesting insight into the workings of the spiritual realm and heavenly places. Daniel was experiencing a vision, when the angel Gabriel appears to him, touches him and then tells him,

> *"Do not fear, Daniel, for from the first day that you set your heart to understand, and to humble yourself before your God, your words were heard; and I have come because of your words. But the prince of the kingdom of Persia withstood me twenty-one days; and behold, Michael, one of the chief princes, came to help me, for I had been left alone there with the kings of Persia. Now I have come to make you understand what will happen to your people in the latter days, for the vision refers to many days yet to come."* Daniel 10:12-14

Notice that Daniel's prayers were heard the very first day he set his heart to seek God. Daniel's prayer and fasting moved Zion to release angelic ministry to respond to Daniel. When the angel Gabriel breaks through, he tells him that the prince of Persia withstood him for twenty-one days. Michael, one of God's chief princes came to offer assistance and bring the breakthrough.

What was this withstanding and resistance about? There was obviously contention and opposition in the spiritual realm between the forces of heaven and the forces of hell. What grounds did the prince of Persia have that held back heavens' forces. There must have been legal ground for the resistance. The resistance was most likely on the basis of human error or sin that gave these powers ground against them. Maybe there was something in Daniel that caused the prince of Persia to withstand the angel sent form heaven. Maybe it took time to deal with as it was lifted to the courts of heaven and hence Michael was sent with the breakthrough and the aid. We cannot say for sure, but we do know that sin can give place for the devil and create delays, hindrances and even the seizing of answers and blessings.

Developing a powerful prayer life is about learning to prevail in prayer. We must know how to prevail in prayer until the answer comes. Prevailing in prayer involves continuance and perseverance. We need staying power when it comes to prayer. Prayer is not just making the request made known, but it is staying the course and prevailing over everything that comes to defeat our praying. Once we raise our prayers and release our confession the battle is just beginning. To be successful and acquire the answer and blessing we must do something.

> – Keep yourself in the love of God – Keep yourself unspotted from the world – Walk in the Spirit.

> – Resist the enemy – Watch and pray – Offer continual praise and thanksgiving.

We must guard our heart, mind and lips so that we do not give ground to the enemy.

Lastly, hold fast to your confession.

> *"Seeing then that we have a great High Priest who has passed through the heavens, Jesus the Son of God, let us hold fast our confession."* Hebrews 4:14

Many believers fail in prayer either because they don't pray in the first place or they give the enemy ground in the prayer process and don't receive the answers and blessings asked for. Prayer is a labour, a work and a spiritual exercise. Prayer is a skill and demands knowledge of the word of God. It is a combined effort and must be powered and influenced by the Spirit of God. Prayer demands daily commitment and must be seen as essential without compromise.

CHAPTER 20

The Way Experienced

Spiritual Senses

We are unique in creation. We are tri-part beings; spirit, soul and body. God has designed us in such a way that allows us to relate to both the spiritual and physical world. God designed us this way because of our calling and role in the earth. Adam and Eve were designed, authorised and commissioned to advance the kingdom of God on earth. For this to happen, they had access to the presence and glory of God spiritually that through fellowship with God, they would know the knowledge, wisdom and power of God, so that they might walk in obedience and produce the kingdom of God on earth. Their earthly life would be a matter of implementing all they had received by God in the Spirit.

Dual Capabilities

To fulfil our calling, God created us with dual capabilities. We have spiritual senses by which to relate to the spiritual realm and we have physical senses by which to relate to the natural world about us. In the beginning, heaven and earth were one, joined. We know this because Adam and Eve had access to Eden, to the presence of God, to angels, and to the tree of life. After the fall, everything changed. They were banished from Eden, the presence of God, the tree of life and in fact, all of heaven. Angels were stationed to guard the way in case Adam and Eve took of the tree of life and humanity were lost forever to the curse of sin and death. Revelation 21 and 22 reveals God's ultimate plan and purpose, heaven and earth free from the curse, united and in complete harmony.

Minds and Hearts Darkened

The fall brought an immediate spiritual change for humanity. Our spiritual connection was lost and we were put in the dark. Our minds were darkened and our spiritual life seriously damaged as we were cut off from our Father's house and spiritual blessings and sources (Ephesians 4:18). Cut off from Zion, heaven, we were taken captive by the devil, spiritual powers and their evil influences. Many people are attuned to the spiritual realm and these spiritual powers through wrong means such as spiritism, mediums, witchcraft, palm reading, crystal balls, occult practices, divination and many other illegitimate means. One thing is clear about our spiritual life, by default we are all separated and alienated from Zion, heaven. None of us have access by our own merit. Unless God reaches out to us, we are cut off, in the world, without God and without hope (Ephesians 2:12).

Spiritual Restoration

Great news, God so loved the world He sent His only Son to redeem us and open up the *way* back to Zion, heaven, the Father's house and restore our spiritual life and senses. Adam's sin brought both spiritual and physical death. The finished work of Jesus has provided for our spiritual resurrection now, and when Christ returns, he will resurrect our physical bodies which will become immortal and incorruptible (2 Corinthians 15:53-56). Our spiritual life then has been restored and we now have access to the Father to worship in spirit and in truth (John 4: 24). Salvation has reconnected us spiritually to Zion and the Father's house. Our spirit has been given access to engage with our Father in heaven through the Spirit.

For this to happen we must understand how our spirit functions and operates.

The writer of Hebrews points out the '*division of soul and spirit, joints and marrow*' (Hebrews 4:12)

Paul says that we can live and walk in the Spirit (Gal 5:25). It's clear then that we can experience spiritual life. It's possible to live, walk, worship, minister and serve with our spirit (Romans 1:9).

The word of God identifies and refers to our spiritual senses.
It speaks of the spiritual sense of taste "*Oh, taste and see that the Lord is good.*" Psalm 34:8. And of the spiritual sense of hearing, "*He who has an ear, let him hear what the Spirit says*' Revelation 2:7. It speak of spiritual sight "*the eyes of your understanding being enlightened*" Ephesians 1:18. It speaks of smell "*For we are to God the fragrance of Christ among those who are being saved and among those who are perishing. To the one we are the aroma of death leading to death, and to the other the aroma of life leading to life.*" 2 Corinthians 2:15-16. And finally, the word speaks of the spiritual sense of touch "*And when I saw Him, I fell at His feet as dead. But He laid His right hand on me, saying to me, 'Do not be afraid; I am the First and the Last.'*" Revelation 1:17.

At the beginning of Jesus' ministry, He stated His purpose. In Luke 4:18-19, Jesus said,

> "*The Spirit of the Lord is upon Me, Because He has anointed Me To preach the gospel to the poor;*

He has sent Me to heal the broken-hearted, to proclaim liberty to the captives and recovery of sight to the blind, to set at liberty those who are oppressed; To proclaim the acceptable year of the Lord."

Notice that Yeshua/Jesus came to preach good news, heal our hearts, set us free and liberate us.

He also came to recover the sight of the blind. Whilst Jesus healed physical blindness, the greatest need of people is to be healed of spiritual blindness. Spiritual blindness is prevalent in the church today. Peter spoke of believers who were short-sighted, even to blindness (2 Peter 1:9). Paul prayed for spiritual sight in Ephesians 1:18 and Jesus in Revelation 3, told the Laodicean church they were blind and naked. He counselled them to *'anoint their eyes with eye salve that they may see* (vs 18).

Jesus is our prime example. He only did what He saw the Father do and He only said what He heard the Father say (John 5:19; John 12:49-50). Jesus lived, walked, ministered, battled and served in the spirit. He constantly exercised His spiritual senses and came under the anointing, ministries and gifts of the Holy Spirit. **Jesus experienced the supernatural because he walked and lived in the Spirit.**

Jesus ministered both in the spiritual realm and the natural realm in a balanced way. He knew that his earthly success was because of his heavenly engagement. He moved in tune with the Spirit. Jesus gave an example of living and walking in the Spirit. This was a vital part of His coming to earth, we must have an example of spiritual living. Jesus shows us how to do it. He knows that we cannot fulfil our heavenly calling without a working model.

In the Old Testament, prophets were called 'seers' (1 Samuel 9:9). They had the ability to see into the spiritual realm and receive visions and words from the Lord bringing strategies for victories to the people of God. **Samuel was a seer**. His spirit and spiritual senses were attuned to God from being a young boy. He heard the voice of God and was shown what he must do all through his ministry.

Elijah and Elisha were seers too. In 2 Kings 6:14-17, the Syrian king sent his army to bring Elisha to him. As the morning came, Elisha's servant looked out and saw the vast army surrounding them, and asked, what they were to do? Elisha prayed, and asked, 'Lord open his eyes that he may see.' Immediately, the Lord opened his eyes and he saw horses and chariots of fire on the mountain surrounding Elisha. Elisha went on to command blindness on the Syrians.

There are many more that were caught up in the spirit like David, Ezekiel, Daniel and many of the prophets. They saw visions and heard the word of the Lord. They encountered angels and demons and because they were seers, they were able to bring about God's will and purposes in their times. The spiritual realm and heavenly places are real and teeming with activity both demonic and divine. If we are blind, not only will we not see it, we won't know what to say and do!

The New Testament also gives examples of those who engaged the spiritual realm and heavenly places. Jesus prioritised his spiritual life. His followers are to be like Him. Peter was. Peter had visions, heard the word of the Lord and the word of angels. John too. He knew how to be in the Spirit. He both heard and saw and received from the risen saviour Yeshua, as well as the ministry of angels. If we are truly in the Spirit, we should be seeing and hearing and receiving and engaging. We cannot fulfil our heavenly calling without being in the Spirit. We too have a heavenly calling to work with the Lord, the Holy Spirit and angels. We don't worship angels, but we are to work with them! This is only achievable in the spirit.

How to be in the Spirit

"If we live in the Spirit, let us also walk in the Spirit." Galatians 5:25

We must develop our spiritual life. The fruit of the Spirit are produced as we learn to live and walk and invest time in the Spirit. They are not natural qualities but spiritual qualities.

The more time we invest in the spirit, the greater the production of spiritual fruit and spiritual gifts will develop and manifest. Equally, the more time we spend in the flesh, the more the works of the flesh will develop and manifest.

Faith

To live and walk in the spirit demands the use of faith.

"For we walk by faith, not by sight." 2 Corinthians 5:7

Faith is the substance of things hoped for and the evidence of things unseen (Hebrews 11:1). How do you see the 'unseen?' through faith. Faith believes the word of God and all that it says on the matter of heavenly places. Faith receives the truth and acts upon it. But how does faith come and how is it developed?

"So then faith comes by hearing, and hearing by the word of God." Romans 10:17

Faith comes by opening up and exposing your heart and mind to the word of God. As you develop an appetite for the word and begin a healthy intake of hearing and listening through various available means, faith is produced and developed. Faith is not static but it should move you to action.

"While we do not look at the things which are seen, but at the things which are not seen. For the things which are seen are temporary, but the things which are not seen are eternal." 2 Corinthians 4:18

Seeing the unseen means opening up your spiritual eyes, the eyes of your understanding, your inner eyes. It means using your imagination, which is your mind's eye! **This is not making up your own images but on the contrary, those already revealed in the word of God**. We must be guided and directed by the word of God. Our mind's eye should be set on what God says about Zion, heaven and heavenly places and things. We are encouraged to look on the things unseen. We've revealed both heavenly places and heavenly things in this study. The word of God is rich in describing the spiritual realm, along with heavenly places and things. The more we look at it, the greater the reality, the greater the faith, which leads to fulfilling our heavenly calling.

Confession

To live and walk in the spirit demands confession.

Faith without works is dead (James 2:17). Getting into the spirit involves faith in our hearts and confession in our mouth (Romans 10:10). As we grow in the revelation of the word concerning heavenly realities and practice seeing them with the mind's eye it should lead to confession and thanksgiving unto God for sending Jesus to open up the new and living way back into the Father's house and presence. **Faith plus confession brings us into whatever realities and benefits are available.**

The Mind is Key

To live and walk in the spirit also demands the use of the mind.

"...and be renewed in the spirit of your mind." Ephesians 4:23

The mind is key to being in the spirit. Our minds must be renewed by the word of God. But notice, that we are to be renewed in the spirit of our mind. This is a clue about how to access the spiritual realm. **Activating our spirit is linked to our mind.** We must develop the spiritual part of our mind. The word of God has a lot to say about the mind and about developing a spiritual mind. How does it work? Look at the diagram below and learn.

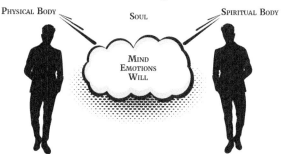

The mind activates both the physical body and the spiritual body.

> *"For as he thinks within himself, so he is."* Proverbs 23:7 NASB

Every physical act stems from a seed thought. 'I think I'll do this' 'I think I'll eat this' or 'I think I'll go here'. We are a product of our thought life – any activity we desire to do starts within our mind. The mind guides our physical body and physical life. Our mind determines the actions and directions of our lives. We speak our mind. Our minds take us into the world of food, recreation, rest, work, play, sport, entertainment and everything else in the natural world that we want to engage in. It's about focus. Whatever you focus on, your physical body will pursue. In the same way, the mind activates our spiritual life and body/form.

> *"If then you were raised with Christ, seek those things which are above, where Christ is, sitting at the right hand of God. Set your mind on things above, not on things on the earth. For you died, and your life is hidden with Christ in God."* Colossians 3:1–4

As we focus our mind on spiritual truths (the word), and realities of the things above, where Christ is, we enter the spiritual realm and our spirit man engages in prayer, worship, and spiritual service. Spiritually, we have access to heavenly places that include Zion, heaven, as well as the heavenlies. **We currently cannot access the spiritual realm in our physical body because of its fallen state, but when we are resurrected and receive our glorified body, like Jesus, we will have access to both realms.** For now, it's in the Spirit that we enter Zion, worship God, join our High Priest in intercession, come under the glory and inspiration of the Spirit of God and His ministries and gifts, present praises, sacrifices, gifts, receive direction, guidance, and minister the new covenant through the blood of sprinkling. It's in the spirit that we use our spiritual authority against the enemy. To function with our spiritual senses, we must learn how to silence our natural senses. I believe that the more we learn to live and walk in the spirit, that more of the heavenlies will open up to us.

In our next study we will look further at how to be in the Spirit. We will also be looking at developing a spiritual mind, at how to silence our natural senses, the meditative process and tuning in with spiritual senses along with the role and ministry of the Holy Spirit. Once we learn how to do this, we can begin to function in the spirit with the Spirit, with our spiritual senses attuned. This will lead to the development of spiritual fruit and the gifts of the Spirit in us and through us.

We must be renewed in the spirit of our mind. We must also understand how important the mind is in getting into the Spirit. We get into the Spirit by faith. We are to look upon the things unseen, the things God tells us in His word about the spiritual realm and the things above in Zion, heaven. As we focus on the truths of the word of God, and envision the things above, it should lead to confession. As we come into agreement with God's word about what Jesus has done for us in opening up a new and living way, it becomes really power-ful when we confess those truths.

As we meditate and focus on these truths we are lifted into the Spirit and the reality of heaven and all that is there. We are told clearly to come 'boldly before the throne of grace', which is in heaven. The apostle John was in the Spirit and ac-cessed heaven and saw the throne, the golden altar, the risen Jesus, the Spirit of God, angels and so much more. Jesus has opened up heaven for us right now but we can only access it in the Spirit.

Developing a Spiritual Mind

To live and walk in the Spirit also demands developing a spiritual mind.

Another important factor on getting into the Spirit is devel-oping a spiritual mind.

> *"For those who live according to the flesh set their minds on the things of the flesh, but those who live according to the Spirit, the things of the Spirit. For to be carnally minded is death, but to be spiritually minded is life and peace. Because the carnal mind is enmity against God; for it is not subject to the law of God, nor indeed can be. So then, those who are in the flesh cannot please God."* Romans 8:5-8

The human mind is naturally set on the things of this world. The mind by default is focused on the physical, natural realm and so is ignorant and blinded to spiritual realities. A spiritual mind is a mind that is aware of heavenly things and is set on the truths and realities of them. A spiritual mind has invested time reading, studying and meditating on spiritual certainties. It takes commitment to develop a spiritual mind, especially when our minds are exposed to the cares and affairs of this life. Many believers are stuck in natural, worldly, fleshly and even carnal mind sets that are keeping them from living and walking in the Spirit. In fact, the enemy loves to tempt us and set us up to be carnally minded and in the flesh. Notice that being in the flesh and being in the Spirit is decided on which direction our mind is set.

Meditation

To live and walk in the Spirit demands practicing meditation.

Meditation is vital for being in the Spirit. The bible has a lot to say about meditation. Meditation is focused thinking. It's not about emptying your mind but about filling your mind with all that's written in God's word.

> *"This Book of the Law shall not depart from your mouth, but you shall meditate in it day and night, that you may observe to do according to all that is written in it. For then you will make your way prosperous, and then you will have good success."*
> Joshua 1:8-9

The bible promises that meditating on God's word will lead to prosperity and good success. One reason is that meditation bring you into the Spirit and positions you to receive from God.

> *"Blessed is the man who walks not in the counsel of the un-godly, nor stands in the path of sinners,*
>
> *Nor sits in the seat of the scornful; But his delight is in the law of the Lord, And in His law he meditates day and night."* Psalm 1:1-2

The blessed man is one who meditates on the word day and night looking for godly counsel. It goes on to say in verse 3 that meditation is likened to a tree that draws life giving water and nourishment. It bears fruit and its leaves are ever fresh and it prospers. Meditation is the way into the Spirit and receiving spiritual nourishment from heaven.

Listen to David.

> *"Meditate within your heart on your bed, and be still."* Psalm 4:4
>
> *"When I remember You on my bed, I meditate on You in the night watches."* Psalm 63:6

Daniel also came to visions whilst meditating on his bed.

> *"In the first year of Belshazzar king of Babylon, Daniel had a dream and visions of his head while on his bed."* Daniel 7:1

When Peter was praying at 12 noon, he fell into a trance and meditative state and came to a powerful heavenly vision (Acts 10). **Jesus died to open up spiritual living and walking for us.** He has provided everything we need to confidently and boldly come into the Father's house and experience the glory. Praise God, through Jesus we no longer fall short of the glory of God!

Meditation brings us into the spiritual realm. As we focus on spiritual realities and exercise our faith confessing the word and all that Jesus has done to get us there, we activate our spirit man and spiritual senses to engage with the heavenly places. It takes time and commitment to develop it but it is so worth the effort. We should prayerfully and praise-fully use the approach to get into the spirit and enter the Father's house.

> "Enter into His gates with thanksgiving, And into His courts with praise. Be thankful to Him, and bless His name." Ps 100:4

As we meditate on approaching God and the spiritual truths that support this, and begin to vocalise them, our confessions will transport us into the Spirit and lead us into the heavenly temple. This is just the beginning of being intimate with the Father. This should also be accompanied by meditative prayer. We should ask the Father to open our spiritual eyes and ears. Exercising our faith, meditating on spiritual truths and focusing our minds will deal with competing and distracting thoughts and will help us get into the Spirit. Once there, we must silence our natural senses and rely upon our inner, spiritual senses to tune into the Spirit. We should also 'wait on the Lord'. This takes time and should not be rushed.

Silencing Natural Senses

To live and walk in the Spirit demands silencing natural senses.

Many believers struggle with distractions when it comes to prayer. They struggle to focus. Their mind wanders all over the place and competing thoughts take over and before they know it, they have stopped praying. Trying in your own strength and will power not to think on pressing issues, the cares of life and other responsibilities is near impossible. When believers attempt this, they end up condemning themselves and feel worse for failing.

The whole experience can be one of struggle and failure from start to finish. It only takes a couple of failed attempts in order to throw in the towel. I like to get to the quietest place in the house, lock the door, turn off anything that would distract me and shut down my natural sense of seeing and hearing. I have invested in a heavy sleep mask that I wear when approaching God in the Spirit. I find it helps to focus.

The best way to deal with competing and distracting thoughts is not to try and empty your mind but to fill your mind with spiritual thoughts. Meditating on the truths of the word of God grips your mind and holds your attention. Recalling the approach to the throne and the golden altar, through the cross, the finished work of Jesus, the divine exchange, the ascension to the gates of Zion, onto the streets of gold and towards the holy hill of the Lord, into the heavenly temple, etc. becomes a powerful way that leads you into the spiritual realm.

When you do this and focus your mind and confession it leaves little room for your mind to be distracted. The house, the bills, the job, the children, and the chores pale and vanish for a time. Add to this envisioning yourself on this journey makes it even more powerful. Your faith will soar. Getting there is one thing, now we have to learn how to 'tune in' to the voice of the Spirit and if you can receive it, angels and heavenly places. The more you take this journey and practice it, the more your spiritual senses will develop. We should be still, be quiet, be open, and be sensitive. We should begin to communicate inwardly using our spiritual senses: our inner voice and inner ears. This is where meditative prayer really kicks in.

Meditative prayer is when we internalise our praying. We begin to use our inner man, our spirit and its spiritual senses to commune with the Father. Meditative prayer will put to use asking, seeking and knocking. Meditative prayer is about enquiring of God. We should ask God, 'Is there anything you want to show me or say to me, right now, Lord?' And then, wait silently for God to respond. This is where prayer becomes a dialogue, a two-way interchange of communication. We should also know and understand how the Father speaks to us so that we can learn to tune in and receive His voice.

Tuning in to The Spirit

To live and walk in the Spirit demands building a relationship with the Holy Spirit.

The role of the Holy Spirit is to search the deep things of the Father's mind and reveal them to us. In this, the Holy Spirit is the great revealer. Jesus had this to say about the ministry and role of the Holy Spirit.

> *"And I will pray the Father, and He will give you another Helper, that He may abide with you forever — the Spirit of truth, whom the world cannot receive, because it neither sees Him nor knows Him; but you know Him, for He dwells with you and will be in you."* John 14:16-17

Jesus called the Holy Spirit, the Spirit of truth. He went on to say that He would be the Helper and would dwell with us and be inside of us. This means that the Spirit would work within us to reveal the truth. But there's more. We should also 'wait on the Lord'.

> *"And I will pray the Father, and He will give you another Helper, that He may abide with you forever —   the Spirit of truth, whom the world cannot receive, because it neither sees Him nor knows Him; but you know Him, for He dwells with you and will be in you."* John 14:16-17

> *"I still have many things to say to you, but you cannot bear them now. However, when He, the Spirit of truth, has come, He will guide you into all truth; for He will not speak on His own authority, but whatever He hears He will speak; and He will tell you things to come. He will glorify Me, for He will take of what is Mine and declare it to you. All things that the Father has are Mine. Therefore, I said that He will take of Mine and declare it to you."* John 16:12-15

God is always speaking. He is the Word! Words are constantly proceeding from the Father (Matt 4:4). Notice that Jesus said that he had many things to say but it would take the ministry of the Holy Spirit, to guide into all the truth. The Holy Spirit speaks what He hears and tells us things to come. He also takes of what is the Lords' and declares it to us. The Spirit 'speaks' and 'declares' not His own agenda but only what He hears. Wow! It's the Holy Spirit that brings the mind of God and the mind of Christ to us. The Holy Spirit brings the vision and voice of God to us.

> But as it is written: "Eye has not seen, nor ear heard, Nor have entered into the heart of man, the things which God has prepared for those who love Him." But God has revealed them to us through His Spirit. For the Spirit searches all things, yes, the deep things of God. For what man knows the things of a man except the spirit of the man which is in him? Even so no one knows the things of God except the Spirit of God. Now we have received, not the spirit of the world, but the Spirit who is from God, that we might know the things that have been freely given to us by God. These things we also speak, not in words which man's wisdom teaches but which the Holy Spirit teaches, comparing spiritual things with spiritual. But the natural man does not receive the things of the Spirit of God, for they are foolishness to him; nor can he know them, because they are spiritually discerned. 1 Corinthians 2:9-15

God reveals His heart and mind by the Holy Spirit. Jesus said the Holy Spirit will *be with you* and *be in you.* It's the Holy Spirit's role to search the deep things of God and make them known to us. Where does this happen? Inside, within us, in the spirit of our mind. The spiritual man, the one who invests time in developing spiritually, receives the things of the Spirit of God. The natural man, the one who is more focused on the natural life and senses, cannot receive the heavenly ministry of the Spirit because in his mind, he thinks its foolishness and so he is closed.

Jesus said the Holy Spirit will teach us, lead us and guide us in to the truth. As we enquire of God, we can expect the Holy Spirit to lead us and guide us in the spiritual realm. The Holy Spirit brings quickens us and directs us in the use of spiritual gifts in many situations that we enquire about. Here in this passage, it is showing the importance of working with the Holy Spirit. Jesus didn't do or say anything until He had heard the Father through the Holy Spirit. So, how do we hear the Holy Spirit within us. He uses our own 'inner voice.'

The Holy Spirit speaks to the spirit of our mind. We must by reason of use, exercise our spiritual senses to discern the word and voice of God, and good and evil (Hebrews 5:14) Remember, Jesus said, '*My sheep know my voice.*' Getting to know the voice of God is a learned practice. Actually, we can have a number of voices at work in our mind: our own voice, demonic voices, the world, and God. How do we know the voice of the Lord? It will always line up with the written word. It will promote the will of God. It will always be full of grace and truth. The whole purpose of the new covenant is that God wants to put His word in our hearts and minds (Hebrews 8:10).

If we want to receive from the Holy Spirit, we should humble ourselves with reverential fear. We must firstly establish living and walking in the Spirit. We should establish holiness, as He is the 'Holy' Spirit. We should be worshipers in spirit and truth. We should invite the Spirit of God to speak with us and reveal the Father's mind. We should be careful not to grieve Him or make Him jealous (Ephesians 4:30; James 4:4). We certainly should not 'quench' the Spirit and nor should we insult Him (1 Thessalonians 5:19; Hebrews 10:29). We are exhorted to be filled with the Spirit.

> "*And do not be drunk with wine, in which is dissipation; but be filled with the Spirit.*" Ephesians 5:18

To be filled, means to be 'controlled' by. If someone is filled with anger, it means that they are *controlled* by anger. We are to be filled with the Spirit repeatedly, daily even hourly. We know that Jesus broke away from the busyness of ministry in order to be filled with the Spirit and come under His anointing, inspiration, revelation and power as He revealed the Father's works and words. Jesus was skilled at hearing and seeing by the Spirit. He invested lots of time, daily, tuning in and listening to the Father's voice by the Spirit.

Jesus also ministered in the spiritual realm as well as the natural realm. What are we to expect when the Spirit speaks and reveals the Father's mind and voice to us? Well, the works and words are received in either 'open visions' or 'closed visions'. The Spirit communicates with 'impressions', 'images', 'perceptions', 'visions', 'dreams', 'images', and with the 'still, small voice.' We should be open and patient at first as we are learning and practicing to use our spiritual senses. It does take time to develop, so we shouldn't be discouraged and we should never give up. Once we know how to be in the Spirit, we are one step closer to being led of the Spirit and empowered with spiritual gifts. We'll look more at this as we study the gifts of the Spirit and how they operate.

CHAPTER 21

Spiritual Gifts

Divine Glory

Satan fell from Zion but Jesus was sent from Zion. His mission was to restore the kingdom of God on earth. Adam didn't lose religion, he lost the kingdom and the spiritual life needed to engage it and come under the divine glory; inspiration, revelation and power needed to fulfil the commission and establish the will of the Father on earth.

Another part of Jesus' mission was to model what living, walking and ministering was like connected to heaven and walking in the power and authority of the Holy Spirit. Jesus was baptised in the Spirit. He lived under an open heaven and was in league with the Father, the Spirit of God and angels. Everything Jesus did was through the gifts of the Spirit. He did nothing independently nor did he do anything out of His deity. He lived as a man reliant upon the Spirit of God. We must understand this otherwise we won't operate in spiritual gifts.

"Have this mind in you, which was also in Christ Jesus: who, existing in the form of God, counted not the being on an equality with God a thing to be grasped, but emptied himself, taking the form of a servant, being made in the likeness of men" Philippians 2:5-7 ASV.

Jesus' mission was also to establish the new covenant in His blood, whereby we could be forgiven, washed, cleansed, and made righteous in order to have spiritual life restored and be reconciled to the Father. His mission was also to triumph over the world, the flesh and the devil and provide a victory that would make us overcomers so we could share his throne, power and glory (Revelation 3:21). His mission included raising us up to the enthroned life as priests and kings so we could enter Zion, His rest and access the glory. Lastly, Jesus' mission was to return to Zion and open up a new and living way whereby we could rise and join Him in His present and continuing ministry as High Priest and Mediator of the new covenant (Hebrews 10:20).

Jesus' successful mission from start to finish means that we can function exactly as He did on earth and do the greater works that He spoke of by accessing the glory of the Father through the Spirit of God and secure the aid of angels. This brings us to the operation of the gifts of the Spirit.

The Holy Spirit is the third *person* of the Godhead. He is co-equal, co-eternal and co-existent with the Father and the Son. He is omniscient, omnipotent and omnipresent. He is responsible for managing the anointing and revealing and communicating the revelation, inspiration and power of God. He is the one who anoints, fills, endows, authorises, equips, teaches, guides, leads, reveals, inspires and empowers us to minister the kingdom and will of God.

He is the one who leads us in intercessions. He is the one who empowers the church for spiritual victories over Satanic and demonic powers. He is the one who convicts the world of sin and righteousness and future judgment (John 16:8-11). He is the one that through His spiritual gifts, inspires and empowers the believer to minister to broken people and bring them to God through the gospel and the new covenant.

He is sensitive and can be ignored, insulted, grieved, quenched and resisted. He will not force Himself upon anyone but when the character is humble and the conditions are right, He will bring His operations into play. He will not and cannot work where the believer is in the flesh and in bondage to the world, the flesh and the devil (Galatians 5: 16,17). He works with those who have established the crucified life and have risen as overcomers and ascended to the enthroned life. He is called the 'helper' and as such is available to help us know, grasp, understand the thoughts and the ways of the Father.

He is the helper and the one who is sent to help us be Christlike and do the greater works that Jesus said we would do (John 14:12,16).

Through the Spirit's help we can access the same glory that Jesus accessed and minister the same ministry that Jesus ministered and move in the same anointing and gifting that Jesus moved in. **Jesus is the way, the truth and the life and as such has made the same help, He received by the Spirit available to us.** Jesus has restored and opened up the way for you to be filled with the Spirit so you can experience the glory of the Father and manifest supernatural power and authority. The Spirit is the promise of the Father and is for all who are afar off (Acts 2:38-39).

Spiritual Temples

We have been made temples of the Holy Spirit. In the old testament, the Spirit of God came 'upon' the individual and inspired and empowered them to speak or act. But it was a temporal experience until the next time. After Jesus had died, the Spirit would be sent and this time because of the provision of Christ, the Spirit would not only come upon them but be *in them to abide* as comforter and helper.

> *"Do you not know that you are the temple of God and that the Spirit of God dwells in you? If anyone defiles the temple of God, God will destroy him. For the temple of God is holy, which temple you are."* 1 Corinthians 6:19-20

> *"Or do you not know that your body is the temple of the Holy Spirit who is in you, whom you have from God, and you are not your own? For you were bought at a price; therefore glorify God in your body and in your spirit, which are God's."*

Notice that the Holy Spirit is '*in you.*' This is important as it means that we must develop our inner, spiritual life to be in harmony with Him and hear Him. God has given us His Spirit that we may freely know the things that only the Spirit can know and communicate (1 Corinthians 2:10-12). However, if we don't take time to be open to Him and invite Him to minister, He won't. If we ignore His presence, He will remain silent within.

We must daily exercise our spiritual senses and practice inner silence and meditative prayer in order to hear the Father's voice and see the Father's works. The gifts of the Spirit are spiritual communications bring revelation, inspiration and power to us. The gifts of the Spirit are needed in order to minister to the church and see her built up, edified and equipped for ministry. The gifts of the Spirit are needed to defeat the enemy and win spiritual battles in the heavenlies so that we can be effective on the ground. The gifts of the Spirit are needed in order to minister the gospel of the kingdom to broken lives, that are captive or oppressed and need liberating and healing. Ministry without the gifts of the Spirit can never achieve the good, acceptable and perfect will of God.

Jesus' ministry was powerful and effective because of the Spirit of God.

> *"The Spirit of the Lord is upon Me, Because He has anointed Me To preach the gospel to the poor; He has sent Me to heal the broken-hearted, To proclaim liberty to the captives And recovery of sight to the blind, To set at liberty those who are*

oppressed; To proclaim the acceptable year of the Lord." Luke
4:18-19

The ministry of the early church was powerful and effective because of the Spirit of God.

> *"But you shall receive power when the Holy Spirit has come upon you; and you shall be witnesses to Me in Jerusalem, and in all Judea and Samaria, and to the end of the earth."* Acts 1:8

The early church did greater works than Jesus in that the ministry had multiplied and *many* were operating in the gifts of the Spirit. The apostle Paul cast out devils, healed the sick, raised the dead, spoke in tongues, prophesied, and in fact, moved in all the gifts and so did Peter and many others. They had 'unusual miracles' manifesting through them (Acts 19:11-12). Why? Because they were operating under the order of Melchizedek and as a spiritual temple and royal priesthood and the Spirit of God and angels were actively at work daily.

Understanding the revelation of the tabernacle of David will get you into the Spirit. Understanding and grasping the revelation of the order of Melchizedek will get you operating in the Spirit. When this happens, everything changes, a spiritual shift takes place and you will begin to reach the level of spiritual maturity demanded to live and walk in the Spirit.

In the Spirit

When the early church was established it was functioning as a spiritual temple and spiritual priesthood. The early church adopted the Davidic order of worship which included psalms, hymns and spiritual songs (Ephesians 5:19; Colossians 3:16; James 5:13). **They operated in the same anointing as Jesus and performed greater works by the same way Jesus had, by the Spirit of God.**

Unfortunately, over time the devil deceived the church and robbed her of the truths that caused her to move in the glory and power of God through the Spirit until the church had become a religious institution void of the glory and the power of God. Now in the last of the last days, God is revealing and releasing this powerful revelation into His church for His end time strategy of saving the gentiles and bringing to pass His restoration and regeneration of all things through releasing Christ from heaven (Acts 3:21).

David operated in the Spirit under this divine order. Jesus operated in the Spirit and under the order of Melchizedek and so did the early church. The contemporary church is being transitioned in our time and is being brought into the revelation of the Davidic order of ministry in the Spirit as well as operating under the eternal and spiritual order of the royal priesthood after the order of Melchizedek.

In this season the church is going to come into both the former and latter glory in one last display of spiritual power that will release the glory of God and bring in the final harvest and so hasten the return of the Lord Jesus Christ from heaven for the restoration of all things.

How will it happen? The church is being lifted into the Spirit and is about to come under the divine glory and power of God and move in every spiritual gift of the Holy Spirit once again. In a vision, while I was in the Spirit, I saw a huge conveyor belt reaching from the ground up to heaven. I saw angels lifting up huge stones on to the belt so that they were transported up off the ground and into heaven. I heard the Lord say, *'I'm lifting my people into the Spirit. I'm raising up my spiritual temple!'* Praise God! In this season the Lord is building the house and not man (Psalm 127:1).

In another vision, I saw a huge catapult in the Spirit being drawn back and released. I heard the Lord say, *'I'm catapulting my church into her future.'* God is about to do a speedy work in bringing the church into her destiny and true calling. The glorious church without spot and blemish is about to be seen and come into her heavenly calling and operations. When the church is repositioned and lines up to the word of God becoming the spiritual temple and priesthood, she is going to come under the glory and the outpouring of the former and latter rains will flow. This is going to be a move of the Spirit of God greater than anything witnessed in human history.

"*Not by might nor by power, but by My Spirit,*" *Says the Lord of hosts.* Zechariah 4:5

The Seven Spirits of God

The ministries and gifts of the Holy Spirit are essential in ministering the kingdom of God. God is raising up His spiritual temple and priesthood and for her to function she must be in tune more than ever with the Spirit of God. In our studies, we have clearly shown that through His provision and merit, He has opened up Zion, the city of God, heavenly Jerusalem and the sanctuary that is above. Jesus is the way to the throne and the altar and to every spiritual resource and blessing.

In the book of Revelation, John introduces us to the seven Spirits of God.

"*Immediately I was in the Spirit; and behold, a throne set in heaven, and One sat on the throne.*" Revelation 4:2

John goes on to describe the brilliance of God's throne but then says this in verse 5, "*Seven lamps of fire were burning before the throne, which are the seven Spirits of God.*"

These seven lamps of fire burning are the seven Spirits of God. Seven is the number of completeness and perfection. Only the Holy Spirit can bring to the church and the world the complete and perfect revelation of the Father. He is the Spirit of truth who proceeds from the Father (John 15:26). One of the symbols of the Holy Spirit is that of fire. John the Baptist said that Jesus, when He comes, would baptize with the Holy Ghost and fire (Matthew 3:11).

The Menorah or seven branched lampstand that was set in the holy place gave illumination for the priests to minister. It is symbolic of the ministry of the Spirit of God. The Spirit of God is the main branch and the six candles that are fed from the oil in the stem reveal the operations of the seven Spirits of God to give complete and perfect revelation of the Father and His kingdom.

> "There shall come forth a Rod from the stem of Jesse, And a Branch shall grow out of his roots. The Spirit of the Lord shall rest upon Him, The Spirit of wisdom and understanding, The Spirit of counsel and might, The Spirit of knowledge and of the fear of the Lord." Isaiah 11:1-2

The seven Spirits of God are revealed here in Isaiah: The Spirit of the Lord, the Spirit of Wisdom, The Spirit of Understanding, The Spirit of Counsel, The Spirit of Might, The Spirit of Knowledge, The Spirit of the Fear of the Lord.

It's important to note that the Holy Spirit works with those who are humble and surrendered. When I learned of the seven Spirits of God, I began to humble myself and ask for the Spirit of God to mentor me in spiritual living. I invited each of the Spirit's operations to work in my life. All I can say is that the gifts of the Spirit were activated in my life. We are exhorted not to be ignorant of spiritual gifts as well as to desire them. God says that His people are destroyed through ignorance and the lack of knowledge. It's time to learn about and begin to desire and pursue spiritual gifts.

> "Now concerning spiritual gifts, brethren, I do not want you to be ignorant." 1 Corinthians 12:1

> "Pursue love, and desire spiritual gifts, but especially that you may prophesy." 1 Corinthians 14:1

> "Even so you, since you are zealous for spiritual gifts, let it be for the edification of the church that you seek to excel." 1 Corinthians 14:12

We must make sure that our motive for operating in the gifts of the Spirit are for the greater good of the kingdom and not for personal gain and acclaim. The Holy Spirit will only glorify Christ not us! As we come boldly before the throne of grace with expectant desire and seek God, we should expect to come under the ministry of the seven Spirits of God. Remember, the kingdom of God is within you (Luke 17:21), in other words, you access it from within, through the spirit of your mind.

As we learn to develop and activate our spirit and spiritual senses, we will learn through the art of stillness and meditative prayer to receive from the Spirit. **We must grow in exercising spiritual senses, so that we experience both closed and open visions.** Closed visions are experienced as we silence our natural senses and operate in meditative prayer. Closed visions are experienced through our spiritual senses. Peter had a closed vision as he fell into a trance at noon as he prayed upon the rooftop. His spiritual senses were active and he saw the vision of God and heard the voice of God (Acts 10).

The apostle John had closed visions as he came into the Spirit in the book of Revelation. Open visions are experienced with our spiritual and natural senses at work. A good example is the first martyr, Stephen. As he was being stoned to death, he had an open vision through both spiritual and natural senses at work.

> But he, being full of the Holy Spirit, gazed into heaven and saw the glory of God, and Jesus standing at the right hand of God, and said, "Look! I see the heavens opened and the Son of Man standing at the right hand of God!" Acts 7:55-56

Closed visions are usually experienced as we seek God privately and open visions are experienced as we learn to stay in a prayerful and spiritual state. Jesus operated in both closed and open visions. Much of Jesus' ministry was performed with open visions as He followed and obeyed the Spirit's prompting. The apostles also had learned this practice. We too, must learn practice and exercise our spiritual senses. The more we do, the more we will experience both closed and open visions.

This is key to operating in spiritual gifts and being led of the Spirit.

Now to the operation of spiritual gifts. As we have seen, Jesus operated in spiritual gifts and did nothing independently of himself. He 'emptied' himself and took on the form of a servant and was made in the likeness of a man. Jesus developed his spiritual life and senses. This explains how He could see the works of the Father and hear the words of the Father.

We know that the ministry and role of the Spirit is that of helping us to receive from the Father. He does this by searching the deep things in the mind of the Father and revealing them freely to us when we seek Him (1 Corinthians 2:9-15). We must practice tuning in through the approach and using meditative prayer. We must hear the voice of the Father. Remember, He is the Word not the silence! He speaks, His Word is forever proceeding from the throne so if we'll put in the time we will hear.

Once we hear, we're on our way to experiencing the gifts of the Spirit. One reason that many believers don't operate in spiritual gifts is that they have neglected to develop their inner life, their spiritual senses. The Spirit is 'in you' and so if you want to hear Him, silence your natural senses and tune in with your spiritual senses.

The gifts of the Spirit are what we can call the 'communications' of the Spirit. In other words, as we seek the Father and bring circumstances and situations to Him, enquiring and asking for direction, expect the Holy Spirit to communicate spiritual gifts in order to deal with whatever matter needs dealing with. Also, the more open you are and practiced and experienced you become, be open for the Spirit to communicate spiritually and inwardly and lead and direct you. **As you do, you will begin to realise that what the Spirit reveals will be the operation of spiritual gifts.**

> *"Do not be deceived, my beloved brethren. Every good gift and every perfect gift is from above, and comes down from the Father of lights, with whom there is no variation or shadow of turning."* James 1:16-17

It's important to know that every good gift and every perfect gift is from above, and comes down from the Father of lights but is communicated to us by the Spirit of God. The

Holy Spirit knows perfectly the Father's mind, will and purpose and He also is the Power and authority of God. The Spirit releases spiritual gifts or communications to us and it is up to us to have obedient faith and step out to perform what the Spirit reveals to us. **This is how spiritual gifts work. They are received in the spirit of our mind, inwardly and then acted upon by us in faith.**

Let's understand some key thoughts about spiritual gifts and then look at how they operate.

Spiritual gifts come down from the Father of lights. The Father is the source of spiritual revelation, inspiration and power. **Spiritual gifts** are spiritual communication brought to us by the Holy Spirit. The role of the Holy Spirit is to communicate the inspiration, revelation and power of the Father's glory. Know that the Father allows the Spirit to distribute them as *He wills.* **Spiritual gifts are spiritual**. They come from the Spiritual realm and from the Spirit of God. They are not natural gifts in any way as we shall see. **Spiritual gifts** must be understood. Paul tells believers not to be ignorant of spiritual gifts. You cannot function in them if you don't know them or are ignorant of them. **Spiritual gifts** must be desired. If you don't desire them you won't pursue them and if you don't pursue them you won't attain them. **Spiritual gifts** are not to be confused with the fruit of the Spirit. The fruit of the Spirit develops as you establish living and walking in the Spirit. The more time you invest, the more of the fruit of the Spirit will develop and manifest in your life. Love is the Key fruit of the Spirit and all the others develop out of love. Faith is the Key gift of the Spirit and all the others demand the gift of faith. **Spiritual gifts** are for every believer and every believer can move in every spiritual gift. It isn't true that no one believer can have all the gifts, in fact the opposite is true. All the gifts are available and accessible to each and every believer as the nature of the ministry demands their use. **Spiritual gifts** are for men and for women. God promised to pour out His Spirit on both men and women, young and old (Acts 2:17-18). **Spiritual gifts** are vital for spiritual effectiveness in spiritual warfare, in building up and edifying the church as well as in evangelising the world.

Today, the gifts of the Spirit are minimised and misunderstood. Some believe that they were given to the apostles for establishing the church but then were taken away, when the church was established. There are many that consider the gifts of the Spirit foolish and some believe that because they are gifts, they are optional extras and can be declined.

It is clear from Scripture that the gifts of the Spirit, though gifts, are absolutely essential and vital for the church to come into the 'greater works' that Jesus spoke of and function supernaturally as to fulfil her heavenly calling and mission. The mission of the church demands the gifts, operations and communications of the Spirit to empower the church for supernatural service. She cannot effectively fulfil her calling without the gifts of the Spirit.

The reason a lot of ministry is ineffective is because the gifts are not relied upon. Ministry can be done without them. The ministry, roles and gifts of the Spirit are still in operation as long as the church is in the world and should be known, desired and pursued.

> *"Then Peter said to them, "Repent, and let every one of you be baptized in the name of Jesus Christ for the remission of sins; and you shall receive the gift of the Holy Spirit. For the promise is to you and to your children, and to all who are afar off, as many as the Lord our God will call."* Acts 2:38–39

They Promise still stands and means that the gifts are still available for any believer who will seek them, desire them and create the right conditions for them to function. Spiritual gifts are not for personal fame or acclaim but come into operation when a believer is set in the body of Christ as God has willed. They operate when a believer desires the profit of all.

The gifts flow when there is unity in the Spirit and where there is mutual surrender and submission to God, and one another. Lone rangers and free spirits who operate independent of the church and aren't accountable rarely operate in spiritual gifts. They are given through the Spirit for the profit of all by those who are committed to all.

Now let's see what they are and how they work.

> *"Now concerning spiritual gifts, brethren, I do not want you to be ignorant: You know that you were Gentiles, carried away to these dumb idols, however you were led. Therefore, I make known to you that no one speaking by the Spirit of God calls Jesus accursed, and no one can say that Jesus is Lord except by the Holy Spirit. There are diversities of gifts, but the same Spirit. There are differences of ministries, but the same Lord. And there are diversities of activities, but it is the same God who works all in all. But the manifestation of the Spirit is given to each one for the profit of all: for to one is given the word of wisdom through the Spirit, to another the word of knowledge through the same Spirit, to another faith by the same Spirit, to another gifts of healings by the same Spirit, to another the working of miracles, to another prophecy, to another discerning of spirits, to another different kinds of tongues, to another the interpretation of tongues. But one and the same Spirit works all these things, distributing to each one individually as He wills."* 1 Corinthians 12:1–11

Paul calls the gifts of the Spirit 'the manifestation' in verse 7. In other words, the gifts are communications that manifest God's spiritual knowledge, power and anointing. Again, in verse 11, the gifts are 'distributed' to each one individually as He (the Spirit) wills. **This simply means that when the attitude is right and the conditions are right, the Holy Spirit will manifest and distribute the necessary gifts to the individual that are needed to minister. The gifts are not given as permanent endowments but are manifested and distributed as and when needed.**

Categories of Gifts

According to this passage, there are three categories of spiritual gifts.

1. Revelation Gifts

Within this category we have, the word of wisdom, the word of knowledge and the discerning of spirits. In these gifts, **God imparts a fragment of His own knowledge, wisdom and discernment to us.**

The word of wisdom is a revelation of what to say and what to do under the anointing of the Spirit. Wisdom is the application of knowledge. It is knowing what to say and do with the knowledge revealed. We must obey the word of wisdom the Spirit gives to us and act in faith.

The word of knowledge is a revelation of a truth or fact associated with a certain situation disclosed. It is knowledge of what is going on behind the scenes in the spiritual realm. It's knowledge revealed by the Spirit and does not come from our head or own knowledge base.

The discerning of spirits is the revealing by the Holy Spirit of what spirits are at work in a given situation, or area, demon, angelic or human. Once revealed, the Spirit will release the word of wisdom to know what to say or do.

2. Power Gifts

Within this category we have, the gift of faith, the gifts of healings and the working of miracles. In these gifts **God imparts a portion of His own divine powers and abilities to us**. It is not human but divine ability. These gifts demonstrate the power of God especially in the market place.

The gift of faith is a deposit of supernatural belief and confidence in the revelation of God that causes us to speak or act upon what is before us. Faith without works is dead. Faith must speak or act to bring about the desired results. The gift of faith causes us to speak forth or act on information given.

The gifts of healings are supernatural deposits of healing power and virtue given to heal the sick and cast out devils. Healing and deliverance often work together. Sometimes Jesus healed a person and sometimes he cast out a demon and healing came. The fact that there are 'gifts of healings' plural, means that the Holy Spirit can release gifts that cover the need for a variety of healings.

The gift of the working of miracles is a natural act that is supernaturally charged and produces wonder and glory to God. Jesus performed many miracles and so did many in the early church. God worked unusual miracles through the hands of Paul as if the miracle itself wasn't unusual.

3. Inspiration Gifts

Within this category we have, prophecy, different kinds of tongues and interpretation of tongues.

In these gifts **God imparts His anointing to bless the church and build her up in the work of the ministry.** These gifts allow God to speak a relevant message into the church or believer's life.

The gift of Prophecy releases the mind of God for the church, a ministry or a believer. It is different to the office of a prophet in that again it is a fragment or portion needed at that time. The gift of prophecy is for edification, exhortation and comfort. It can also carry a word that reveals God's plan for the future.

The gift of tongues is the speaking forth a word or message from God of edification, exhortation or comfort under the anointing of the Spirit. It is a supernatural utterance or proclamation by the Spirit that cannot be understood with the natural mind.

The gift of the interpretation of tongues is the speaking in one's natural language as to interpret or reveal the message spoken in tongues. Tongues and interpretation equal prophecy.

The Gifts in Operation

To illustrate the gifts in operation I'd like to share a few personal experiences that I have had in the Spirit and hopefully show how the gifts work. I have already shared some of these but this time I'd like to show the gifts of the Spirit working through these experiences.

The Four Trumpets

As I was praying and seeking the Lord, I was in the Spirit and a vision of a fortified wall or stronghold opened up before me with four windows cut out. I could see a trumpet in each of the windows. I asked the Lord what it meant and He told me that the four trumpets represented the revelation of the old testament, the revelation of gospels, the revelation of the new testament letters and the revelation of Revelation. He said that there were four demons, Doubt, Deception. Disbelief and Fear, who had stolen these revelations and had introduced doctrines of demons in their place. I was enraged and livid and asked what could be done. The Lord told me to approach the wall, rebuke the demons and call upon angels to recover the trumpets, have them returned to Zion, sprinkled with the blood of sprinkling, and then presented on the sea of glass for redistribution. I simply obeyed. As soon as I did this, the Lord spoke to me and said, 'Dennis, I'm going to release the revelation of the four trumpets into your life and ministry.'

Let me identify the gifts of the Spirit at work in this vision: First, the word of knowledge was given me regarding the stronghold and the trumpets and what they meant. Secondly, I was given the gift of the discerning of spirits – Doubt, Deception, Disbelief and Fear by the Spirit. Next, the word of wisdom was given as the Lord told me what to say and do. Lastly, I received the gift of faith and obeyed the Lord, doing what He told me to do and saying what He told me to say.

From that moment, the Lord began to release the revelations of the trumpets into my life and ministry. Here in this one vision four of the nine gifts of the Spirit came into operation.

Altar Ministry

Coming to the end of a Sunday morning service, I had invited the church to come to the altar for prayer. As different believers lined up across the front of the church, I began to pray over them. I had prayed for about two believers when the Holy Spirit said, 'Dennis give me a chance!' I was stunned for a moment and stepped back. I had already prayed what I felt led to pray but then when the Spirit spoke, I apologised and asked the Spirit to take over. As I approached the next person, a vision opened up above them and I began to prophesy over them. This happened along the prayer line as the Spirit released the gift of prophecy as well as the gift of the word of knowledge.

Deliverance

Deep in prayer and in the Spirit, I was seeking God about a relationship that has broken down and had become a great burden to me. The person had cut me off and wouldn't respond to calls and was extremely hostile even though I hadn't done what they thought I had done. The person was really sick and the doctors were saying that they were a car crash and on the brink of death. As I was in the Spirit, I lifted it to the Lord and asked Him to take me to the person in the Spirit so I could help. Immediately a vision opened up and I saw hundreds of jet black, slimy snakes slowly moving in and out of each other. I didn't see, but I knew this person was underneath them. The Spirit told me that the person had a spirit of rage, murder, lust and associated devils at work against them. He told me that the chief devil was rage and that murder followed rage. He then reminded me of the words of the Lord when he said that whoever is angry without cause is guilty of murder. I rose up in the Spirit with a righteous anger and named each of the devils revealed and commanded them off this individual. Without realising it, I had pointed my fingers at them when I spoke and immediately the scripture came to mind where Jesus said He cast out Satan with the finger of God. As soon as I did this the Lord said, 'Dennis, you have just done something in the Spirit.' The next day, I was praying for this person again and came into the Spirit. As I did a huge wall was before me. I asked the Lord what it was and He told me it was a wall of offence. He went on to tell me that the person was deeply offended and that was another reason for their hardness of heart. I asked for His help. Immediately, I was dressed in white armour and the sword of the Spirit was in my right hand. I looked to my left and my right and I was flanked by mighty angels. Next, the Lord told me to go to the wall and strike it three times in His Name. Now, this person hadn't responded to me for over twelve months. As soon as I obeyed, and did what the Lord said, my phone which was by my side rang. It was this person. From that moment the relationship was healed and today is stronger than ever.

Here again, the gifts of the Spirit were clearly at work. In the altar call, I heard the voice of the Spirit within asking me to give Him a chance. As I obeyed, the gift of prophecy and the word of knowledge began to flow. In the Deliverance vision, the gift of the discerning of spirits was given to me to know what I was up against. Next, the word of knowledge was given as to the facts surrounding the issue. The gift of the word of wisdom was also given to me so that I knew what to do and what to say and lastly, the gift of faith to step out on what the Spirit had showed me and directed me to do and say. The gifts of the Spirit resulted in supernatural ministry that brought blessing, deliverance and victory.

The need of the hour is that believers come under the Spirit of God and receive and manifest the gifts of the Spirit. I believe that God wants to release strategies for victories through the house of prayer. For this to happen, we need to equip the church for the work of the ministry. No more time can be wasted, as the world rolls steadily and speedily to the Day of the Lord, the spiritual temple and priesthood must rise up in the Spirit and come under the glory and power of the Spirit of God and manifest supernatural ministry as Jesus and the early church did.

You cannot walk somewhere that you don't live. It's time to live, walk, war and minister in the Spirit. Jesus has opened up a new and living Way so that we can perform greater works than He did. It's all possible by establishing spiritual life and senses, I believe that the greatest season of the church is upon us. Are you ready? Are you hungry for more? Are you ready to become an overcomer? Are you ready for the enthroned life? Are you ready to become a royal priest with Jesus and minister the new covenant? Are you ready to live and walk in the Spirit? Do you desire the gifts of the Spirit? Are you willing to take your place? The city of God, Zion, heavenly Jerusalem is fully open and accessible. We are no longer short of the glory of God. Everything is in place awaiting the church and the believer to rise up in the Spirit and come under the glory of God so that it can be manifested in the heavens and in the earth. The kingdom is waiting, the church is waiting and the world is waiting. Follow Jesus and embrace the Way, the truth and the Life!

Contact Details

If you've been impacted and blessed by this book
please contact Pastor Dennis.

d-ryan1@hotmail.co.uk
admin@tclc.co.uk

Trafford Christian Life Centre
107 Barton Road
Stretford
Manchester
M32 9AF

Tel: 0161 7185248
tclc.co.uk

Printed in Great Britain
by Amazon